# DESIGN RESEARCH MASTERY

## How to Lead Research That Builds Buy-In and Great Products

BIS Publishers

BIS Publishers
Timorplein 46
1094 CC Amsterdam
The Netherlands
bis@bispublishers.com
www.bispublishers.com

ISBN 978 90 636 9954 3

For my parents — thank you for teaching me the value of hard work and to always go after my dreams.

For Chris, Jackson and Heidi — thank you for giving me wings to pursue those dreams.

"Becoming a customer-centric organisation requires more than just insights: it takes influence. Alongside a fresh perspective on research in the age of AI, this book shows you how to drive change, build stakeholder trust and navigate the politics of design. If you want your research to matter, start here."

**— Jim Kalbach**

Author of *The Jobs To Be Done Playbook* and Chief Evangelist at Mural

"With *Design Research Mastery*, Sara Fortier has given us frank and actionable advice to propel design researchers forward in a pivotal moment for design and technology, where research is more critical (and misunderstood) than ever."

**— UX Magazine**

"With hard-won experience, Sara Fortier offers more than just research tactics. She delivers a framework for human connection that drives meaningful change, rooted in the belief that great research starts with deep listening, and earning trust through understanding. *Design Research Mastery* is a guide for lasting, positive impact — not just on products and services, but on the people and teams you serve."

**— Gerry Scullion**

Director at Humana Design and Founder of This is HCD

"With empathy and clarity, Sara empowers researchers with the tools they need. This is the book to read when you're ready to conduct exploratory and generative UX research that makes a difference — adding value to both your organisation and your career."

**— Cory Lebson**

UX Research Consultant and Author, *The UX Careers Handbook*, 2nd Edition

"This book transforms user research from simple storytelling to compelling storyselling, making it indispensable for designers at every stage of their career. With its blend of theory and hands-on advice, this is the book I wish I'd had when starting out. It's both a roadmap and a source of inspiration for the next generation of design leaders."

**— Wonjoon Chung**

Associate Professor, School of Industrial Design, Carleton University

"This book is an excellent and accessible overview of what it takes to drive success in design research. It serves as an invaluable guide for applying a user-centered approach in real-world contexts, where alignment with business goals and organisational objectives is essential. The book also covers some of the most common and practical research methods used by design researchers and importantly shows how to effectively translate data into usable insights and compelling design storytelling."

**— Bjarki Hallgrimsson**

Associate Professor, School of Industrial Design, Carleton University

# Contents

1 **PREFACE: WHY I WROTE THIS BOOK** 02
- Future-Proofing Your Career 03
- The Design Research Knowledge Gap 05
- The Mountain That We Have to Climb 07
- The Secrets to Project Success 08
- How to Use This Book 08

2 **GAINING STAKEHOLDER BUY-IN:** Grow Influence and Build Trust 11
- The Circle of Influence 12
- How to Grow Your Circle of Influence 15

3 **GAINING STAKEHOLDER BUY-IN:** Communicate the Value of Your Work 28
- Design Leadership Skills That Get Results 29
- Meet Decision Makers Where They Are 30
- Start Small and Educate Allies 38

4 **DESIGN RESEARCH FUNDAMENTALS** 42
- The Importance of Human-Centred Design 43
- Design Research and the Design Process 43
- Key Purposes of Design Research 47
- Facets of Design Research 47
- The Six-Stage DRM Process 52

5 **LEADING SUCCESSFUL PROJECTS** 56
- Project Planning 57
- Project Initiation 68
- Project Execution 70

6 **RESEARCH PLANNING:** Research Goals and Methods 76
- Craft Research Goals 78
- Develop Research Themes and Questions 81

7 **RESEARCH PLANNING:** Defining and Recruiting Users 94
- Determine User Groups 95
- Choose the Recruiting Criteria 98
- Choose the Number of Participants 100
- Choose a Recruiting Method 102
- Recruiting and Screening Materials 105

8 **IN-DEPTH INTERVIEWS** 112
- Interview Planning 114

- Developing Interview Questions 118
- Interview Scheduling 126
- Skills for Conducting In-Depth Interviews 129

9 **OBSERVATIONS** **136**
- Observation Planning 139
- Logistics and Participant Prep 146
- Field Kit: An Essential Tool 149
- Tips for Smooth Observation Days 153

10 **DIARY STUDIES** **162**
- Diary Study Planning 167
- Creating the "Diary" for Your Study 172
- Pre- and Post-Study Interviews 176
- Tips for Robust Diary Studies 177

11 **WORKSHOPS** **182**
- Key Workshops in Design Research 183
- Workshop Planning 190
- Tips for Workshop Flow 192
- Workshop Time Management 195
- Post-Workshop Follow-Up 196

12 **MAKING SENSE OF DATA:** Analysis and Synthesis **200**
- Why Learn the Fundamentals? 202
- Recommended Theory and Approaches 203
- How to Make Sense of Data 205

13 **DESIGN STORYTELLING:** Creating Impactful Research Deliverables **220**
- Great Design Storytelling 221
- Develop Design Artefacts 224
- Communicate Insights: Crafting the Report 232
- Build Feature Roadmaps 240
- Tips for Better Insights Reports 242

14 **DESIGN RESEARCH RISING:** The Future of Design Research **248**
- What (or Who) is Behind the Mastery? 251
- The Emerging HCD Unicorn 252
- The Bridge Between Humans and Tech 255
- A Force to be Reckoned With 256

**ACKNOWLEDGEMENTS** **257**

**INDEX** **258**

Preface

# WHY I WROTE THIS BOOK

## And Why You Should Read It *

"Continuous effort — not strength or intelligence — is the key to unlocking our potential."

— Winston Churchill

# Introduction

Design research projects aren't exactly known for always succeeding or going the way we planned them to. They can be difficult to get off the ground, complicated to organise, time-consuming to run and frustrating to defend to every stakeholder who wants to know why you couldn't just look at a marketing survey or ask AI. But if we become true design research experts, we can inspire the kind of product and service innovation that creates amazing experiences for users, and propels careers and organisations to new levels of achievement.

I've written *Design Research Mastery* to go beyond your standard design research guide. It's an industry manual for elevating your career, effecting meaningful change and running research projects end to end. Mastering design research methods and learning how to conduct research well is, of course, paramount (and I will absolutely get into that in detail). But before we dive into all the tools, planning and processes involved, we need to talk about why so many design research projects fail to effect change — why we don't see our solutions implemented, and why our work gets overlooked or put on the back burner. Only then can we start to rewrite the narrative.

The truth is, we can drive ourselves crazy running around interviewing users and organising diary studies. But the findings, insights and design recommendations we draw from our research will be pointless if: a) they aren't actionable (i.e. they're not feasible or they don't clearly address key problems in the product or service) and b) they aren't listened to or accepted by the people making the business decisions.

These facts are tough to accept and even tougher to problem-solve. That's why I want to help. Because the UX and service design industry is full of talented people who are capable of creating impact. And to do that, you need to create opportunities for the kind of research that uncovers game-changing insights.

## THE INTENTION OF THIS BOOK IS TO:

- **Speak to those who are passionate about human-centred design** and want to do more design research, but feel frustrated, undervalued or unsure of how to gain support for their work (This includes UX researchers, UX designers, service designers, product managers, or any multidisciplinary practitioners looking to play around in the field of human-centred design)
- **Help those same people build trust with stakeholders and convince others of the value of design and research**, so they can gain more opportunities to conduct research and drive change
- **Give them the tools to lead successful research projects and deliver amazing insights** that can transform products and services for the better

# Future-Proofing Your Career

It seems like people in the tech space are running into more and more existential questions about the value of their work and the future of their careers. As I write this book, there are tools emerging daily that claim to outright replace UX, service design and design research processes entirely. This is leaving practitioners in our industry unsure about what's next for them, and it's also raising some doubts about investing time into learning or improving these processes, when so many of the steps involved are already being optimised or executed with AI.

While I'm not done developing in my career (we never are), I've been in the field long enough to know that new technology and new changes to the way we work are totally normal, expected and workable. It can be scary at first, but remember that tools are just tools — they need people to wield them. The longevity of your career is not going to be defined by the tools you used or didn't use. Instead, it'll be defined by the quality of the working relationships you build, the tangible value you bring to organisations and the users they serve, and the ways that you evolve your strategic and creative mindset.

Here are the key reasons why this book will help you conduct impeccable design research in the AI era.

- **AI can make you work faster, but you need established expertise to use it effectively.** Yes, AI is already revolutionising the way we do our work. It's taking all of the time-consuming tasks in design research and helping us to make them more efficient — recruiting and scheduling participants, and conducting data analysis, visualising findings, etc. BUT, if you don't know what prompts to give AI, what feedback to give it when it outputs a wrong or inaccurate answer, or even how to tell when an answer is wrong or inaccurate, then it will make your work sloppy... and you'll perpetuate the bad rap that design research already gets. So, no matter which tool you're using, you need to know your stuff first, before you can augment your speed with new technology.

The upcoming chapters are designed to help hone that expertise, and fill in knowledge or experience gaps, so that you can be highly strategic (and confident) in your work and your use of AI.

- **Empathy is innately human, and it's a central part of researching and designing for human needs.** Design research is a key component of the human-centred design (HCD) process. And a core tenet to the philosophy of HCD is empathy and understanding for the people affected by the product or service we're studying. Machines can never develop true empathy — so as practitioners, you need to embody that "empathy" factor. It's your job to represent the feelings, pain points and needs of your users, and you can only do that when you talk to them and learn from them. (Never forget this, and don't let your stakeholders forget it, either.)

  This book will teach you how to study your users or customers in a highly empathic and unbiased way that creates tangible and actionable results for the businesses you work with.

- **To make an impact, you need to grasp complex contexts.** A critical part of the work you do in design research is understanding the nebulous and ambiguous information in front of you, connecting the dots and finding a way forward. You need to read between the lines, gathering information from all the different areas of the business, stakeholders, and of course users... and you need to understand when to probe deeper, when to pivot, and when to push forward, based on what you're hearing, and what your goals are. This isn't something AI can grasp completely on its own.

  The chapters on research planning (6–7) and making sense of data (12) should be especially helpful in training this uniquely human design research "muscle."

- **AI can't herd cats (or build strong relationships).** The reality of this work is that it's all about people. You study people, and you work within groups of people (teams and stakeholders) to understand what you need to research, why you're doing the research and where it adds value in the transformation of a product, service or organisation.

  Inevitably, when you're working to effect real change, you deal with a lot of misaligned opinions, differing priorities and political dynamics. In UX, service design and design research, we often joke about herding cats, and the lessons we've had to learn in facilitating conversations and initiatives between people that have different ideas of what should be done or what's important. No tool can do this for you end to end. It's up to you to form positive relationships, listen to stakeholders and gently align all of your collaborators toward a common goal.

  This is why stakeholder management is a key throughline in this book... although, I encourage you to see it less as "management" and more as collaboration.

- **Strategy and storytelling will become your superpower.** Finally, when you put together your abilities to hold both empathy and context, and you become an expert in stakeholder alignment, you'll find power in your capacity to translate research findings into something highly valuable and tactical. This, combined with design storytelling, is the magic of design research — it's what allows your project to move from research findings to insights, and from insights to meaningful action. It's what wows stakeholders and compels them to make real changes to their products and services, and to make better experiences for their users.

Telling a compelling and motivating story requires an emotional connection to the research, as well as a strategic perspective on what will best serve your users while also driving incredible value and a return on investment (ROI) for the business. Once you have this, you become a master of design research.

In this book, I'm giving you every piece of advice I've collected over the course of my career to help you build long-term sustainability in your career, so you can keep doing the work you're passionate about AND ensure that your work actually has an impact, whether it's AI-assisted or not.

As a first step, let's look at why it's so hard to conduct successful design research and convince stakeholders of its value.

## The Design Research Knowledge Gap

Better experiences make for a better world. Most people working in UX, service design and design research have a deep-seated ambition to make an impact. So, naturally, when we join a new team or project, we tend to start out feeling creative, optimistic, curious and excited to make things happen.

But then, that starts to shift. We start hitting roadblocks and challenges: shifting priorities from leadership, feature releases disrupting our work, technology limitations, team silos, tight budgets that constrain our research, logistical barriers to connecting with real users, and stakeholders who don't see the point in our work. All that can leave us confused, discouraged, frustrated or burnt out, and it can get in the way of accomplishing anything meaningful.

Why does this shift happen?

The problem is, there's a gap between our formal training and the actual demands of the industry. I've read a lot of great books about design research while in school and throughout my career. They've helped me absorb the fundamentals and the broader steps involved, and they've often inspired me with examples of really innovative projects. But none of them prepared me for the demanding, multi-skilled work involved in actually effecting change.

*How you feel at the start of a new project:*

*How you feel a little later, when reality settles in:*

Let's take a look at the "expectation versus reality" for the experience of conducting design research in the industry.

| **What we think design research is** (What schools teach us) | **What design research really is** (What no one teaches us) |
|---|---|
| • Plan research activities and recruit users<br>• Conduct research with users to understand their needs<br>• Uncover insights and pain points<br>• Conceptualise solutions and recommendations<br>• Collaborate with multidisciplinary teams<br>• Create design and research artefacts like journey maps, personas and reports<br>• Conduct co-design workshops<br>• Present findings | All of the things in the left column, PLUS:<br>• Stakeholder alignment and expectation management<br>• Project management and product management<br>• Change management, training and communication<br>• Facilitation of difficult conversations<br>• Negotiation between the business and the user<br>• Systems thinking (seeing the forest for the trees)<br>• Avoiding being replaced by robots |

Practitioners in the UX and service design space simply aren't trained for all of these extra responsibilities ahead of time, but we're almost always placed at the centre of change, where those responsibilities fall on us. And success in the "real world" depends on handling them well.

When we don't, we prove the nay-sayers right, and we end up spinning our wheels, unable to do the good work and research that leads to change. It's a vicious cycle that's hard to get out of, and it can be enough to burn you out and send you running from the industry into a different career path. (But please, don't run. Trust me.)

# The Mountain That We Have to Climb

Does all of the above seem daunting? Well, it doesn't have to be this way. I'm just one example of the truth in that. If you're persistent and you apply the advice in this book, there are substantial rewards in your future.

Imagine getting approved budgets, resources and time to do the research you're passionate about, and running successful projects end to end with ease and confidence. Imagine captivating executives with your design storytelling and seeing your insights turn into real-life solutions that make a big difference in users' lives. And imagine being invited to talk strategy with executives and facilitate workshops that effect change on the organisation level, eventually becoming a valued leader of research-based design initiatives. It's all possible if you can demonstrate project success and prove the value of what you do.

I didn't start my career serving big-name clients and ushering in digital transformations left and right. Silicon Valley was tough, and starting my own agency was tougher. I weathered that journey with a mix of grit, trial and error, some foundational knowledge from school and a LOT of informal self-education.

I know how frustrating it is to be a designer or researcher out there in the world. It really can feel like you're Sisyphus pushing the rock up the mountain. You struggle to convince your directors and leadership of why you should be allowed to even start your research project, only to have it get cut partway through, because no one sees it as a strategic priority or understands its advantages. Or, you complete the project, but your insights and suggestions are brushed aside, your beautifully designed PDFs are put in a folder where dreams go to die (never to see the light of day again) and your future project proposals are declined. The rock goes up so high, only to start slipping down again.

It's important to acknowledge how hard this work can be when you feel like you're the only one trying to make a difference. But hopefully, you keep going. Because there are lots of great ideas out there to discover, and you're not wrong when you look at a product or service and think, "There has to be a better way." The world needs people like you to keep pushing forward.

With this book, my goal is to lighten the load. I want to empower more practitioners to get where they want to go faster, so you can start to see all those amazing things I listed come true for you... so that you can make experiences better and easier for those around you, and ultimately make the world a better place to live in.

## The Secrets to Project Success

Now that we've established the big "why" behind this book, we should address the "how." There's a huge difference between knowing how to run design research projects and knowing how to run *successful* research projects that make an impact. I will help you learn to do the latter.

As you read each chapter, you'll notice sections called "Action Advice" and "Alignment Advice." They're there to help you make the most out of each stage of your project by focusing on what matters to the decision makers.

They're centred around two factors that drive project success:

**Action:** You'll need to empower your stakeholders to invest in your research in the first place. You'll also need to inspire effective decisions about their products and services by providing them with actionable insights.

**Alignment:** Gaining alignment with your stakeholders is essential. You'll need their weigh-in and cooperation throughout your research project, so you can ensure that you're delivering on their goals, building trust and managing their expectations.

## How to Use This Book

This book is chock full of examples, practical advice, anecdotes from my own experiences, and methodical step-by-step guides for planning, conducting and analysing design research. (Anyone who works in the field of UX or service design should be able to find some nuggets in here, no matter your level of experience.)

I've intended for it to be a dual-purpose book. It should act as:

**A manual** for conducting each of the four key design research methods

**A success guide** for making an impact in the professional world (by winning over the hearts and minds of the decision makers and stakeholders who can approve, review and act on your research)

You can read this book **cover to cover**, to enrich the work and activities you're already doing, or **as a reference book**, to pick up when you need:

- **Ideas for how to build trust with stakeholders** and engage with them effectively (if you're not seeing movement on your projects)
- **A guide for planning effective research** when you're in the early stages of a project or haven't started yet and you want to make sure you're set up for success
- **Organised end-to-end guidelines** that you can use ad hoc as you move through any phase of a design research project, for detailed research method instructions, checklists and tips
- **A source of inspiration** if you've been doing the same process for too long and want a different perspective

As you read this book, my hope is for you to not only excel at specific design research methods, but also learn when and how to bring stakeholders and project team members on board (and fully appreciate why that's crucial). This will allow you to consistently solve real problems that users have, make their experiences easier or less frustrating, and build a long track record of undeniable successes in influencing high-level decision-making. That's the dream, and it's achievable. I've seen entire Fortune 100 company roadmaps change as a result of successful design research insights!

# 2 GAINING STAKEHOLDER BUY-IN

## Grow Influence and Build Trust

"Be so good they can't ignore you."
— Steve Martin

# Introduction

I couldn't launch into the "how" of conducting successful design research without first talking about stakeholder buy-in. It's not hard to find projects that need research, but it can be very hard to find stakeholders who will actually allow you the time and budget to conduct it. To convince them, you need to become an expert at stakeholder management and championing the "why" behind your research. That's what I'll cover in these next two chapters.

So many designers and researchers I talk to are really passionate about the work — they want to dive right into doing interviews and observations to understand user needs and then get going on conceptualising amazing digital solutions to the problems they uncover. In reality, that eager passion to transform products and services isn't always welcomed with open arms. After all, each organisation has its own ways of working and thinking. Stakeholders might already be convinced that they know all of the pain points without talking to users, or they may have already decided on a new direction for the business. Someone coming in from the outside trying to break that mould by suggesting to do research could easily be sidelined.

So, even though eager researchers just want to do the work they were trained for (i.e. sparking amazing digital transformations), they end up spending a lot of their time convincing people to let them do it. It's an exhausting part of the job, for sure — and it's also necessary.

But you don't have to push that boulder up the mountain alone. I'm going to help you approach it one step at a time. This chapter will teach you the mindset you need and concrete tips on how you can grow your influence, so that you can clear a path for the research you love with less struggle. You should refer to it in tandem with chapter 3, which will walk you through how to communicate the value of your work to the stakeholders that you're planning to sway.

# The Circle of Influence

To catalyse innovation through your research, (or to get your research project greenlit in the first place), you need to establish influence in an organisation. The first step in growing that influence is understanding what level of influence you already have, what level of influence is realistic to achieve, and what uncontrollable factors you'll need to deal with along the way.

This concept of a "circle of influence" comes from the book, *The 7 Habits of Highly Effective People,* by Stephen Covey, a well-known American educator, businessman and motivational speaker. While he uses this model to teach readers about personal development, I'll be using it as a framework within the world of design research. The circle of influence is a great tool for reframing your perspective when you're trying to get more support for design research because it reminds you to take a step back and look at the bigger picture. It can also lessen the frustration that comes along with constantly convincing people that your work has value and purpose.

Covey's model is broken down into three circles: your circle of control, your circle of influence and your circle of concern. I'll explain what each circle represents within a UX or design research context.

## STEPHEN COVEY'S CIRCLE OF INFLUENCE

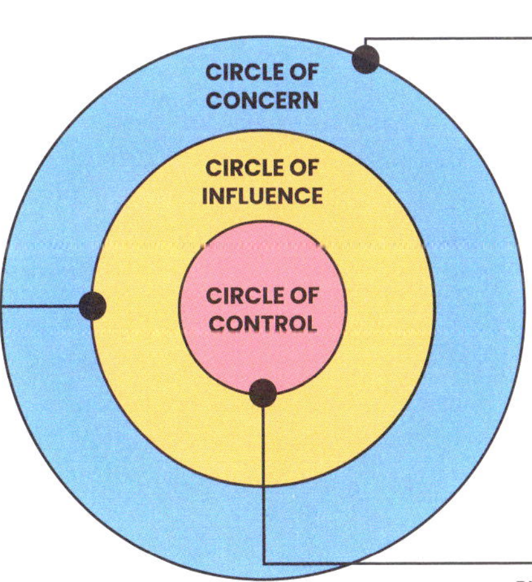


### CIRCLE OF CONCERN

**Wide range of concerns and no control**
The circle of concern contains the factors in an organisation that you have no control over.

Your circle of concern could include:

- Your organisation's values
- Their benefit and healthcare programs
- Their leadership team
- Their financial circumstances (layoffs, budget cuts, etc.)
- The behaviour, thoughts and feelings of those around you

### CIRCLE OF INFLUENCE

**The circle of influence** describes the factors that we can do something about, or indirectly control to an extent. As you gain influence in an organisation, you have the potential to affect more things.

Your circle of influence could include:

- Your team
- The projects you work on
- UX processes and practices used in your team
- Your organisation's understanding of design and research
- The stakeholders you interact with
- Your client or organisation's products and services
- User and customer experience
- Aspects of company culture

### CIRCLE OF CONTROL

**What we can directly control**
The circle of control refers to the factors that are in your direct control as an individual within the organisation.

Your circle of control could include:

- The quality of your work and deliverables
- How you choose to react to what others do and say
- Your knowledge of human-centred design
- The thoughts and feelings you have about your work and working relationships

Covey's model is so effective because it helps to distinguish between the things we can control and the things we can't, so that we can focus our energy where it matters — in this case, toward gaining stakeholder buy-in for research.

He teaches that focusing on your circle of concern actually shrinks your circle of influence. On the other hand, focusing on your circle of influence reduces your circle of concern.

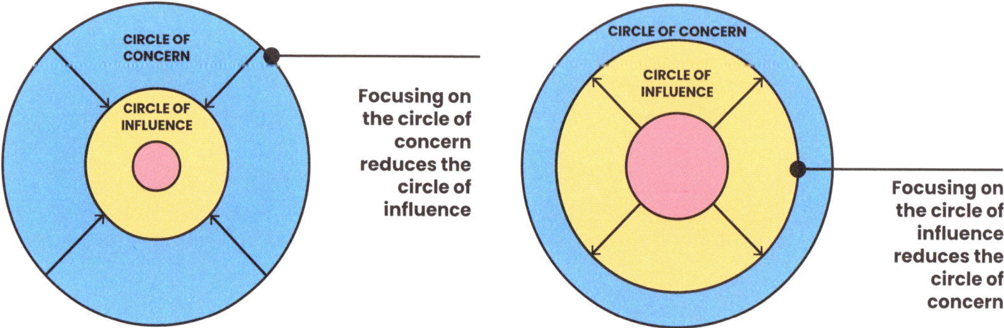


For example, say that you bring up the idea of doing some user interviews to a decision maker, and they shut the idea down during a team meeting. This makes you feel angry and defensive. So, you start to tighten your grip by saying defensive statements to contradict that individual, and maintain control of the plan. This reaction could actually discourage cooperation, have a negative impact on morale, and you could lose influence within your own product team.

On the other hand, if you're focused on growing your circle of influence, you're more likely to stop yourself from reacting defensively and focus instead on the things you can control — like your own thoughts and feelings about the situation. (Spoiler: I'll dig further into techniques for this in the final chapter.) You can choose to be positive and open-minded, take other ideas and perspectives into consideration and address concerns by incorporating other people's ideas into your plan. What concerns does this decision maker have, and why? What could you do to accommodate or address those doubts?

You might even decide to take the conversation offline, brainstorm solutions with your research team and/or stakeholders, and open a new discussion once you've worked together on a new plan. You never know — you could stumble onto an even better idea than the one you had.

To understand how this concept can be used to help you gain buy-in and grow your influence at work, I've mapped the different levels of an organisation within the circle of influence starting from the centre and moving outwards:

- **Your team**
  At this level, you can influence the tactical project.

- **Your department/division**
  At this level, you can influence the products and services your division works on.
- **The organisation**
  At this level, you can influence the organisation's strategy.

**CIRCLE OF INFUENCE IN THE ORGANISATION:**
(Think about influence in this way)

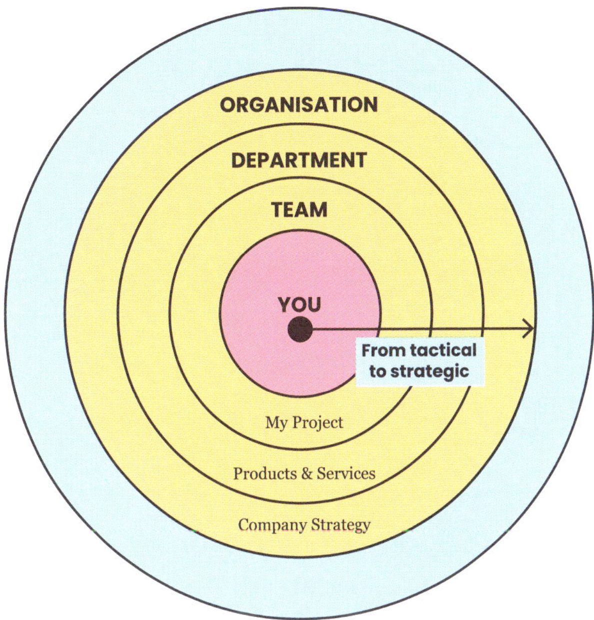


**You need to master each sphere one by one and work outwards from the centre.** This is a key part of using the circles of influence. If you try to grow your influence at the department level before you've gotten the support of your team, for instance, you could end up greenlighting an initiative that your team isn't on board with, or offending a key player. And that could cause a ton of other complications that might get in the way of your research advocacy.

As you follow this strategy, your circle of influence will start to grow, your circle of concern will start to shrink, and the type of work you're doing will go from more tactical (at the team level) to more strategic (at the organisation level). This will happen naturally, because as you establish yourself as a leader, others will gravitate toward you and see how you bring value to almost any conversation. They'll want to include you in more meetings and decision-making processes because they'll realise they love the way you think.

As you set out to increase your level of influence, it's normal to feel a little uncomfortable or intimidated. But the potential benefits outweigh the discomfort. If you use the strategies coming up in this section, you'll see the design recommendations from your research get implemented, you'll help your organisation place more value on design and research, and you'll gain more opportunities to lead projects and advance your career. You'll also find yourself being invited to higher-level strategic meetings, becoming a delegate for your design team and shaping the business roadmap.

# How to Grow Your Circle of Influence

Now that I've covered the high-level process and benefits of growing your circle of influence, let's look at how you can make that growth happen in your day-to-day reality as a design researcher.

## FOCUS ON YOUR CRAFT

When you first start working with a new team or organisation, it can be tempting to jump in and criticise an existing product or dictate what research should be conducted to improve the user experience. But doing this will alienate your stakeholders and make it harder to gain opportunities for research. Instead, if you want to capture your stakeholders' attention, you have to first prove that you're good at what you do. No one will take you seriously unless they see that you're an expert in your own right. So, before you even think of trying to influence others or champion design and research, you need to show your stakeholders that you're an expert, through the quality of your work, your knowledge of human-centred design and your deliverables. These things are directly within your circle of control, so they should be your starting point.

This means constantly examining what you're doing and pushing to improve your skills. You have to truly care about every bit of research you conduct, every deliverable you produce, every discussion you lead. "Sharpen the saw," as Covey says. Keep an eye on the details. Strive to be a master at each research method that you use, so that you yield consistently actionable insights every time. Plan your projects inside and out, and keep close tabs on them.

## UNDERSTAND THE BUSINESS

Every bit of work we do in design research serves as a means to an end, and that end is usually the growth or improvement of the business or organisation we're working with. To master stakeholder buy-in, you need to fully investigate the context of that business's needs, understand what priorities are important to your stakeholders and examine how their organisation sees and uses UX or service design to deliver on their goals.

The next section focuses on three strategies for improving your understanding of the business side: putting business needs first, focusing on stakeholder priorities, and using the design maturity scale.

### PUT BUSINESS NEEDS FIRST

In design research, your aim is to help organisations identify new opportunities to improve a user experience for the good of the — wait for it — business.

You read that right. Consider the business needs first, and how a solution might impact the bottom line, and you'll be able to win over any stakeholder. As designers and researchers, we tend to fixate on user needs, and as a result, we lose executives. They can't always see that what's good for the user is good for the business.

Of course, as the researcher, you innately care about the user. That is your job — to find out what they need, what bothers them and to advocate for them. BUT, you should always be thinking about the context of the business or organisation you work for.

Below are some tips to help you take on this mindset and reexamine your priorities.

- **Get curious about the way the business works.** Embrace that curiosity, even if all you have to look through are dry and dull annual reports or huge quarterly review decks full of business jargon. In my experience, there are gems buried in those bullet points. Reading annual reports has helped me see how design research could help transform those companies. It's also helped me understand what internal lingo I should use and which priorities I should link to my proposed research activities, so I can develop the "why" when I'm pitching new ideas.
- **Think of your work as "win–win."** Remember that user and business needs aren't mutually exclusive. If the overall business strategy is sound, the organisation and its users will be set up to benefit each other. When you understand which key performance indicators (KPIs) need the most improvement based on an organisation's greater goals, you can use your research to identify the reasons why performance is low in those areas. Then, you can make suggestions to improve not only the user experience in question but also boost performance and, potentially, profitability.
- **Plan to do a regular "sanity check" on your day-to-day progress.** You might not want to hear it, but everything you do should serve the end goal of helping to boost targeted KPIs and ensuring that your organisation gets ROI from your research. Of course, you will achieve this through a deeper understanding of the user, but it's important not to get lost in the weeds or let your users' thoughts and feelings take you too far on an unrelated tangent. Always look to your research goals and how they relate to the business. (Check out chapter 6 to read more about setting effective research goals.)

## FOCUS ON STAKEHOLDER PRIORITIES

If you want to take your stakeholders' needs to heart and serve them effectively, you'll need to fully understand what their high-level strategic priorities are, what they really care about and how to talk to them in a way that gets their attention. Otherwise, you could end up asking the wrong questions or studying the wrong things in your research. The end result will be ineffective insights and insignificant recommendations. Ultimately, this will devalue the work you're doing in the eyes of stakeholders, and you'll start to lose their trust. It'll be much harder to gain influence in the organisation or get more opportunities for doing research. Not an ideal scenario by far.

Get to know your executives and stakeholders with the same enthusiasm you have for getting to know your users. Let them know that you care about what they care about, and that your priority is to uncover information that will help them and the business shine. That's when your research will have real power. To investigate and familiarise yourself with stakeholder priorities, I recommend holding a stakeholder workshop (chapter 11), conducting informal stakeholder interviews (chapter 8) and doing some preliminary desk research.

Research + Business Priorities (illuminated by your stakeholders) = **IMPACT**

## USE THE DESIGN MATURITY SCALE

Design maturity describes an organisation's understanding of human-centred design and to what extent they do or don't value design and research. (It's synonymous with UX maturity, but covers a larger umbrella that includes service design.) The Design Maturity Scale is a great tool to help you think about where a business is starting from, what kind of resources they have and what attitude they have toward design internally. This will give you important clues for how to grow your circle of influence without rubbing stakeholders the wrong way or trying to do too much too fast.

There are a few different models out there that address design maturity, but, here is the **Design Maturity Scale** that I use:

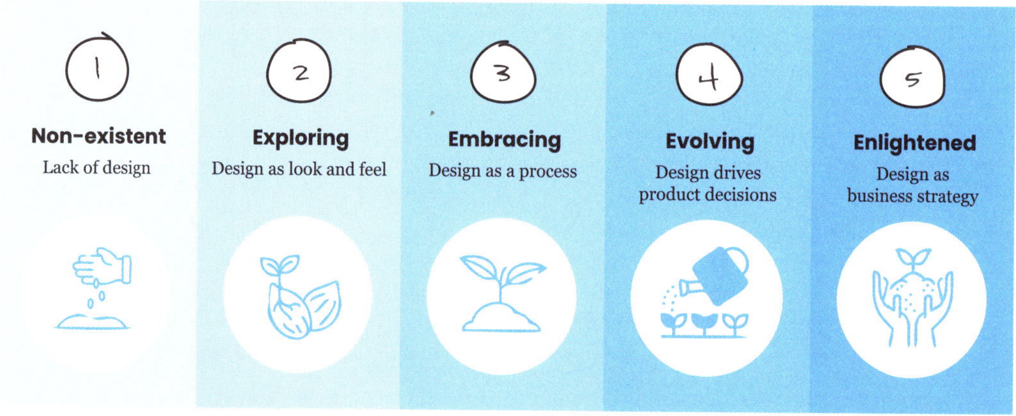


Here are some high-level steps to follow as you gear up to gain influence.

- **Identify your organisation's design maturity level.** Conduct a design maturity assessment to investigate how well the organisation understands and utilises the human-centred design process. Is it surface level, somewhat integrated, or truly a part of how the organisation approaches every day work?

- **Set your own expectations based on that level.** If your organisation is on the low end of the maturity scale, you obviously won't be able to just walk in and convince them to approve a budget for a six-month-long, large-scale research project. Set yourself up for success and save yourself frustration by managing your own expectations about what you'll be able to accomplish at the start. Keep the next rung on that design maturity scale in mind as a goal to work toward.
- **Tailor your approach for conducting research.** This includes what research you plan to do, how you plan to communicate and even who you communicate to and when. For example, with a low maturity organisation, you'll likely need to start with small wins and bite-sized projects first.

(**Note:** For more details about the Design Maturity Scale, see the online resource listed at the end of this chapter.)

## NAVIGATE COMPANY POLITICS

Once you have a good idea of how your organisation values design research, it's time to start investigating the power structures and dynamics within the organisation and finding your champions/decision makers. Niven Postma famously said, "Office politics are about relationship currency and influence capital." I couldn't agree more.

I've coached design and research practitioners of all levels who say things like, "I'm kind of above office politics," or "I'm a straight shooter. I'm just going to tell it like it is, and be honest." But creating real impact in the context of design research means exercising your diplomacy skills and sometimes softening the message to help your audience hear it. Being aware of the politics in your organisation will help you navigate them and avoid unnecessary friction as you push toward understanding user needs, design transformations and positive change in general.

To navigate company politics, you'll need to start from the centre, like I mentioned earlier in this chapter, with your team. Then, once you've successfully gained influence at the team level, you'll have opportunities to influence stakeholders at the department level, and eventually the organisational level.

Here are some key steps to navigating office politics:

- **Seek to understand:** Always seek to understand those around you first, then seek to be understood. Start by asking questions and listening. This is how you start to build great working relationships — by showing people that you appreciate their perspectives. Then, when you do voice your own thoughtful and well-informed opinions about the product or service that you want to improve, people will feel more seen by you, and they'll make the same effort to understand your point of view.
- **Seize opportunities:** Once you've got the "lay of the land," look for ways you can help, and actually start adding value (even if the ways you can help aren't research-related). Do this every chance you get! People will start to see you as a useful contributor and recognise your voice in meetings. If you're given a chance

to participate in an initiative or to do some initial research, or you see an opening where you can contribute in some way, don't hesitate. Seize the opportunity, and do it justice by doing a great job.

- **Take initiative:** As you start seizing opportunities to engage with stakeholders, you should also demonstrate your ability to proactively think of the business's needs and find new (and potentially surprising!) ways to be helpful, even if that helpfulness doesn't immediately translate to improving the user experience. The key is to prove the value of your skills, ideas and perspective by focusing on how you and your work can be of service, instead of blatantly pushing your agenda to greenlight research projects straight out of the gate.

Next, I'll outline some key ways that you can seek to understand, seize opportunities and take initiative at three levels: in your team, your department and your organisation.

## Navigate Your Team

Whether you've just formed a new team or you're joining an existing team as an outsider, avoid making any assumptions about the people who'll be working closely with you. If you can express interest in them, learn their working styles and win them over, they'll turn into your biggest supporters.

| | |
|---|---|
| 1 **Seek to understand** | • Where is the team doing well?<br>• Where are they struggling?<br>• What do they need to do their jobs effectively?<br>• Who's been there the longest?<br>• Who has influence? |
| 2 **Seize opportunities** | • Attend meetings where you can meet more team members.<br>• Facilitate workshops and lead meetings with organised agendas. |
| 3 **Take initiative** | • Identify process-related issues and offer to help with improving them.<br>• Try to conduct research below the radar, if your team's budget allows and it won't create problems.<br>• Be on the lookout for small ways to add value to your team. |

## Navigate Your Department

Once you've grown your influence at the team level, you can start to look for ways to influence your department and the products and services they work on.

| | |
|---|---|
| 1 **Seek to understand** | • What departments does the organisation have?<br>• What are their goals?<br>• Are there any conflicting or competing goals between departments? |
| 2 **Seize opportunities** | • Get involved in high-visibility projects.<br>• Find ways to talk about your work and tie it back to strategic goals. (More on this in chapter 3!)<br>• Speak up in meetings where there are executives and stakeholders present, once you're sure that you understand the business. |
| 3 **Take initiative** | • Present solutions, not problems.<br>• Ensure that your suggestions are clear, actionable and tangible. Your executives and stakeholders shouldn't need to read between the lines.<br>• Help them see how your insights relate to potential design concepts, and how those concepts can impact the business. |

## Navigate Your Organisation

Finally, once you've grown your influence to the department level, you'll be given more opportunities to be involved at the organisation level and across departments. You'll have earned these opportunities by establishing yourself as an expert in the eyes of stakeholders, and as the type of person who can think strategically and bring value to any conversation.

| | |
|---|---|
| 1 **Seek to understand** | • What are the business goals?<br>• What are the strategic priorities and initiatives?<br>• Who are the leaders?<br>• Read the annual report and watch the town hall meetings. If you find yourself stumbling on boring or confusing business jargon, reach out to a stakeholder who has time to answer your questions, or ask AI. |
| 2 **Seize opportunities** | • Share internal case studies or projects that you've led to success. Refer to them in meetings often or even post them in the hallways.<br>• Offer to do "roadshows" of your work. If you see that other teams are curious about a recent project you completed, offer to take an hour and present the project to them and their |

| | |
|---|---|
| | group. You never know what new research could come out of it. Don't squander this opportunity when it's given to you — roadshows are often the single best way to showcase great design research AND get buy-in for more projects that are cross-departmental. |
| 3 **Take initiative** | • Evaluate and measure the ROI of your research. Do some benchmarking to compare the numbers (e.g. task durations) before the organisation implemented your suggestions with what they look like afterwards.<br>• Build a business case for new research. Reach out to the data team or business analysts when you have free time and get relevant stats that you can reference.<br>• Do some desk research to uncover new initiative ideas. These new ideas should be geared toward business goals/pulling ROI. Include evidence to back them up. |

## FIND CHAMPIONS AND DECISION MAKERS

As you navigate the different levels of your organisation and systematically grow your influence, you should also be searching for key people who already have a significant amount of influence, and aligning yourself with them. There are two types of people within an organisation who can help enable your work: champions and decision makers.

**Champions** appreciate the work that you do, and are willing to advocate for it to others in the organisation. They should be positive, charismatic and open-minded people who can often be heard talking about innovation and change. They might be visionaries with big ideas or "do-ers" within the organisation who are excellent at getting things done. (You want both types of champions on your side.) Ideally, they'll also be influential people who hold sway across different departments and regularly attend meetings with colleagues outside of their immediate teams. Be on the lookout for people who are well-connected to decision makers and able to influence "higher-ups."

All that being said, remember: influence doesn't necessarily equate to powerful positions. Your champions don't have to be directors or C-suite executives, but they should know people in those roles. Make sure to foster and nurture your relationships with potential champions. Ask them what they're currently focused on, where they think the company is going, etc. Offer to help them on a project, even a small one, so they can get to know you and your work.

**Decision makers** have the power to greenlight your projects and initiatives. They may be in more senior roles, or they may have been at the company longer than others (although that's not always the case). They're budget holders (but they won't necessarily be your direct manager or boss), and they're in directorial, VP or C-suite level positions. They should have many of the same qualities as a champion... and, of course, it's possible for a champion to also be a decision maker.

Find ways to introduce yourself to them. Don't be shy — leaders are just people. If you see them in a meeting where you happen to be a fly on the wall, shoot them an email after the meeting to introduce yourself. The right decision maker will be interested in finding new opportunities that move the needle for the organisation (and that make them look good in the process!).

The decision makers and champions that you choose will need to understand and appreciate the value of design research and your value as a leader in the field. They might not always come to the table with this mindset at the outset. You'll need to persuade them by doing great work and educating them on why you'll be able to help the organisation meet its goals. (More on this in chapter 3.)

## BUILD TRUST

Another major part of gaining alignment and growing your circle of influence is trust. While I've personally found that building trust comes naturally (we generally want people to trust us), it takes time. That's where a steady approach and patience comes in, because this work is so important to the success of your projects and ultimately your career.

Just think about a scenario in your own life, where you trust someone implicitly to get a job done, and because of that you can let your stress fall away. As humans, we seek out people we trust for advice, and when someone we trust brings up a hard truth, we listen. At the same time, trust can easily be broken. A missed meeting or deadline, a forgotten communication, or a slight deviation from our typical selves or personalities can all create cracks in the foundation that we build with our stakeholders. This might sound daunting, but it's actually simple. Do what you say you're going to do, follow up often, show that you care and do a good job. AND, if you mess up, focus on a speedy repair. Own your mistake as quickly as possible and don't let it happen again.

### GROW YOUR INFLUENCE AT WORK

Become the **informal leader** of your team

TEAM

Become the **expert** for your stakeholders

DEPARTMENT
TEAM

Become the **trusted advisor** on all things related to user and customer experience

ORGANISATION
DEPARTMENT
TEAM

**TRUST**

From here → To here

As you build trust, you'll evolve from an informal team leader, to an expert within your department, to a trusted advisor within the organisation. You'll prove to your team, stakeholders and organisation leaders that you have their best interests in mind and that you'll deliver on their goals. That's the position where you'll find that anything is possible, where you'll have the highest level of influence and your research will have the biggest impact.

Trust enables teams to move more quickly. Building trust with your stakeholders means you'll be granted more buy-in for your research and more opportunities to impact product and service strategy. When teams don't have trust, collaboration falters or stops, communication lacks clarity, priorities shift constantly, team members disengage, leaders micromanage, and you start to lose autonomy (i.e. your circle of influence shrinks). In other words, you really don't want this to happen.

Here are five strategies for building trust with your stakeholders throughout any design research project. You can also use these as general guiding principles to apply to your stakeholder interactions outside of a project context.

**Collaboration:** When you bring people along, include them and ask for their thoughts and opinions. This shows that you care about what others have to say. It also shows that you're a team player and helps stakeholders and team members get used to hearing your voice. Work with team members and stakeholders to develop goals, plans and approaches for the research. Make it known that you're taking their opinions into consideration, and brainstorm ideas and solutions together in meetings and workshops.

**Expectation setting:** When you set the expectation ahead of time for how a project will play out and for the issues that could come up, you're doing two things: 1) you're showing your expertise, because you've been there, and done that, and you know what a typical project looks like, which automatically builds trust, because people trust experts... and, 2) you're avoiding potential pitfalls. When you warn people ahead of time about what will or could happen, this puts them at ease and prepares them for inevitable bumps in the road.

For example, they won't be surprised if participant recruitment takes a long time because you'll have already told them that could happen. Set expectations about the time and resources you'll need to complete your work effectively and get results. Establish a governance team, and be clear about how much time you'll need from them. Identify potential risks related to your projects, and develop risk mitigation strategies. (See chapter 5 for more on this!)

**Planning:** Along with expectation setting, you should create a solid plan. Research planning is important (as I say in chapter 6) because it offers an opportunity for you and your stakeholders to establish and align on a single source of truth for what your design research goals are, and how you'll achieve them. On the stakeholders' side, they can weigh in to ensure that the research plan connects to business goals. This involvement also creates accountability, so they'll pay closer attention to what's being planned. On your side, you can ensure that the research plan is sound and will actually yield actionable data and insights that will help the business.

Create a detailed plan for your research based on goals relevant to the organisation. Include a high-level roadmap with priorities and key milestones outlined, and make sure everyone involved agrees with the plan and the research approach. Develop and distribute a clear-cut project schedule and provide weekly updates on the plan as it evolves.

**Communication:** This is a no-brainer. Communicate, and be responsive — respond to all messages promptly, and don't let your stakeholders wonder about anything. Focus on expressing your ideas in clear and concise ways. Touch base with stakeholders whenever something important comes up, and show them they can count on you. Err on the side of overcommunicating, never going too long without checking in. Remind everyone of the vision, goals and objectives often, and use presentations and weekly meetings to maintain alignment. Make a point of establishing which stakeholders should be copied on which emails.

Another excellent communication practice: bringing up issues and red flags early on without being asked! Be honest and communicate if things are falling off-track, and if priorities need to be shifted, communicate with the team and stakeholders to get realigned. Never forget that your stakeholders' product or service is on the line (and their annual bonuses might be, too). Make them look good by ensuring the project runs as smoothly as possible.

**Working in the open:** Involve stakeholders in reviewing early works-in-progress (WIPs) and refrain from hiding your process and work behind a curtain. It will help them see and appreciate all the work and thoughtful thinking that went on behind the scenes, without any smoke and mirrors. This transparency helps to build trust. Take a participatory approach, and ask for stakeholder feedback and input at frequent intervals. You don't need to apply all of their feedback — you can use your expertise and push back (with clear and tactful justifications) if needed. Make sure to also work in shared spaces and with shared tools. Include your stakeholders whenever you can... except in situations where their presence might influence a research participant's answers.

Again, building trust won't happen overnight, but apply some patience and persistence, and it'll happen.

# Conclusion

While the UX and service design disciplines have grown significantly over recent years, a lot of business people and stakeholders involved in product and service design still don't fully understand research or why it's important. But that doesn't mean your circle of influence needs to stay small. With the right set of strategies and some confidence, even if that confidence is faked at first, you can build trust with stakeholders and help them see how research with real users can further their goals.

Ultimately, business leaders and the people working for them will want to make informed, data-driven decisions about the products and services they work on. Once they see the power of design research, the right decision makers will want to team up with you.

**Online Resources:**

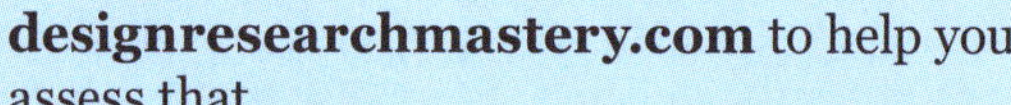

As I mentioned earlier, understanding your organisation's level of design maturity is key to growing influence and building trust. I've included a resource at **designresearchmastery.com** to help you assess that.

What you'll find:

- Design Maturity Guide

# Key Takeaways:

1. **To grow your influence, you need to first hone your craft and meet your own high standards.** If you want more people to listen to your suggestions, establish yourself as an expert. The best way to do that? Commit yourself to being truly excellent at your craft and "sharpening the saw." If you're really good at what you do, people will see you as an expert and they'll turn to you for advice.

2. **Utilise Stephen Covey's circle of control, influence and concern to understand how you can affect change in the organisation.** Move from the inside of the circle outwards, as you master your team, department, and organisation — growing your influence gradually from a tactical level to a strategic level.

3. **Instead of just focusing on the user, dedicate time to understanding the business and its current state.** Most products and services exist not only to serve users but to create a profit or make some kind of impact at the organisation level. Learn about those business needs as well as your stakeholders' specific priorities.

4. **Navigate company politics, instead of ignoring them or hoping they don't exist.** Seek to understand, seize opportunities and take initiative at at all levels in the organisation. Find your champions and stakeholders.

5. **Building trust is one of the most important parts of gaining stakeholder buy-in for your research.** When your stakeholders trust you, you can make design research initiatives happen faster and more effectively, and you'll have a higher chance of project success. That success can lead to even more opportunities. Again, the goal is to move from an informal team leader, to an expert within your department, to a trusted advisor within the organisation. You can build stakeholder trust by employing collaborative strategies, setting clear expectations, planning your research thoroughly, maintaining high standards of communication, and working in the open.

# GAINING STAKEHOLDER BUY-IN

## Communicate the Value of Your Work

"Good design is good business."
— Thomas J. Watson Jr.

# Introduction

When you're conducting design research, your job is to be the catalyst for change through the power of your insights. But before you can do the amazing work you're trained to do and prove to your stakeholders just how powerful those insights can be, you have to convince them to let you do research in the first place. Organisations are not always ready to question or closely examine their existing products, services and processes, even if the stakeholders or executives in charge say they welcome change.

As you work to gain influence within your team, department and your organisation based on the strategies in chapter 2, you should equip yourself with strong, well-thought-out arguments in favour of research, so that you can advocate for its value. That's what I'll cover in this chapter.

To be the best advocate possible, you'll need to exercise key design leadership skills and speak to your stakeholders and decision makers in a way that captures their interest. You'll also need to find ways to educate the stakeholders around you about the value of design research, and employ a realistic, gradual strategy for getting design research projects off the ground.

I'll dive into each of these approaches in detail, and provide you with related tips.

# Design Leadership Skills That Get Results

Before you start talking about design research to anyone who'll listen, you need to set the stage and present yourself as a leader. In this discipline, that means adopting some key design leadership skills. These are often called "soft skills." People who learn them become convincing negotiators and better design leaders. They can help you get what you need out of organisations, companies and people, and ultimately help you get buy-in for your research. This book will guide you in exhibiting these skills at each stage of a research project.

**Advocacy:** This one goes without saying, but it deserves some emphasis. If you want people to invest in design research, you need to be effective at communicating its value to your stakeholders, and any other leaders that have influence over your potential project. This involves understanding your cause on a deeper level, projecting confidence and being persistent. As design research advocates, we have to "fight the good fight" and push every day to make our voices (and the voices of our users) heard.

**Diplomacy:** Because of the cross-functional nature of design projects, you, the researcher, need to work well with lots of different types of people from different disciplines, like marketing, engineering, product management, etc. You'll also need to manage stakeholder expectations throughout your project when inevitable issues come up and normal pivots happen. To perfect the art of diplomacy, you'll need to be both assertive and tactful, learn to read the room and balance business requirements with user needs.

**Empathy:** Empathy is central to design research, but researchers typically think about empathy in relation to users. To be a true leader, you need to place just as much emphasis on holding empathy for your stakeholders and team members. It's important to understand what might be going on in their world, and the pressures they may be facing that can ultimately affect the success of your work. To fully embrace this mindset, I recommend doing an empathy mapping exercise, but focused on your stakeholders instead of on your users. (For an empathy mapping template, see the resources linked at the end of this chapter.)

**Facilitation:** In this case, I'm not talking about conducting co-design workshops within your project team, although that type of facilitation is also crucial. Here, I'm talking about a higher level of facilitation. This includes navigating difficult conversations in meetings, dealing with opposing perspectives and reining people in when they're digressing – even if those people are intimidating executives. Practitioners who can easily summarise next steps and action items, or steer a ship back on course when there's conflict, disagreement or uncertainty (and do all of this while maintaining positive relationships), are seen as great leaders.

**Organisation:** You might not immediately associate being organised with being a leader, but researchers who hold influence come prepared to take on any challenge, whether they have a team for support or they're working solo. They're able to keep files and materials organised and easily accessible, and they can handle many moving parts at once without missing a beat.

Ultimately, great design leaders excel at planning and structuring work and priorities, not just for themselves, but also for their teams and their stakeholders. They know their projects inside and out, and are able to consistently demonstrate this to their stakeholders, building an unshakeable level of trust. Just as I alluded to in chapter 2, once they know you've got things under control, they'll be more likely to understand when or if problems arise, and they'll feel confident giving you more responsibility.

**Storytelling:** As a researcher, you need to be a great storyteller and understand how to captivate an audience. All of your hard work conducting research adds up to that moment where you deliver insights to your stakeholders in a report or presentation. Weaving a story through your insights can help your stakeholders stay engaged while absorbing copious amounts of information. It can help them empathise with users and ultimately decide to act on your recommendations. They may also be less likely to forget about your recommendations! Jerome Bruner, a well-known American cognitive psychologist, famously said that stories are 22 times more memorable than facts.

If you commit to delivering appealing, professional research deliverables that tell a compelling story, you'll be more likely to impress executives, have your work passed around to decision makers and get your insights acted on. They'll be able to understand and resonate with the truths you're uncovering and be more willing to take your recommendations for innovation and product/service improvement seriously. (For a walkthrough of insights reporting best practices, see chapter 13.)

# Meet Decision Makers Where They Are

When you start growing your influence outside of your direct team, you're going to be striking up conversations with people who have very different ways of thinking about and talking about their priorities.

If you want to help your executives and stakeholders understand the value of design research, you don't want to leave them feeling confused or at odds with your vision. In chapter 2, I walked you through strategies for understanding the business needs of your organisation and your stakeholders' priorities. As you learn about those needs and priorities, you want to prove that they matter to you, and that your work is focused on helping stakeholders achieve their goals. The strategies I unpack in this section will help you do all of the above effectively.

## USING LANGUAGE TO YOUR ADVANTAGE

Designers and researchers aren't taught how to speak in terms that executives and business leaders understand and care about. Early in our careers, instructors and other designers or research professionals assess our design acumen by how well we know our design jargon, our methods and our philosophy. But these are not the same things that a Chief Technical Officer (CTO) cares about, for instance.

In fact, in my experience, executives who are subjected to design jargon tend to sigh, eye-roll and flat-out ignore designers during meetings. They might purposefully leave those practitioners out of pivotal conversations or refuse to approve their projects. The best way to avoid these pitfalls and ensure that people are really listening to you: learn the way your stakeholders talk and start talking like they do.

I remember the moment I started doing this. I was a few years out of school and was starting to get annoyed by people telling me I was "green." (This type of comment usually comes from seasoned, jaded folks who are quick to judge your ideas as naive.) So instead of excitedly launching into all the cool things I thought we should study and the amazing journey maps we could create, I focused on listening. I was lucky to attend a few meetings with executives, and I decided to dedicate my attention to really hearing them — what they worried about, what words they used, what their motivators were. I realised we had the same goals, and all I had to do was connect my enthusiasm about investigating the user experience to their motivators (like customer churn, market share, etc.). Communicating from a place of mutual interest was much easier than I'd thought and I started to slowly build up trust and influence that would propel my career forward. It started first with listening, and THEN speaking.

Here are some tips to help you strike up meaningful conversations with your stakeholders:

- **Drop the jargon.** In UX, service design and in a lot of tech-related disciplines, we love talking about wireframes, personas, journey maps, service blueprints, etc. But stakeholders might not be familiar with these terms, and might feel alienated by them.
- **Talk in terms of results, not deliverables.** The tactics and ground-level activities in your research project are your responsibility. Focus on the potential outcomes of your work, and what effects you could bring about for their organisation.
- **Identify your differences and adjust.** Take note of the phrases and words you and your stakeholders use to refer to the same things, and alter your vocabulary to match.

I've put together some examples of ways that you might change your language:

| Designer/Researcher Term | | Stakeholder/Business Term |
|---|---|---|
| Users | → | Customers |
| Pain Points | → | New Opportunities |
| Poor Experience | → | Low Satisfaction |
| Better Experience | → | Higher Retention |

## CONNECTING YOUR RESEARCH TO ROI

While every business is different, return on investment is always going to be a top priority and concern. Businesses need to be profitable. Even in public sector organisations, stakeholders have to be conscious of where their money is going, and be able to assess whether the results justify spending tax payer dollars — in fact, they often face more scrutiny.

So, if you want to convince your stakeholders of the power of design research and get them to listen, connect the research you want to do with their "why," i.e. the business impact. This section highlights specific actions that will help you communicate this connection effectively.

**Investigate the current state, and use hard numbers.** Decision makers deal in numbers to set goals and measure their growth. The majority of the design research you'll conduct will be qualitative, and stakeholders might view qualitative data as "fluffy" or not concrete enough to help them make business decisions. Your best chance of captivating them is to dig into analytics. Find someone in the organisation that can share their key performance indicators and historical performance data. Compare that performance to industry benchmarks, and investigate the current benchmarks the organisation is using. How are things measuring up? What areas are lagging? Then, start looking at ways design could help boost weaker areas.

You should also look beyond these KPIs for neglected areas that are costing them money or where they're not living up to their full potential. For example, are they examining their internal business processes? Are those processes clunky and inefficient? Could they save money by improving them?

To help you, here are some real life examples of KPIs to look into:

- **Support call volume and cost:** How many customers are calling in for technical support? How much does it cost the company every time they receive a support call?
- **Support call duration:** How long are calls on average, and how long does it take to resolve issues by phone?
- **Claim processing time:** How long does it take to create a claim, review a case file or process an application?
- **Customer churn and user drop-off data:** How many customers are "dropping off" (i.e. discontinuing their transactions with the business)? How has the churn rate changed over time? When are customers dropping off? Where in their journey do users decide to cancel their membership or not renew, and why?
- **Churned revenue:** Beyond the churn rate, what's the revenue impact of those lost customers? (This is typically calculated by considering the average monthly recurring revenue, average contract value or lifetime value of churned accounts.)
- **Duration of key business processes:** How long are they taking, and is that

amount of time necessary? Could it be reduced from two weeks to 48 hours with some well-designed changes?

- **Number of people involved in key business processes:** If there are a lot of different people involved, there's a high chance that teams are working in silos and doing duplicate manual entry work. There probably isn't a clear sense of where the process connects between one person and the next.
- **Number of tools being used in key business processes:** Are users having to use 11 different pieces of software to get one job done? If so, there might be an opportunity to streamline the process.

These are all numbers that you can start investigating and using as benchmarks to compare the current state to a possible future state where processes, products and services are improved. (And you can move towards those improvements by employing design research.)

**Pull industry stats and citations that highlight the value of design research.** Do some digging on your side to find studies, reports and arguments about the financial benefits of design and research. Make sure to cite reputable sources, like Forbes, Harvard Business Review or other popular sources in your area. You should be able to confidently stand behind these quotes. (For a list of useful stats and facts that tie design research and design thinking to ROI, see the link to online resources at the end of this chapter.)

**Compile all of this evidence, keep it on hand and wait for your moments.** Chances are, you won't be given an explicit opportunity to present a business case to leadership in your organisation. If you are given the chance, make good use of the industry stats mentioned above, triple check your slides and rehearse what you're going to say. Seize the opportunity and thank your lucky stars! Otherwise, if you're like most of us and you're not getting formal opportunities to argue for design research, you'll want to look for small opportunities to speak up in meetings and bring up some of the points you've collected. Make sure they're highly relevant to the conversation.

**Example 1:**

You might be sitting in on a call, muted and listening, when an executive points out that they're losing a ton of customers at this one point in their acquisition funnel. They express some frustration and they start making some guesses as to why the churn is happening. That's where you could unmute, jump in and suggest that design research will help them find out the real reason for the churn. (And, ideally, you'd back up that fact with an example of a company that leveraged design research to solve a related problem.) Again, you can't be afraid to speak up. You'll need to find your voice in those rooms and project confidence.

**Example 2:**

There can also be power in bringing up personal experiences you've had with similar products and services. Not too long ago, I was on a project with a client and they were guessing at some of the reasons why their Net Promoter Score (NPS) was low. I had actually just recently had my own interaction as a customer with that same business, and it was so bad that I had wanted to leave and take my money elsewhere. I brought up my anecdote on the call with the executives and explained exactly what had happened. They were very intrigued. I told them, "Now you've heard my story, and you have an idea as to why your NPS score could be low, imagine if you could talk to 20 or 30 other people like me and find out the real truth behind their ratings. How powerful would that be for changing things internally and keeping more customers?"

The execs knew the answer, and ended up signing on for more research as a result. You see, sometimes, it's about reminding executives and stakeholders (who tend to be far removed from the experiences of their users) exactly what a frustrating experience could look like, and helping them recognise that they are not the user. This invaluable reality check can really inspire them to find out exactly what is going on.

## COMMON BUSINESS DRIVERS

To help you prepare for conversations about ROI, here are some examples of common business drivers that effective design and research can impact. The more of these you can tie your work back to, the better. Bringing these up will also make stakeholders understand that you care about what they care about, and that you've put a lot of thinking into how you can help.

- **Reducing risk for product launches:** So much money and time goes into product and new feature launches, and expectations are usually high. At the same time, there's a lot of room for failure, especially if an organisation isn't taking direction from user feedback before sinking their money into an idea. Your business case can show them how design research could prevent wasted resources: by finding out if a product, service or feature is solving a need up front, instead of finding out late and scrambling to fix things post-launch.

- **Increasing market share:** Growth is a universal priority for businesses, especially those that are backed by investors. Connect design research to that growth opportunity and explain how deepening their understanding of user needs and pain points will allow them to win more of the market (because great products attract more customers).

- **Reducing customer churn/increasing customer retention:** Generally, the cost of gaining a new customer is higher than keeping an existing one. Savvy leadership will never underestimate the value of their retention rate, especially if they're providing a subscription-based service. (These are also key KPIs that most businesses, especially SaaS companies, will already be monitoring closely.) Conducting research can illuminate the customer journey and help you identify specific parts of the product or service that need to be improved, so you can reduce customer churn at those touchpoints.
- **Getting to market faster:** Investing in design research at the start of the project might feel like you're slowing product development down, but in reality, you'll speed it up, because you'll be designing the "right thing" from the start. You'll uncover hidden user needs and unique opportunities for innovation or that might have flown under the radars of competitors. Your stakeholders can use this information to get new ideas out to market sooner, gaining an advantage and avoiding the frustrating delays they might have experienced if they'd built their products and services based on assumptions, with no real research to back up their decisions.
- **Streamlining business processes:** KPIs related to internal productivity and operational efficiency ("lagging indicators") can create just as much impact on ROI as those more related to future performance and customer growth ("leading indicators"). If you can point out preventable loss from out-of-date or redundant internal systems, you can make a great argument for doing a research-based transformation.

## HANDLING STAKEHOLDER OBJECTIONS AND FEARS

When you pitch the idea of investing in research, you're not going to be met with a resounding "yes" every time. Your stakeholders might express objections and fears that seem to poke holes in your argument. To give yourself the best chance of success, you'll want to come prepared with tactful, reassuring and carefully considered responses to the objections and fears that your stakeholders are likely to bring up. This is a typical practice in sales, and it can also help you gain buy-in for research.

These are the most common objections and fears I've run into throughout my career, with scripts for responses that have proven effective.

### Common objections to conducting design research:

| Objection 1 | Response |
|---|---|
| "We already know what our users want." | **We are not our users.** It's very important to remember this. Instead of making business decisions based on our assumptions, we should make them based on real data. By doing this research, we'll understand our users better and find their unmet needs, so that we can find new areas of opportunity and improvement. |

Creating empathy maps and looking at business analytics can only take us so far in understanding users. We don't live in their heads. We can't truly empathise with them or predict their needs when we're working from assumptions. Nothing can replace the value of actually talking to users and coaxing truthful, non-biased responses out of them.

| Objection 2 | Response |
|---|---|
| "We don't have time to do all of that research." | I understand, however, doing research up front will actually save us time and money in the long run. It will take more time to fix issues after the product (or service) is launched than it will to make sure we're designing the right product from the beginning. |

If you've seen launches fail first-hand because of a lack of user understanding, feel free to bring up that experience, and express your confidence that you can help them avoid running into the same issue.

| Objection 3 | Response |
|---|---|
| "Our customers don't want to talk to us. How would we even find people to participate in this research?" | That's a valid concern, but there are several ways we can identify and enlist customers for help. I recommend we provide a monetary incentive for participation, and I can develop an achievable recruitment plan to get people involved. |

This response reassures stakeholders that you're an expert at what you do, and that you know how to find people that will participate in research. Make sure to display total confidence when addressing this objection.

**Common fears about research:**

| Fear 1 | Response |
|---|---|
| "I don't want to bother or annoy our customers." | Customers who sign up to participate will be very happy to be asked their opinion, and to get a chance to impact your product or service. In fact, being invited to participate in the research will make them feel valued, and it will increase their loyalty. |

Stakeholders often worry that asking for their customers' help will turn them off and develop a negative relationship. But in reality, users and customers are generally happy to be included and valued for their input. I've been conducting research for well over a decade, and this has been my experience across the board.

| Fear 2 | Response |
|---|---|
| "What if our customers say something negative? Will that reflect poorly on me or my team?" | Design research is meant to uncover pain points. This is a normal part of the process. In fact, the goal is to find them. Having this knowledge can put you ahead of your competitors. Pain points are a gold mine of opportunity for new features, products and services that will bring in more customers. |

The stakeholder you're talking to probably has some KPIs or professional goals attached to how well a project is doing and how that project is perceived. They might be afraid that your research will reflect poorly on them and that they'll be blamed for any deficiencies. This can be a major deterring factor for conducting research, so addressing it and reassuring them should be a priority.

| Fear 3 | Response |
|---|---|
| "I need to be part of those conversations with users so that I know what's happening and can make sure we're staying on track." | Your presence in the interviews may actually hinder our ability to uncover the best insights. It might create biased responses or self-censoring on the part of the user. To ease your concerns, let's build the interview protocol together and have regular debriefs. |

Your stakeholders might be afraid of losing control of the project. If they're the ones greenlighting it and if goes wrong, they might feel like their reputation is at stake. I've had stakeholders ask to sit in on user interviews or even ask to conduct the interviews themselves.

Bring them into the process while establishing some boundaries. Reassure them that they'll be kept in the loop the whole time, and that you're not going to work in silos or suddenly pull out some big shocking reveal. Debriefing at regular intervals can help a lot. You might even find them asking for less frequent debriefs over time, as their trust in you grows.

## Start Small and Educate Allies

Now that you're prepared for common stakeholder objections to research, you can start (gently) pushing to conduct research. Avoid overdoing it with your first research initiatives. It's very hard to go from "zero to 100," especially with organisations that have low design maturity.

Stakeholders need to dip their toes in, and you need to make some measure of progress, even if it's slow. Focus on small, incremental wins at the beginning until you can build some momentum.

Try out these approaches to help stakeholders warm up to the research process.

**Ask to do some quick informal research.** Don't show them a potentially overwhelming six-month-long research plan to start off with — you'll work up to that. Instead, propose a shorter study, maybe six weeks long. That might mean you only interview 8–10 trusted users to start with. But it will be enough to prepare a light insights report and a couple of personas, to give them a taste of how useful design research can be. Come prepared with a plan, and make sure to show off any interesting ideas and perspectives that you come across.

**Pitch validation research.** This tends to be a more approachable type of research to start with for organisations with lower design maturity, because it identifies issues in the current state without the same insinuation of full-on digital transformation, or the scary thoughts of "starting over" that people sometimes associate with discovery research. Put together a short, simple proposal outlining what you want to do and how the results will benefit the business. For example, you might start with a round of usability testing examining an existing feature that could benefit from incremental improvements.

**Keep an eye out for any opportunity to do research.** Was there a recent drop in numbers for a department's KPIs? Are people confused about why the numbers dropped? Try to work your way into that conversation.

Once you've figured out how to speak your stakeholders' language and you've conducted some successful preliminary research, you can dive into educating them about the value of the work you've done — and the potential value of the work that you hope to do going forward. Even if the organisation in question sits high on the Design Maturity Scale, there's always room for more education. After all, you're a new perspective coming in with fresh eyes and an eagerness to do your research and plead your case.

Here are some good tactics for creating awareness:

- Add case studies to the organisation's intranet
- Print and post-up your design artefacts on the walls in the office
- Host town hall meetings or ask to present in one
- Share interesting blogs and articles
- Put together webinars or lunch-and-learns and promote them

Again, this process won't happen overnight. You'll need to slowly build education and awareness over several months, but there will be signs along the way that it's working, including positive feedback from colleagues and more questions coming at you during meetings.

# Conclusion

Researchers who conduct successful projects have to wear a few different hats. Researchers who go on to be accomplished, strategic leaders wear even more. Even though you might feel removed from the "business" side of day-to-day operations, everything you do as a researcher has the potential to make a big strategic and financial impact. Once you fully appreciate that, and you've done some research on your organisation, you'll be ready to develop tactics and arguments supporting the true value of design research.

Whatever you do, remember that research conducted in isolation from business objectives and decision makers isn't research that will make an impact. No matter how exciting and meaningful an insight is to you, it won't translate well to your stakeholders if it's not aligned with their priorities.

**Online Resources:**

I've put together a couple of resources that can help you advocate for the value of design research and empathise with your stakeholders — both are at:

**designresearchmastery.com**

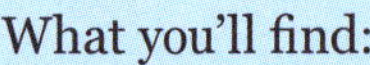

What you'll find:

- Design Research ROI Examples
- Empathy Mapping Template

# Key Takeaways:

1. **To become a stand-out design leader that stakeholders will listen to and respect, you should practice and build these key "soft" skills:**
   - Advocacy
   - Diplomacy
   - Empathy
   - Facilitation
   - Organisation
   - Storytelling
2. **To advocate effectively for your design research projects, you need to meet decision makers where they are and relate to their perspective.** Some strategies that will help you in this are:
   - Avoiding design jargon and talking in terms of results
   - Connecting your research to ROI (in actual numbers)
   - Speaking to common business drivers (like reducing churn and getting to market faster)
   - Handling stakeholder objections and fears with confidence
3. **When it comes to fighting for your design research initiatives, make sure to start small and build from there.** Giving an organisation a taste of what you can do is a persuasive tactic, but if you try to do too much all at once, you could scare stakeholders away. Choose your moments wisely and inch your way in gradually with modest but effective research projects.
4. **You can create allies and attract champions for design research by educating people about your work.** Make use of one-on-one interactions, webinars, lunch-and-learns, company intranets and town hall meetings to share resources (like relevant case studies and articles) as well as clear examples of your previous research and how it added value.

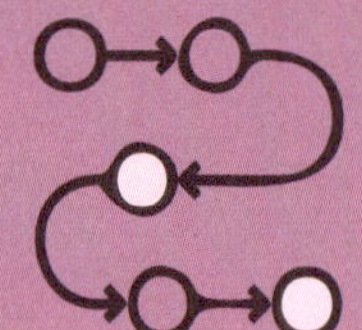

# DESIGN RESEARCH FUNDAMENTALS

"Everything is designed. Few things are designed well."
— Brian Reed

# Introduction

Back in chapter 2, I emphasised "focusing on your craft" as an essential component to gaining influence within an organisation. If your stakeholders see you as an expert, they'll be more likely to listen to you and even help you gain buy-in for your research from other key decision makers. Being an expert at your craft includes knowing your design fundamentals off by heart, having a deep understanding of what human-centred design really means, and being strategic about the role that you, the design researcher, can play in that greater process.

Revisiting these core concepts with a "beginner's mindset" can help you plan and conduct research in ways that's highly relevant to your overall project objectives, and avoid wasted effort from using the wrong research methods at the wrong times.

If you're already very confident in this area, you might want to use this chapter as a reference for educating your champions and allies, and enhancing the design maturity of your organisation. Either way, I recommend at least skimming through the sections, so you know why I'm emphasising certain parts of the process, and so you know what I'm talking about when I reference the "Six-Stage DRM Process" later on in the book.

If you come from an interdisciplinary background or you don't have formal training in design, this chapter can help you communicate your ideas more clearly to project teammates, with added knowledge about the greater design process and how your research fits in.

# The Importance of Human-Centred Design

Design is everything. I'm not just saying that because of the part it's played in changing my life and propelling my career forward. I literally mean that design is essential and inescapable in our daily lives. Every human experience is designed intentionally or not, whether it's an interaction with a product, service, a public space, a roadway, or even a traffic sign. Some fun examples I often reference are:

- **Push/pull doors:** Which way does the door open? How can something so simple make you feel inept?
- **Renewing driver's licenses and car insurance:** Why is this so annoying and unclear every time?
- **Using a can opener:** My hand hurts and the can isn't fully open...
- **Shopping in a grocery store:** Where is the oat milk?
- **Finding your way through an airport:** Stressed at the airport, rushing to make your connecting flight? Where is security for international connections?
- **Visiting the emergency room at a hospital:** Who doesn't love the long and inaccurate wait times, the smells, the sounds, the wall colours and the uncomfortable chairs?

This list might have awoken some emotions in you, but these experiences are all part of the average human existence. They might be good, they might be bad, and in most cases, they could be designed to be much better.

**Human-centred design (HCD) is an approach to design that places the needs, behaviours and challenges of human beings at the forefront of the design process.** Design research is a key component of this approach and to the design process as a whole, because it uncovers those needs, behaviours and challenges, which then inform the transformation or improvement of products and services. There are countless different types of humans in this world, and it would be impossible to understand every single one of them. The emphasis on humanity here is about relating to human user groups and stepping into their shoes... via well-conducted research.

# Design Research and the Design Process

"Design" is a big umbrella term — there are many different kinds of design, including the design of physical products, space design, wayfinding design, etc. While airport layouts and push/pull doors are fun analogue examples for understanding HCD at a fundamental level, this book concentrates on design research that informs the design of digital products and services. And that's the lens I'll also be using throughout this chapter.

The form of design research I'm talking about is useful for any practitioners whose work is based in "digital transformation" and redesigning digital touchpoints. It can also be incredibly helpful for understanding end-to-end user and customer experiences with non-digital touchpoints... but, of course, a common motivation for businesses to investigate non-digital touchpoints is actually to figure out how to "digitise" them in a way that enhances those experiences and helps the bottom line.

There are five phases of a typical design process:

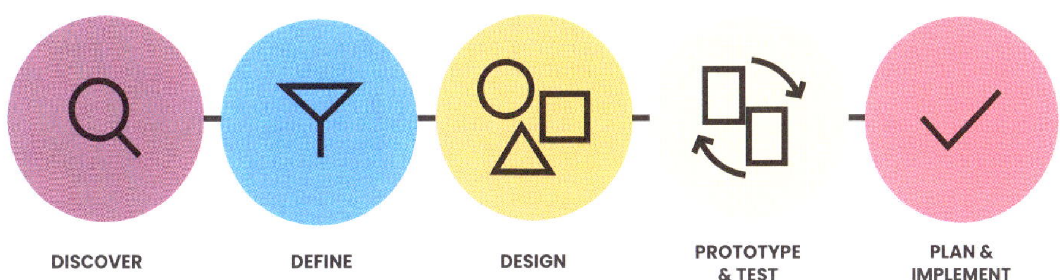


As a refresher, let's walk through the design phases at a high-level, keeping in mind that **the "discover" and "define" stages are the focus of this book.** Putting enough time and effort into these two phases upfront will help you ensure that your product or service solves the true needs of users, because you'll be designing based on real user data instead of assumptions.

| | |
|---|---|
| **Discover** | Conducting research to uncover problems with a product or service, or to find out the "why" behind a known problem |
| **Define** | Making sense of the data from your research, framing the data into insights and defining in detail the design problem(s) to be solved |
| **Design** | Conceptualising ideas for solutions and translating those into actual designs, from low-fidelity to high-fidelity |
| **Prototype and Test** | Turning concepts into non-final working versions (prototypes) and validating the design(s) with users and stakeholders, through things like usability testing or rapid prototyping sessions |
| **Plan and Implement** | Bringing your designs to life by creating feature roadmaps, working with product and engineering teams to develop them, generating assets and design systems, etc. |

In reality, the design process isn't completely linear. It's iterative, and many phases or stages will end up happening in parallel. For example, after you design something, you should prototype and test it, iterate on the design, test the new iteration(s), and so on.

Now, I couldn't talk about the design process without giving a nod to the famous "double diamond" created by the British Design Council. And it's important to review because I'm proposing a spin on it later on in this chapter.

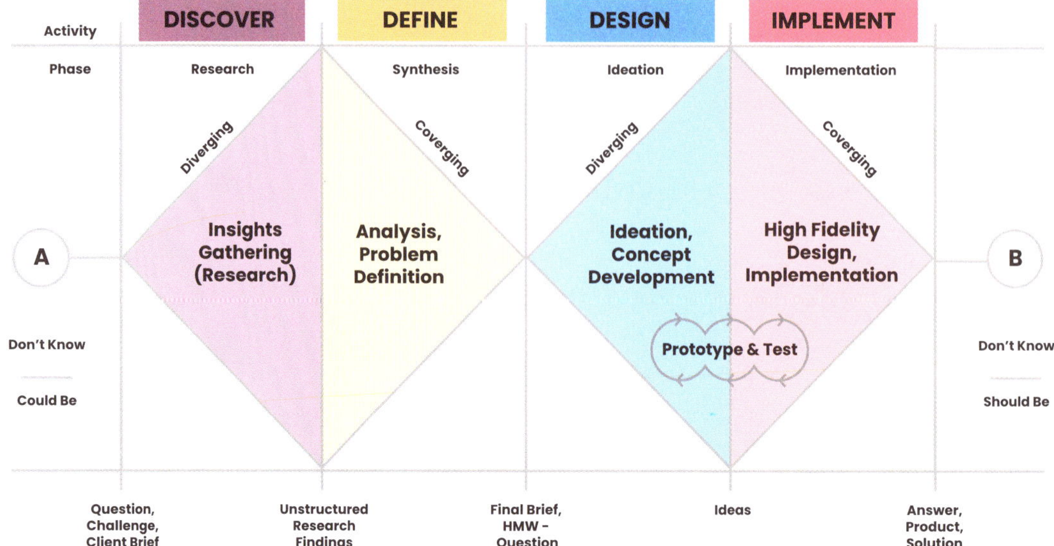


In the first half of the first diamond, you start in the "discover" phase, where you're **diverging (opening)** by doing research and gathering insights. Then, in the "define" phase, you're **converging (closing)** through data analysis, framing insights and defining the problem.

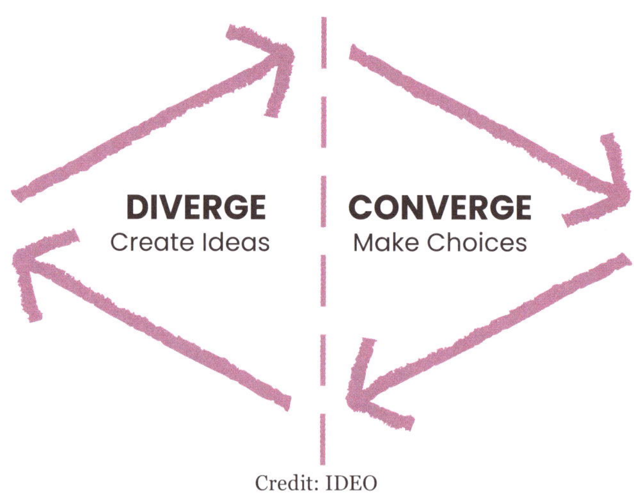


Credit: IDEO

In the second diamond, you're diverging/opening up again in the "design" phase as you ideate and brainstorm, come up with concepts, and maybe do some rapid prototyping. Then, you're converging again as you enter into the "implement" phase, where you're narrowing your concepts down into more high fidelity designs, you're testing prototypes with users, and you're working with product teams and engineering to bring the final designs to life in the form of an application, website or service.

# The "Fuzzy Front End" of Design

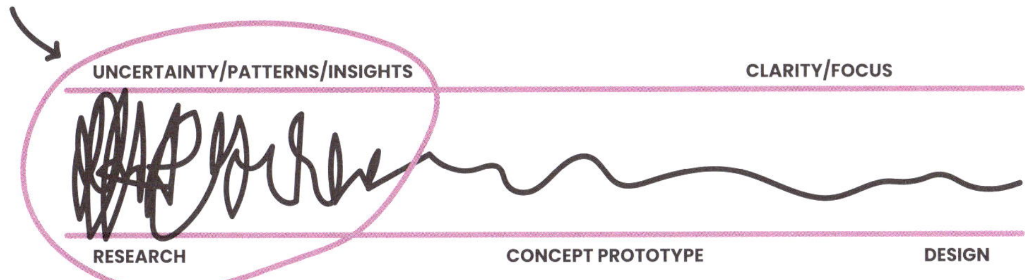


Chances are, you've seen the diagram above before — it's called the "design squiggle." It was created by Damien Newman and it's meant to demonstrate those very uncomfortable moments of divergent thinking at the beginning of the design process, where the direction of your design project is uncertain. We call this uncomfortable and ambiguous space the "fuzzy front end" of design. As design researchers, we live for the most part in this space... which is what we should be doing, because it's where game-changing, ground-breaking ideas start.

The problem is, the "fuzzy front end" gets a very bad rap with stakeholders in general, because:

- **Most practitioners struggle to keep their stakeholders in this space long enough to do the research required for gaining game-changing insights.** This demands a level of project management, trust building, and expectation setting that isn't really taught in design schools.

- **Few are able to conduct research (planning, execution and analysis) with enough rigour** to generate the kind of insights that stakeholders can confidently rely on for major business decisions.

- **Many lack the guidance needed to turn insights into tangible outputs that motivate stakeholders** to change their product or service (or that actually get stakeholders excited about doing so).

This entire book is really about thriving in that discomfort, and helping you overcome the challenges above. Stakeholders genuinely (and understandably) hate this part. They want the solution right away, and they'd prefer not to spend any time at all in this space.

But this space is where innovation happens. You can't have innovation without embracing the messy, overwhelming feeling of not having a clear direction. To do this, you, the researcher, also have to **trust the process**. When you're working on a project, you might sometimes be thinking, "Ugh I'm crossing my fingers that this research is going to give us the insights we need," because you're completely underwater with all of the data you've collected, unsure whether anything useful will come out of it. Remind yourself and your stakeholders that the process exists for a reason — and that when you follow it properly (as outlined in this book), you'll get the information you need to improve the experience being studied and help the business.

The line of the design squiggle WILL become less squiggly over time, as you move into the "define" phase and you gain genuine clarity on the problem at hand and how to best solve it. The outcomes of this process will be clear, actionable and even inspiring for your stakeholders. It'll teach them to trust that research can deliver value and ROI.

# Key Purposes of Design Research

**Design research is research *for* design.**

**Design research is research conducted with the goal of improving a designed experience.** The improvement we're working toward could be a new product or service or it could be a transformation of an existing one.

"Improving a designed experience" is pretty broad and ambitious, as far as goals go. But to get to the "how," we can break this purpose down into smaller, achievable parts. As researchers, there are four key purposes that we'll pursue through our research process.

1. **Explore:** We need to explore the current state of a product or service and uncover information about its users, including their motivations, behaviours, goals, tasks, actions, challenges, pain points and needs.
2. **Empathise:** We need to get to know our users and understand who they are as humans on a deeper level. We also need to relate to the stakeholders involved in the product or service we're examining, and understand their needs.
3. **Innovate:** Through the actionable insights we create, we need to provide inspiration and guidance for stakeholders and designers as they conceptualise new and novel solutions.
4. **Improve and enhance:** This purpose is arguably the most important and most common reason for conducting research. We not only need to inspire new solutions, but we need to work towards making experiences better, more efficient and less frustrating. As researchers, we gather information on the pain points and challenges that users deal with, so that designers can enact digital transformations, fix issues and make products easier to use.

# Facets of Design Research

There are a lot of different and helpful ways to categorise research. Carefully comparing these categories or "facets" can help you decide on the approaches and methods to use in specific scenarios. I'll go through them in this section, and also highlight which of the facets will get the most attention throughout the rest of this book.

In the **legend** below, I've assigned symbols and colour-coding to each facet, for your reference going forward. (Keep an eye out for the symbols in chapter 6 and 11.)

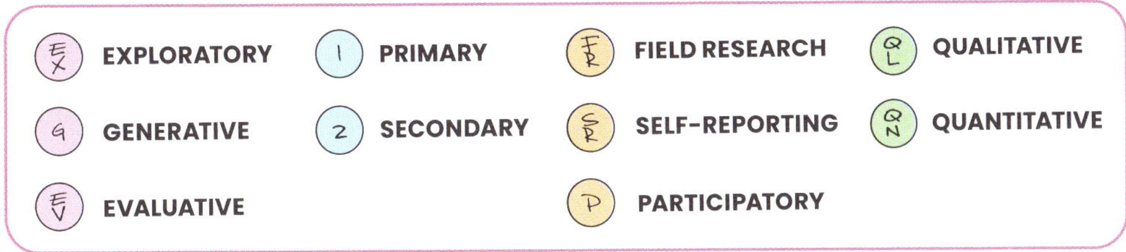


## EXPLORATORY, GENERATIVE AND EVALUATIVE RESEARCH

All of the research you do will fall under one of these three facets. Since this book is intended to be a deep-dive on design research specifically (and not the entire design process), I haven't included any full chapters dedicated to evaluative research methods — those are mostly used during the "design" phase. Instead, I've focused on mostly exploratory and some generative research, which lead into design.

I've mapped out when exploratory, generative and evaluative research methods should be conducted during the design process in the diagram below.

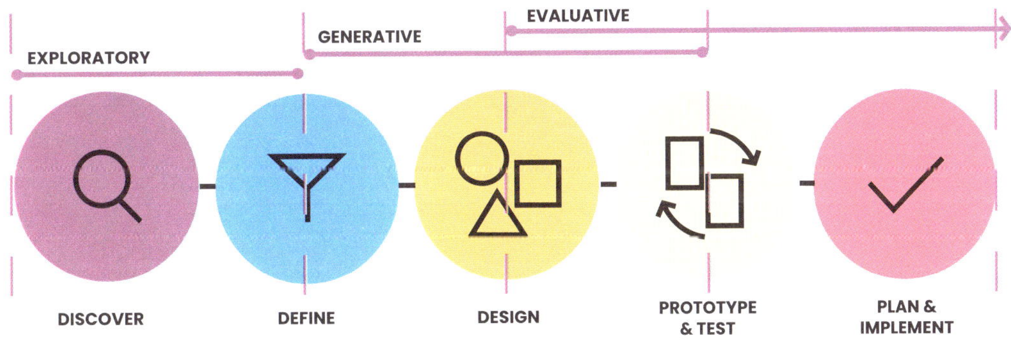


### Exploratory Research

Used for investigating topics or areas of study that we need to understand better; involves uncovering new user challenges, insights, and opportunities for improving a product or service. It's typically used in the "discover" phase and into the "define" phase. (Examples include: observations, diary studies, interviews and literature reviews.)

### Generative Research

Helps with the creation of new solutions to user challenges or pain points through different forms of participatory design; usually includes users and/or stakeholders. It can be used in the "define" phase, all the way through the "design" and "prototype and test" phases. (Examples include: design charrettes, co-design workshops and bodystorming.)

### Evaluative Research 

Involves evaluating the ideas and concepts that you and/or the design team have already come up with, usually by gathering feedback from users and stakeholders as they test out a prototype. Through evaluative research, you can assess the product's ease of use, validate designs or ideas and iterate and improve on what you've created so far, completing loops of your design lifecycle. It often starts in the "design" phase and continues all the way through the "plan and implement" phase. (Examples include: usability testing, A/B testing and service piloting.)

## PRIMARY VS. SECONDARY RESEARCH

All methods of data collection can be categorised as either primary research or secondary research. The methods I emphasise in this book are all primary, because in design research, that's mostly what you're conducting. Secondary research can definitely help as a jumping-off point, but in most cases, your research questions will be so specific that you won't be able to get all the answers you need from someone else's research.

I've put together a chart below comparing the main differences between these facets — you can use it to explain the differences to stakeholders who might be used to conducting secondary research only, or who need some context in understanding why primary research is necessary for your project.

| Primary Research ① | Secondary Research ② |
|---|---|
| Self-conducted (You, the researcher, are collecting data from users by conducting interviews, observations, etc.) | Conducted by others (Someone before you has already conducted research, and you're reading it in journal articles, blogs, books, etc.) |
| Deals with raw data | Deals with analysed and synthesised data |
| Done to gain new findings (There are facts and perspectives you don't know yet that you need to gather) | Done to gather existing facts (Others have put together findings that you can reference) |
| Used to answer your research questions (Your research will be motivated by specific research questions related to your project's goals) | Used to understand answers to other research questions (Research done in a similar area of study can provide context and background to help with your research plan — especially recent research) |
| Requires more time and resources | Requires less time and resources |
| Examples: Surveys, in-depth interviews, observations, diary studies, workshops | Examples: Literature review, jurisdictional scan, trends analysis, document review |

## QUALITATIVE VS. QUANTITATIVE RESEARCH

Impactful design research is mostly qualitative, and that's why I've made qualitative research the star of this book. But even though we know it's powerful, it's generally the least understood by stakeholders. Like I said in chapter 3, decision makers deal in hard numbers, and stakeholders' main concern will be tying data back to the business. It's your job to show them that qualitative data is just as important. (An explanation of data triangulation can help — see chapter 6.)

| Qualitative Research QL | Quantitative Research QN |
|---|---|
| Subjective (for gathering opinions, feelings, behaviours, etc.) | Objective (for gathering statistics, percentage rates, frequencies, etc.) |
| Looks for patterns and themes in the research data | Looks for statistical relevance in the research data |
| Small sample size of participants (e.g. 20 people) | Large sample size of participants (e.g. 1,000 people) |
| Helps with understanding the "why" and "how" behind a problem | Helps with identifying the "where" and "when" of a problem |
| Examples: Interviews, diary studies and observations | Examples: Surveys, A/B testing and analytics tracking |

## SELF-REPORTING, PARTICIPATORY AND FIELD RESEARCH

The last facets of design research in this section are less commonly considered when planning out design research. They're determined by the level or type of participation that the participants have in the research.

### Field Research FR

The participant plays a *passive* role, meaning they aren't deliberately or directly providing the researcher with any data. Instead, they're performing tasks and the researcher is watching and drawing data out from the session. This enables the researcher to recognise and understand the participant's "latent"/unspoken needs that participants may not reveal in self-reporting research. (Examples include: shadowing and fly-on-the-wall observation.)

### Self-Reporting Research SR

The participant plays an *active* role in the collection of data, reporting on their own lived and remembered experiences, opinions and perspectives. They directly provide the researcher with data, by answering general and/or specific probing questions that the researcher poses. (Examples include: interviews, diary studies and surveys.)

### Participatory Research 

The participant plays a *cooperative* role in the research through activities like workshops, which can involve the identification, validation and prioritisation of the problems being studied, as well as the co-creation of potential solutions. This type of research is really useful when conducted with users because it can engage them in solving for their own needs (which they are inherently familiar with) or validating themes and patterns emerging from collected data. It's also great for understanding stakeholder priorities, getting their early feedback on works in progress, involving them in the research, and fostering their accountability and buy-in. (Examples include: co-design workshops, design charrettes and bodystorming — many common generative research methods are also participatory.)

## The Golden Rule of Design Research

The golden rule of design research is: **Mix methods every time.**

Why so many different facets and types of design research? Because different methods will be appropriate for different areas of study, and each one can back up or play off of the others. In design research, there are always multiple ways to investigate people's challenges, motivations, and the contexts in which they live and operate daily... and each could have varying impacts on your understanding of an experience.

For example, you might find it's easiest to rely on self-reporting methods only, like interviews, surveys and diary studies. BUT, with self-reporting methods, participants report on their own experiences, and they may not realise that those experiences could be a lot better. There's a lot of power in mixing self-reporting research with field research and participatory research. With field research, a third party watching the experience will be more likely to notice latent issues and opportunities. With participatory research, you involve people directly in exploring and shaping their own experiences, often revealing ideas they might not have articulated through self-reporting alone, and giving you extra input as you try to solve for their most relevant needs.

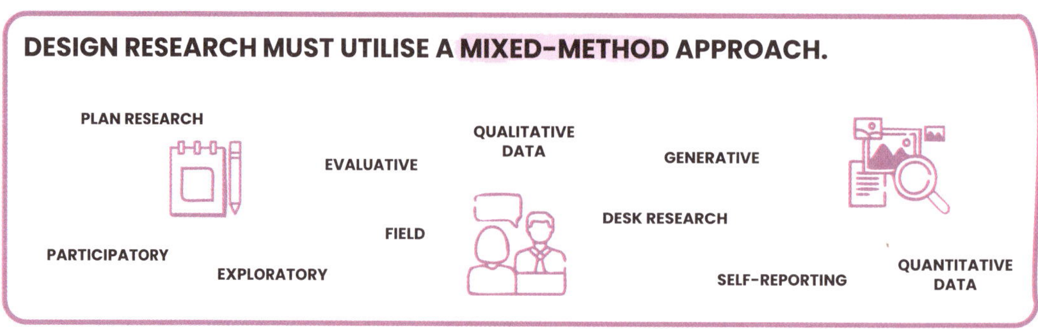

Make sure that your stakeholders understand that mixing research methods and facets will enable more robust and reliable data, making your research outcomes more valuable. (See the section on data triangulation in chapter 6.)

## The Six-Stage DRM Process

After years and years of conducting design research, I realised that building buy-in and actually impacting products and services for the better requires having a wrapper around your research. This includes more than the core processes of participant recruitment, collecting data and analysing it. You need to be looking at the bigger, end-to-end picture, which encompasses strategic planning, conscientious project management, and compelling, actionable communication of your findings and insights. That's why I've come up with the **Six-Stage DRM (Design Research Mastery) Process.**

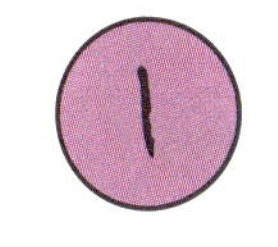

RESEARCH PLANNING

PARTICIPANT RECRUITMENT
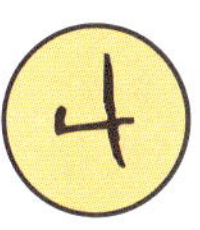

CONDUCTING RESEARCH

MAKING SENSE OF DATA
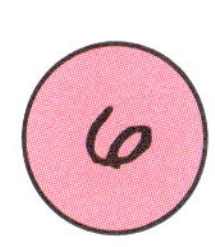

DESIGN STORYTELLING

Here's a brief overview of some activities you can expect at each of the stages covered in this book:

1. **Project planning and initiation:** Identifying design-related business needs, scoping and scheduling, mitigating risk, kicking off, assembling the project plan, ramp-up and preliminary research
2. **Research planning:** Establishing research questions and goals, choosing research methods, developing a research plan, establishing deliverables, defining user groups and determining recruiting criteria
3. **Participant recruitment:** Developing recruiting scripts, choosing recruitment methods, doing the actual recruiting, screening and scheduling of participants
4. **Conducting research:** Executing research methods like in-depth interviews, observations, diary studies, workshops (as well as other methods like surveys and desk research)
5. **Making sense of data:** Coding and analysing the data, refining the design problem, synthesising findings, crafting insights and assembling supporting evidence
6. **Design storytelling:** Visualising findings, co-creating an ideal future state, developing design recommendations, insights reporting, and drafting action plans and roadmaps

Remember the design double diamond? To complement the framework of the Six-Stage DRM Process, I've created a **Design Research Triple Diamond**, with an added diamond on the far left to represent project scoping, initiation and research planning. I've mapped the six stages onto these diamonds to help you put them in context.

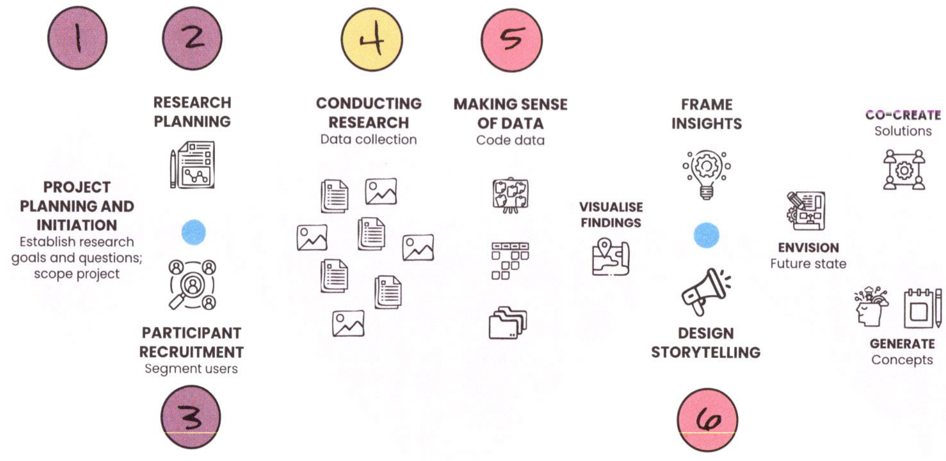


I'll reference this diagram again throughout this book.

# Conclusion

Knowing your design fundamentals inside and out will help you establish or maintain your position as an expert in your craft, and correctly applying them will help you be strategic about how you conduct design research. After all, as researchers, we still have to actively fight the false assumption that we're wasting others' time or using too much of organisations' resources when a shortcut "could suffice." Spoiler: there's no big, secret, free-of-cost shortcut to understanding users. So, let's make the journey worth it for our stakeholders.

**Online Resources:**

Head to **designresearchmastery.com** for a cheat sheet that maps design research tactics across the design process and research stages.

What you'll find:

- DRM 50+ Research Methods & Tools

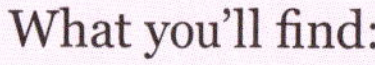

## * Key Takeaways:

1. **Human-centred design places the needs of humans at the centre of digital transformation.** This approach to design requires an in-depth understanding of users through design research.

2. **The design process requires divergent and convergent thinking.** In the "discover" phase of design, you're opening up or "diverging" to find out as much information as you can about a design problem, via design research methods. Then, you'll converge as you start to define/redefine the problem. You'll do this several times throughout the entire design process.

3. **Design research is research *for* design.** Don't forget, the research you conduct is not for research's sake or because you're curious — it's for the sake of improving the design of a product or service, and ultimately the user experience.

4. **Mixing research methods (and research facets) makes for more robust data and more actionable insights in the end.** You definitely want to emphasise primary, qualitative methods for the bulk of your research, but secondary research has an important place in setting context, and some quantitative research (like data analytics) can also supplement your study. Depending on the phase of the design process you're in and what you're trying to learn, you'll also want to use a mix of exploratory, generative and evaluative methods.

5. **The Six-Stage DRM Process is built to remind you that truly successful research is more than just recruiting and talking to users.** It encompasses the end-to-end process, including strategic planning, meticulous project leadership, sound and rigorous methodology, and storytelling that sells your actionable insights to stakeholders. The six stages are:
    - Project Planning and Initiation
    - Research Planning
    - Participant Recruitment
    - Conducting Research
    - Making Sense of Data
    - Design Storytelling

# LEADING SUCCESSFUL PROJECTS

"The key to creativity is to begin with the end in mind, with a vision and a blueprint of the desired result."

— Stephen Covey

## Introduction

This chapter will help you lead your design research projects in a way that ensures success and reinforces the trust you're starting to build with stakeholders as you move through the entire end-to-end research process. A lot of practitioners skip over the essentials I'm about to cover, but without them, your project can crumble pretty quickly. On the other hand, excelling at the leadership and management side will grow your career more than you could have imagined.

If you do a good job and strengthen your credibility in the first few weeks of your project, you'll notice that your stakeholders will loosen the reins. They'll trust that you can talk to their most precious assets (users and customers), deliver your work on time and that you know what you're doing. This will give you more authority and agency to actually lead your project, so you can spend more of your time ensuring that your research yields actionable insights for achieving business impact.

Remember the Design Research Triple Diamond I introduced in chapter 4? Project planning and initiation takes up that whole first diamond. That's how fundamental this process is, in my opinion. It deserves its own diamond, and its own chapter.

A successful project has clear goals based on the business context, aligned teams and an organised plan that manages expectations and risk. That's the standard we need to meet if we want to make a tangible impact every time we conduct research. We can't always wait around for someone else to take the reins, especially if we're the ones championing the research in the first place.

What if you're not a project manager? Well, I'm not one myself, but as a consultant in UX and service design, I had to pick up these skills over time, and they've been invaluable to the projects I've led, and to my career in general. No matter your official title, I believe that to be successful in your work, you need to understand these principles. If you're working "in-house" right now, you might not use all of the steps I've outlined... but even the ones that don't seem relevant now could help you later in your career.

I've broken down successful project leadership into three main stages:

1. **Project planning:** Defining project scope, building a project schedule, and identifying and mitigating risk
2. **Project initiation:** Kicking off the project, assembling your project plan, establishing a governance team, and initial ramp-up research
3. **Project execution:** Monitoring timeline and budget, looping stakeholders into latest developments, problem-solving issues and creating progress reports

The majority of this chapter will focus on project planning (since that part is so intensive), but don't miss the initiation and execution sections at the end.

# Project Planning

Project planning shouldn't be confused with research planning, which I'll cover in the next chapters (6–7). Here, I'm talking about planning out the logistics of the overall research project at a high level — not individual research method logistics.

The assumption going into project planning is that you've done a broad assessment of which research methods and activities will probably be involved, based on the objective your stakeholders have given you. (Flip forward to chapter 6 as needed for help with choosing research methods). This is when you're fleshing out the specifics that will make up the core structure of your project.

# SCOPING YOUR PROJECT

Before you kick off your project with your stakeholders, you need to do some scoping to sort out the amount of work that's required to meet project goals, as well as the restrictions you're working with. There are a few key considerations for project scoping: **project background, timeline and resources**. I'll cover each of these steps in the next sections.

## UNDERSTANDING THE PROJECT BACKGROUND

You'll need to investigate the context and restrictions that you'll be working within, so that the logistics you're proposing to your stakeholders are practical and achievable. There are three background questions I like to ask before I scope a project. These questions will help you get a clearer understanding of how much research will be needed, and what kind.

### What is the main purpose of this project?

You might already know the overarching goal of the project, but you might still be figuring out how this goal relates to the overall roster of products/services/features that the business is outputting and to the market context.

The main purpose will typically fall under one of these three categories:

| Incremental Improvement | Extension of Offerings | Disruption/ Innovation |
|---|---|---|
| Making improvements to an existing product or service (including releasing new features) | Extending a new offering to an existing customer base or user group<br>OR<br>Extending an existing offering to a new customer base/user group | Venturing into an entirely new market<br>OR<br>Creating a new type of offering that hasn't been done before in the market |
| **Less research-intensive** (Evaluative research) | ⟷ | **More research-intensive** (Exploratory & generative research) |

### How much is already known about the problem area?

This question will orient you as far as problem clarity: how much research has been done by the organisation in the past, how much you or your stakeholders already know about the problem area, and whether you're venturing into the unknown or benefiting from the context of previous studies. It will also help you start to think about what timeline you're looking at with your research, so that you can start setting and managing your stakeholders' expectations.

| Well Understood Problem Area | Somewhat Understood Problem Area | Mostly Unknown Problem Area |
| --- | --- | --- |
| **A fair amount of research has been done in the past** (including primary research with users)<br><br>The organisation has a clear understanding of the pain points and opportunities involved | **Some research has been done in the past** (e.g. informal customer interviews, process mapping, surveys, sales team research)<br><br>The organisation understands the high-level pain points and opportunities involved, but **there are still gaps in their understanding** | **No research has been done**<br><br>The organisation **doesn't know** the high-level pain points or opportunities involved |
| Often the case with **incremental improvements to a product/service** | Often the case with **larger improvements or extensions of a product/ service** | Often the case with **product/ service ideas that are new to the market or the organisation** |
| Research needed:<br>• **Secondary research**<br>• **Evaluative research** (e.g. usability testing) | Research needed:<br>• **Secondary research**<br>• **At least one primary research method** (e.g. workshops and/or interviews) | Research needed:<br>• **Secondary research**<br>• **Two or more primary research methods** (e.g. workshops, observations and interviews) |
| Fewer user groups might need to be studied | At minimum, user groups who are the least understood will need to be studied | Most relevant user groups will need to be studied (but the study of certain groups might be prioritised or deferred to future projects, to make initial research more approachable) |
| Research could take up to **4 weeks** | Research could take **8–10 weeks** | Research could take **12+ weeks** |

⟵ ⟶

**Less research-intensive** (Evaluative research)

**More research-intensive** (Exploratory & generative research)

 **Alignment Advice:**

Remember, your stakeholders are not the user. Don't rely too heavily on your stakeholders when you're assessing the question of problem clarity. Depending on the design maturity of your organisation, your stakeholders might think that they understand more about their users' challenges than they actually do. They might be placing too much confidence in a few anecdotes they heard from their favourite customers, a few bad reviews they found, or a high-level marketing survey.

Your stakeholders might have used the product or service themselves, and because of this, they might be convinced that they know exactly what goes on in a typical user or customer's head. (Of course, this doesn't mean that they fully understand the problems that are being tackled in the project. For one, as stakeholders, they're more likely to hold subconscious biases. For another, they're not typically representative of one of the user groups being targeted, let alone all of them.)

If you suspect this is happening, ask questions. "Where did you find those reviews?" "How/when did you get in touch with that customer?" "Can you send those findings to me so I can take a closer look?"

Your stakeholders should absolutely be collaborating with you on the project plan, but never forget that they're also relying on you to be the expert in your field, and to make accurate, helpful recommendations and tell them how much research they actually need to do in order to ensure a successful launch. (Refer back to chapter 2 for more on design maturity.)

### How risky is the launch of the product or service?

With this question, you're making a preliminary assessment of how high-stakes this project is going to be. Generally speaking, the higher the risk, the more crucial your research will be.

| Low Risk | Moderate Risk | High Risk |
|---|---|---|
| A **smaller** amount of money/ time is being invested | A **moderate** amount of money/time is being invested | A **large** amount of money/ time is being invested |
| A launch failure will have **little to no effect** on the organisation's reputation and bottom line | A launch failure will have **some effect** on the organisation's reputation and bottom line | A launch failure could have **a negative effect** on the organisation's reputation and bottom line |
| Associated with **incremental improvements** to a product/service | Associated with **larger improvements or extensions** of a product/ service | Associated with **product/ service ideas that are totally new** to the market or the organisation |

**Less research-intensive**
(Evaluative research)

**More research-intensive**
(Exploratory & generative research)

## DETERMINING TIME AND RESOURCE RESTRICTIONS

When you understand time restrictions or project dependencies you're working with, you can get more specific about what activities and deliverables you'll be able to do or create in that timeframe and what a realistic project schedule might look like. Hopefully, your stakeholders have already given you a sense of what the timeline needs are. If not, ask them when they need research, design and/or implementation to be completed and if the findings of your research might impact any other upcoming projects or product launches they have planned. From there, you can create a "workback schedule."

Your schedule will impact which research methods you'll choose. If you only have 1-2 months, you're going to be limited with how much you can do, so you might suggest sticking to only one research method (e.g. interviews or workshops). If you have 3–6 months, then you'll be able to add in more research methods and you'll also be able to study more participants. But remember, as the expert you can also recommend which approach and timeline is best for the needs of the project.

You should also investigate whether there are any special timeline considerations for your area of study. For example, I once did a project with farmers, and I knew nothing about farming, so I didn't realise that harvest season was in the fall. Thankfully, my stakeholders warned me that recruiting participants during that season might be hard. We ended up moving the project timeline so we could study farmers in the winter, when they were more available. It's always good to ask questions about potential restrictions like this, especially if you're researching groups whose activities might be impacted by seasonal fluctuation.

The next piece of the puzzle is figuring out how much money and other resources you have available to fund and support your research. Here are some factors to consider, so that you can complete your work within scope.

- **Budget:** What is the project budget? How much can you spend on recruitment incentives? How many paid "person-hours" are included in the budget, i.e. how much time can any involved workers spend on the project per month/in total?
- **Human resources:** Who is available to help you? Do you have access to other researchers, designers or subject matter experts who can contribute to your project?
- **Availability:** How many hours do you (and team members) have available to spend on the project during the timeline?
- **Participants:** How many participants will you need to recruit? Do you have easy access to participants or will they be hard to find?

If there's no room in the budget for additional researchers or team members and you have a shortened timeframe, you might have to talk to your stakeholders about pairing down the amount of deliverables they're asking for and/or reducing the amount of participants you're researching. This might sound nerve racking, but trust me, your stakeholders don't want you to promise anything that you can't actually accomplish.

## CREATING A PROJECT SCHEDULE

After you've gotten a good idea of the amount of research needed, and of the timeline and resource restrictions you're working with, you'll be ready to create a draft project schedule for your stakeholders to review. The next section will walk you through this process, but first, I'll give you some examples of typical design research timelines that you can reference as you get started.

The upcoming diagram shows approximately how many weeks you'd need for each of the stages in the Six-Stage DRM Process, based on a design research project that takes 12–16 weeks. This is a pretty standard timeline that I recommend for getting a lot of good research done. A lean project might take 8 weeks, and a medium-sized project will probably be closer to 12 weeks long. A longer timeline for bigger projects is typically 16–20 weeks.

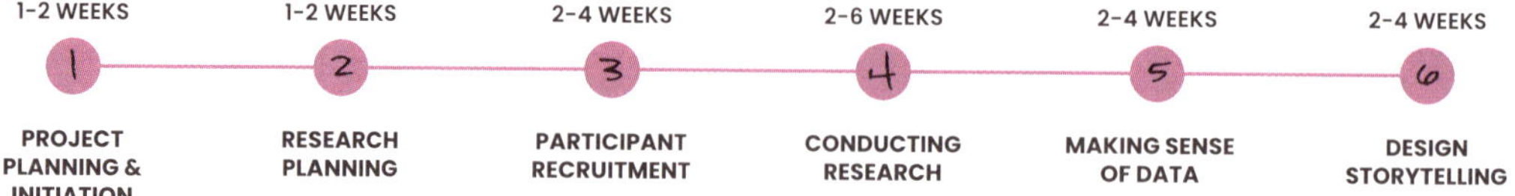


You can reference a breakdown of this timeline with individual activities as well as project schedule template in the "Sample DRM Project Timelines" online resource — see the list at the end of this chapter.

**Sample 12-week project schedule:** This reflects a standard research project that calls for a few research methods to better understand the topic, but doesn't require extensive deliverables.

| | Week 1 | 2 | 3 | 4 | 5 | 6 | 7 | 8 | 9 | 10 | 11 | 12 |
|---|---|---|---|---|---|---|---|---|---|---|---|---|
| **PHASE 1:** Project Initiation | | | | | | | | | | | | |
| Kick-Off Meeting | | | | | | | | | | | | |
| Discovery Workshop | | | | | | | | | | | | |
| Document Review | | | | | | | | | | | | |
| **PHASE 2:** Research Planning | | | | | | | | | | | | |
| Interview Protocols, Recruiting Guide and Criteria | | | | | | | | | | | | |
| Recruiting & Scheduling | | | | | | | | | | | | |
| **PHASE 3:** Discovery Research | | | | | | | | | | | | |
| Secondary Research | | | | | | | | | | | | |
| In-Depth Interviews | | | | | | | | | | | | |
| Co-Design Workshop | | | | | | | | | | | | |
| **PHASE 4:** Data Analysis & Reporting | | | | | | | | | | | | |
| Data Analysis | | | | | | | | | | | | |
| Reporting & Deliverable Creation | | | | | | | | | | | | |

**Sample 16-week project schedule:** This project would be on a larger scale and might require interviews with a larger number of participants. The deliverables might include journey maps, service blueprints, personas and/or reports.

| | Week 1 | 2 | 3 | 4 | 5 | 6 | 7 | 8 | 9 | 10 | 11 | 12 | 13 | 14 | 15 | 16 |
|---|---|---|---|---|---|---|---|---|---|---|---|---|---|---|---|---|
| **PHASE 1:** Project Initiation | | | | | | | | | | | | | | | | |
| Kick-Off Meeting | | | | | | | | | | | | | | | | |
| Stakeholder Interviews | | | | | | | | | | | | | | | | |
| Document Review | | | | | | | | | | | | | | | | |
| **PHASE 2:** Research Planning | | | | | | | | | | | | | | | | |
| Interview Protocols, Recruiting Guide and Criteria | | | | | | | | | | | | | | | | |
| Recruiting & Scheduling | | | | | | | | | | | | | | | | |
| **PHASE 3:** Discovery Research | | | | | | | | | | | | | | | | |
| Observations | | | | | | | | | | | | | | | | |
| In-Depth Interviews | | | | | | | | | | | | | | | | |
| Co-Design Workshop | | | | | | | | | | | | | | | | |
| **PHASE 4:** Data Analysis & Reporting | | | | | | | | | | | | | | | | |
| Data Analysis | | | | | | | | | | | | | | | | |
| Reporting & Deliverable Creation | | | | | | | | | | | | | | | | |
| Final Deliverables | | | | | | | | | | | | | | | | |

When you show your stakeholders a preliminary schedule, it's normal to have some back-and-forth feedback, pushback and adjustments. I can't tell you how many times I've put a schedule in front of a client or other stakeholder and had them ask me right away to condense it, or adjust for vacation times that I didn't know about yet. If and when this happens, don't panic. It's an expected part of the back and forth you'll have with your stakeholders, and it can actually be very useful, because it gives you an opportunity to align and set expectations of when work will be done.

To prepare for the next time you run into this, take a look through these common timeline issues that stakeholders bring up, and see which suggested resolutions could be useful in your specific situation. Make sure you choose solutions that will have the least negative impact on your stakeholders. Come to them with a tactful and well-prepared explanation of why your resolutions will work.

**Issue:** "This schedule is too long. We need to speed up the timeline."

**Suggested resolutions:**

- Reduce the amount of end deliverables
- Reduce the fidelity of a design artefact/deliverable
- Reduce the number of research activities
- Sideline some research activities for a future project

**Issue:** "I need to have some outcomes sooner."

**Suggested resolutions:**

- Prepare a status report with highlights from your research that can be shared early
- Send updates with early findings via email as you go along
- Share earlier, draft versions of deliverables

**Issue:** "I'll be on vacation for two weeks in the summer."

**Suggested resolutions:**

- Push out the timeline to accommodate vacations if possible
- Find an alternate person who can step in (and involve them early in the process)
- Move activities or swap the order of activities based on what's most crucial for stakeholder involvement

It might be tempting to make your activities more rushed in order to fit them in, but resist the temptation to just compress the schedule, if possible. There's always an answer, and a way to get research done. It just means compromising here and there, and getting comfortable with negotiation.

# IDENTIFYING AND MITIGATING RISK

The last major task to do before you get into your project kick-off is putting together a risk mitigation strategy. Why? Because no project is perfect. A risk mitigation strategy can help you manage stakeholder expectations in terms of possible outcomes and delays, and it can create accountability with the stakeholders who are involved. It also makes it easier and way less stressful to problem-solve issues when they do come up. All of this builds more trust with your stakeholders and safeguards your chances of project success.

A **project risk** refers to a potential situation or challenge that could arise during the project, potentially affecting the project schedule, budget, processes, outcomes, etc.

**Risk mitigation** is a project management strategy that involves reducing the likelihood of a risk becoming a reality, and/or reducing the negative impact (or "severity") of a risk when/if it becomes a reality.

Your risk mitigation strategy involves six high-level steps. I'll go through each of these steps in detail below.

## 1. IDENTIFY PROJECT RISKS

Before you can mitigate risk, you need to identify the largest and/or most probable risks that your specific project could be facing. Creating this list will be a balancing act — you want to manage your stakeholders' expectations, but you don't want to scare them away from greenlighting your project.

Every project has unique risks, but there are some that I've seen come up more often in my experience. I've laid out a few below as a jumping off point for your own list of risks:

- **Struggling to recruit enough or the right type of users:** You could run into recruitment challenges, where your recruitment tactics don't yield the "right" mix of people for your research, or you can't find enough people who are interested in participating. (To mitigate this, you would come up with a strategy that involves alternate recruitment methods to keep your project moving — see chapter 7.)
- **Scheduling delays:** You could have trouble scheduling interviews or workshops within the given time, or you might get delayed survey answers or diary study submissions. This can create a ripple effect throughout your project, reducing the amount of time you have for each next step, all the way up to the launch of the product/service.
- **Stakeholder availability:** You might not be able to get timely feedback from stakeholders on key deliverables and milestones because of their busy schedules. This is a very common issue, especially with executives and directors, and it can quickly push your schedule back.

To determine your project's risks, ask yourself what challenges you might have at different stages of your research project that could create a negative impact, whether they're related to project logistics (like recruiting participants), stakeholder absences and availability, or research outcomes. (You can also access a longer list of common research risk examples in the risk mitigation resource linked at the end of this chapter.)

## 2. ASSESS SEVERITY

Once you've identified the possible risks to consider, you should assess how severe the impact would be if that risk were to become a reality. Is the severity:

- **Low:** Won't be very impactful to the project
- **Medium:** May impact project timeline, but won't cause major disruptions
- **High:** Will severely impact the project and has the potential to stop/end the project

In your strategy, you should typically include risks that are in the "medium" and "high" ranges, but if you have a lot of risks in these categories, you should narrow it down to the risks with higher likelihood.

## 3. ASSESS LIKELIHOOD

Similar to severity, you want to categorise how likely the risks are to occur, from low to high likelihood. All risks with "medium" to "high" likelihood should be outlined in your risk mitigation strategy and communicated to your stakeholders asap, regardless of their severity level. Risks with higher likelihood and higher severity should be prioritised, and you should make sure to include specific risk mitigation steps for them.

## 4. DESCRIBE THE RISKS

Give yourself enough time to describe the risk and the potential impact in a clear, concise way that's easy to read. Strike a balance in your wording so that you're not framing things as scary and catastrophic but you're also not glossing things over or "beating around the bush."

## 5. DETERMINE MITIGATION STEPS

The next part of building your risk mitigation strategy is outlining the steps that you, your team or your stakeholders will need to take to either prevent a risk, reduce its likelihood or to reduce the impact once an issue has come up. These steps should also include a plan for escalating issues. Who do you tell, how do you tell them, and do your mitigation steps need approval from stakeholders before they're actioned?

When escalating time-sensitive issues, don't wait for a check-in or for a progress report to come due. After you've established your mitigation steps and practiced risk assessment, you should have an excellent sense of what needs to be flagged right away, what you can handle on your own and flag in a weekly check-in, etc. What I'm saying is, an effective, trustworthy project leader isn't shy or hesitant if something goes wrong.

## 6. COMMUNICATE YOUR STRATEGY TO STAKEHOLDERS

Don't be afraid to talk about this stuff with your stakeholders. They'll probably be happy that you're giving risk mitigation enough time and attention, and that you're not just coming to them with problems, but actionable steps, too. When you present your high-level project plan to stakeholders in the project kick-off, you should include an initial pass of your risk mitigation strategy to get their feedback. Once you've incorporated their notes, share the revision with them, and include the final version in your project initiation document. Get verbal confirmation that everyone understands the possible risks and impact to the project, as well as the mitigation steps involved.

When risks turn into issues, lean on your mitigation steps, escalate issues to the right people and remember that clear, early communication is crucial. Next up are a couple of real-life examples of unfortunate scenarios that have happened to me. My hope is that you learn from these moments, instead of recreating them for yourself!

**Design Research in Reality: *Half-Baked Buy-In***

One time, I was leading a research project, and was happy to have gained what I thought counted as full buy-in from the stakeholder team. (The operative word here is "thought," instead of "knew.") I ran into some difficulties gaining buy-in for the entire stakeholder team, mainly because of busy schedules and other competing priorities. My gut told me that I should pause and get their confirmation anyway, but instead, I let others convince me that the most involved stakeholders could be relied on to represent all stakeholder interests.

When we got to the end of the project and presented our deliverables to the full room of stakeholders, it became obvious that only half of them were on board with what we'd done/created. As it turned out, not all of the stakeholders saw eye-to-eye — in fact, they had competing and opposing goals for the research.

At the final presentation, the team was reamed out by the head of IT, who wasn't pleased with the findings. We realised that our work was being used by one team to play politics with the other team without our knowledge, and we were caught in the middle. If we had done our due diligence and insisted on meeting with the head of IT, we likely would've been able to find this out sooner and adjust the goals and direction of the research to better align all of the stakeholders involved.

**The lesson:**

- **Don't assume that all your stakeholders get along and are aligned.** Do the legwork yourself to involve all interested parties/stakeholders and get any needed signoffs directly from them.

### Design Research in Reality: *Escalation Hesitation*

This story involves one of my least favourite projects from almost a decade ago. I was doing a journey mapping project where I was recruiting people from a survey for interviews. In this case, the client was responsible for sending the survey link out to the customer list based on criteria we developed together. As I started to analyse the survey, I flagged to our main point of contact, a director who was new to their position, that the survey was sent to the wrong list of customers. As a result, a key user group was not going to be interviewed!

I provided some mitigation strategies to that main point of contact, but I didn't escalate the issue to the VP who was supervisor to this newer director. The director expressed that they didn't want to delay the project, so after several emails back and forth (many of which included warnings from us about the possible impact), we complied with the directive to go ahead with the interviews and gather the resulting information.

When we got to the final presentation of the report, I included a caveat on a slide at the outset of the presentation that explained the issue with the target list. The VP had joined us for the first time since the project kick-off... and was furious! As the VP heatedly announced that the research was useless and wasn't conducted with the right people, the director stayed silent. When I mentioned that we had raised the red flag a few times via email, the director threw me under the bus and said that the issue was brand new information, and that they didn't remember having any related conversations.

The fact that I had everything documented via email is what ultimately saved my butt, and saved the consulting firm I was working with from having to eat the cost of the project.

**The lesson:**

- **Always raise flags when you notice issues coming up.** Don't stay quiet or wait until a "good moment."
- **Always raise flags via email, so they're documented, or summarise them in an email after a verbal conversation. Always involve key decision makers on those emails.** Don't rely on your main point of contact to relay your message.

If your main point of contact asks you why you're including higher-ups on your email, explain that it's important for all key decision makers to be made aware of a possible delay/change in project outcomes.

# Project Initiation

All of the work you've done scoping, planning and assessing risk will come together as you realign your stakeholders, solidify your written plan and actually initiate your project. I've outlined key steps that should be completed during project initiation. These will maximise your chance of project success.

**Hold a project kick-off:** Set up a meeting with all of your stakeholders and your project team to get everyone on the same page about the project logistics you've established so far, validate them, and to fill any smaller gaps left in the plan, using an organised slide deck. This is typically the first meeting attended by everyone involved in the project. It's also an opportunity for them to get to know each other and clear up any questions before the project gets started. Again, alignment is central to building trust across the board. (To help you, refer to the DRM Project Kick-Off Checklist at the end of this chapter.)

**Establish a governance team:** A project governance team is a group of stakeholders who oversee a project to ensure that the intended positive outcomes are achieved. They're also key decision makers with accountability for key aspects of the project. This group might include directors, executives, project sponsors, subject matter experts, etc. Some of them will only be involved for deliverable reviews, while others will be required to sign off on all research plans, recruiting criteria, and interview protocols.

Governance teams are extremely helpful in championing your research within an organisation, ensuring that the project plan is followed, and acting as a link between different teams or departments.

**Ramp up/conduct a document review:** After the previous steps are completed, it's time to do some initial research and learn everything you can about the industry, organisation and problem space as quickly as possible, so that you can plan out the actual research and spring into action. This is what we call a "ramp-up" in research. Ramping up is an invaluable skill, because most researchers will find themselves in situations where they get thrown into a project that they know nothing about, and are expected to make magic happen within a pretty short timeline.

**Conduct stakeholder interviews (optional):** When you have the chance, its recommended to hold one-on-one stakeholder interviews once you've gone through your document review (or concurrently with that review), so you can get further background on the project, and, most importantly, so you can better understand their needs and their desired level of influence/involvement in your project. (More on how to conduct interviews in chapter 8).

**Hold a discovery workshop (optional):** Another optional but recommended activity during project initiation is hosting a discovery workshop with your stakeholders and project team. The purpose of this workshop is to quickly gather any known information about your users, including their journeys, challenges, and key characteristics for defining user groups. It also gets you and your stakeholders working together in a collaborative way right from the outset of the project. (More on workshops in chapter 11).

**Document the project plan:** There are different ways of formalising your project plan, but two common types of project management documents you might create are project charters and project initiation documents. They're built to guide you, your team members and stakeholders as you execute on the project and work toward successful outcomes.

A **project initiation document** (PID) is generally used for internal project team alignment, with immediate next steps, communication details and project logistics, including individual roles and responsibilities within your team and the project timeline. I'd typically take my kick-off meeting slide deck, update it with more information and feedback after the kick-off, save it out as a PDF, and rename it as a PID.

Here are the main elements that should be included in your PID before you dive into the research:

- Project background and overview
- Project goals
- Project team roles and responsibilities
- Methodology and approach
- Description and dates of deliverables/milestones
- Tools and technology
- Communication (when, how often, and where)
- Project governance and key decision makers
- Project timeline/schedule (including any planned vacations or significant dates)
- Risk mitigation strategy
- Measures of success

A **project charter** is a strategic document that's generally used for projects where you have multiple groups of stakeholders that need to formally sign off on the project goals, schedule and other high-level decisions. I don't find that project charters are needed for an average-sized project, but they're very valuable on large, multi-year digital transformations. If you're creating one, it's recommended to actually have your stakeholders sign it. (A similar but less formal way of doing this would be to create a team agreement that outlines how you'll work together and who's responsible for what.)

# Project Execution

Project success is not just about the setup, of course. Now that you're ready to ramp up your project, it's important to keep fostering collaboration, trust and alignment all the way through to the end.

As part of this effort, you and your stakeholders should decide on a frequency and format for regular check-ins. (Typically for me, this looks like a 30-minute to 1-hour recurring meeting every week, where we review works-in-progress and discuss project updates.)

Here are some items to cover that will help you keep your check-ins productive, engaging and reassuring for your stakeholders.

- Review recent project developments and milestones
- Highlight what's been going well
- Share works in progress (e.g. early findings or rough deliverables)
- Identify new potential risks and propose mitigation (flagged early)
- Summarise any next steps/actionables from the check-in

**Action Advice:**

**Uphold high communication standards with stakeholders, and don't let them slide.** When you determine the best cadence for meetings and reviews based on the project's needs, make sure to stick to that cadence. Stakeholder requests should ideally be followed up on within a couple of hours — in my opinion, even waiting 24 hours can feel too long on active projects. When you share updates or files, your communication should be clear and concise, and the contents of each email should be structured in a way that's logical and straightforward.

Don't forget that all of your verbal communication with stakeholders should also be followed up with written communication, so that you have documentation of everything discussed. When your stakeholders start to trust you more, they might ask for less communication, and that's fine, but they should still be looped into major project updates and milestones.

The act of communicating with your stakeholders will reassure them that you've "got it covered" and that nothing is going off the rails. In addition to check-ins, I'd send a project status update via email every Monday to report on the progress of the previous week and to highlight what's being done in the new week. Stakeholders will love it! They'll feel empowered knowing exactly what's happening and where they might need to support.

These are the major items that you should include in your project status reports:

- **Activities completed *last* week:** List out any deliverables, big meetings/presentations, or other research activities you and the team started or completed in the previous week; a bulleted list will work fine. Ideally, nothing in your report should be a major surprise.
- **Activities to be completed *this* week:** List out all activities, major dates/milestones or deliverables that you're starting, working on or completing that week.
- **Risks and blockers:** Hopefully, there won't be any risks or blockers coming up for the project, but if there are, flag them, identify their real or possible impact to

the project, and include possible solutions/a risk mitigation strategy. For example, maybe you haven't recruited enough participants yet, and this could cause a delay to the schedule. Or, maybe you haven't been able to get in touch with a key stakeholder to approve a new activity that needs to start soon to avoid a delay. I like to use a colour-coding system to show the level of severity/impact on the project.

- **Project schedule:** I also like to include a link to the project schedule, with a sentence indicating where you're at in the project; If there's been a change, I'll update the project schedule to reflect it, along with the accompanying reason(s) why in the section on risks and blockers.

Lastly, here are some tips that will help ensure that people actually read your report. I've also provided a sample weekly status report in the online resources that are linked at the end of this chapter.

- **Keep your report short and to the point.** It should be focused on need-to-know items, and it should be easily skimmable and point form. Use colour to highlight activities that were completed (in green) or issues/blockers (in orange or red).
- **Use a useful email subject line that's easy to search.** You or your stakeholders may want to reference your status report later. Be sure to title your email something like "Weekly Status Report - [Date]."
- **Always send your reports and status updates on time.**
- **Follow up on any flags and signoff requests that you might have included in your report.** Don't assume "no news is good news." Your stakeholders are very busy and they might have missed your written communication.
- **Always be transparent and honest about project developments.**

# Conclusion

In this chapter, you were setting the stage for your research project by getting better acquainted with your stakeholders and your shared goals, establishing the research approach and restrictions you'll be working with, preparing for potential risk, and assembling all of these details into a core project plan that will act as your guide going forward.

Now, you have the project leadership tools that will help you maintain buy-in throughout your project and convince stakeholders to act on the outcomes of your research.

**Online Resources:**

As promised, here's a list of resources that you can access at **designresearchmastery.com** to support your project leadership. All of them are free to download.

What you'll find:

- DRM Project Kick-Off Checklist
- Sample DRM Project Timelines
- Risk Mitigation Guide & Workbook
- Sample Weekly Status Report

## ✱ Key Takeaways:

1. **An effective project leader puts consistent effort into project planning, initiation and execution.** You don't need to be trained as a manager to take ownership over the logistics of what needs to happen when, how it will happen and who needs to sign off. Stepping up in this way can build deep and long-lasting trust with your stakeholders.

2. **Properly scoping your project requires a solid understanding of your purpose, resources and timeline.** This includes an assessment of how much is already known about the problem area you're going to be studying. Only then can you build a project schedule that your stakeholders will approve and that your team will actually be able to follow. Your schedule might still shift throughout your project, so it's technically never final, but you should take it seriously and do your absolute best to stick to it.

3. **No project is perfect, and things go wrong — which is why you need to develop a risk mitigation strategy.** If you take the right steps, you can reduce the impact of possible delays, challenges and errors. When an issue does come up during the course of your project, don't wait to flag it to your stakeholders. And make sure that you always document flagged issues and warnings via email.

4. **Holding a project kick-off and conducting formal initiation activities will set you and your team up for success.** Also, you shouldn't go into a project kick-off with a finalised project plan. Instead, you should finalise the plan as a collaborative process between you, your project team and your stakeholders. Then, solidify the plan that you come up with together as a project initiation document (PID) and send it to everyone involved.

5. **You should see project status reporting (not just insights reporting) as fundamental to your project success.** Concise, clear and well structured status reports sent at regular intervals will help you stakeholders breathe easier, because they'll know for certain what you're up to, what issues might come up and how you plan to solve them.

# 6

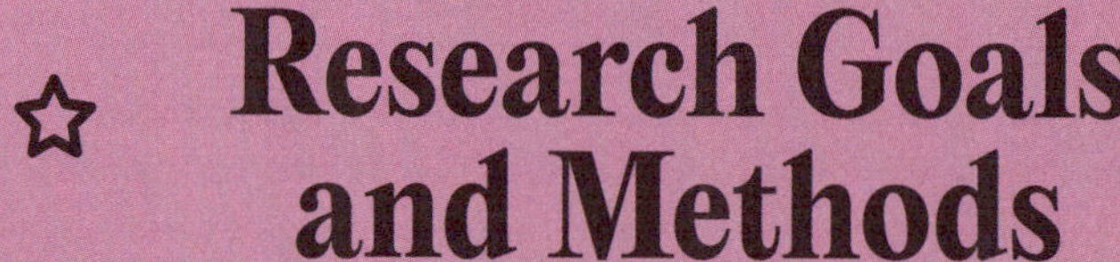

# RESEARCH PLANNING

## Research Goals and Methods

“If you fail to plan, you are planning to fail.”
— Benjamin Franklin

# Introduction

In my experience, research planning is the most important step a researcher can take to ensure that their work actually achieves what it's supposed to achieve, and creates meaningful impact to the product or service in the long run. This early part of the project can sometimes feel boring, tiring and not worth your time. But in reality, if you don't do it, you risk recruiting the wrong participants, collecting the wrong data, falling off schedule and confusing your participants and stakeholders to the point where they could lose trust in you and your project altogether. Poor planning can also create chaos for your research team if you're not all clear on responsibilities or priorities. The tips and strategies in this chapter will help you avoid all of these pitfalls.

Like with project planning, proper research planning is also huge for stakeholder trust: the communication, collaboration and expectation setting you initiate during this stage will help stakeholders believe in your decision-making. Not everything will go as planned during the actual research stage, and pivoting will be smoother if your stakeholders know you're organised and have their best interest in mind. In order to get your insights acted on, your stakeholders need to buy into what you're doing at every stage of the project.

Let's take a look at where we are in the **Six-Stage DRM Process:**

The bulk of your research planning happens after project initiation, as you transition from the first diamond to the second, in the Design Research Triple Diamond.

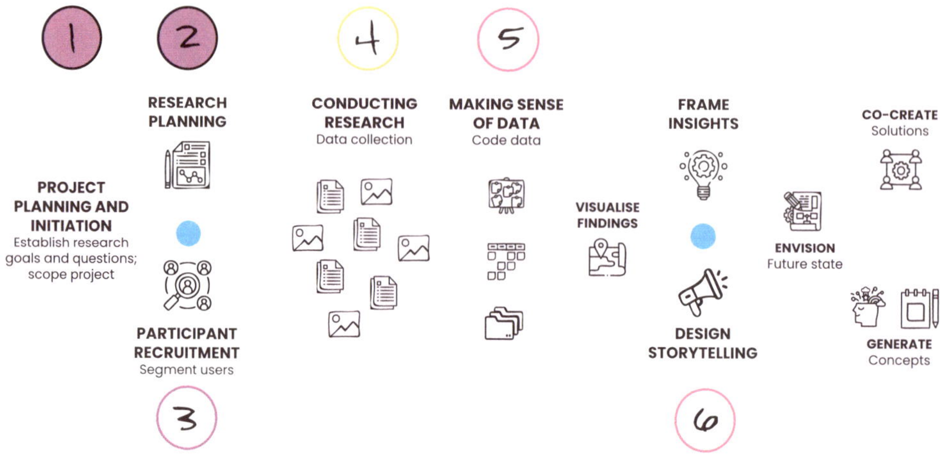


**Your research planning should be thorough, and it should be done before you recruit any participants.** The people you're gleaning data from need to be selected thoughtfully based on your project's needs, so that your data will actually be helpful to your stakeholders – i.e. so that it will yield practical, actionable insights.

## RESEARCH PLANNING PROCESS

Over the years of planning and running dozens of design research projects, I've developed a step-by-step approach to research planning that will help you get and stay organised:

- Craft research goals, themes and questions
- Choose research methods
- Choose participants (e.g. user groups, participant numbers, recruiting criteria, recruiting tactics)
- Write a research plan
- Prepare research materials (such as recruiting scripts, screeners, interview protocols, field kits, consent forms and more)
- Seek approvals and stakeholder feedback
- Recruit participants (outreach, screening and scheduling)

I'll cover some of these steps in this chapter and anything related to participant recruitment will be covered in chapter 7. Together, all of these pieces will culminate in the creation of a research plan, which I'll explain in more detail at the end of this chapter.

# Craft Research Goals

Setting research goals should be a collaborative exercise done with the team and validated with stakeholders. Your goal-setting should be aligned with the business objectives that your stakeholders are concerned with. Establishing this alignment will help you ensure that you're researching an area of interest for your stakeholders, and that you're gathering the kind of insights that will make your stakeholders sit up and take notice.

Your research goals should not be confused with your overall UX or service design project goals. The two types of goals might be similar, but they can also vary from each other depending on the scope of the project.

**Example:**

You might be working on a long-term digital transformation initiative involving several touchpoints and lines of business, but your current design research project may only focus on the customer-facing online service. In this case, your research goals would only reflect what you hope to accomplish by researching customers of the online service.

The goals you set shouldn't be too broad or too ambiguous, and they shouldn't be created in a vacuum — otherwise, you'll be setting yourself up to fumble. I can't tell you how many times I've reviewed a set of research goals that were vague, confusing and essentially useless. If you don't have research goals that actually articulate the outcome you're hoping to achieve, you won't have a "north star" to come back to when you need to realign your stakeholders — because inevitably at some point, they'll go off track or bring in their own perspectives and new ideas that fall out of scope. You won't have a leg to stand on if that scope wasn't clear to begin with. That's why you need a solid set of research goals that gets signed off on by every key stakeholder.

Another big issue that can happen with research goals that are created in isolation? A nasty surprise at the insights reporting stage, when the data isn't well-received because one or more of your stakeholders expected something different. I've been part of projects where the research goals weren't properly set or they weren't done collaboratively, and then at the end of those projects, we were faced with presenting findings to less-than-attentive stakeholders.

Remember my chapter 5 warning stories ("Design Research in Reality") about missed connections with busy stakeholders, and the resulting not-so-fun fallout? Well, the same could happen to you. You might be presenting to a busy executive who only has time to show up to a few meetings here and there, and tunes in at the very end to announce that the research you did wasn't what they wanted. (Ouch.) The idea that you could do all that research and completely miss the mark sounds crazy, but believe me, it happens. That's why you can't skip this step. These goals will be the beacon for your entire project.

To help avoid this, I've put together the **5 Cs of Effective Research Goals**, which can be used as a framework as you plan your project.

**Comprehensive:** They should describe the "who," "what" and "why" of your research exactly, with precise words. If you're doing a study on the home buying experience, instead of saying "the user," refer to them as "the home buyer." One goal on its own might not capture everything, but the sum of your goals should paint a holistic picture of what you're aiming to accomplish with the research.

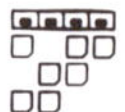

**Clear:** Express your goals in complete sentences and in plain language that anyone can easily understand (avoid using jargon).

**Concise:** Aim for a maximum of 100–150 words per goal. Goal descriptions shouldn't be excessively detailed and your sentences shouldn't be too long.

**Constructive:** The insights you get from your research should be actionable and should help you achieve a better user or customer experience. Make sure your goals are focused on getting that end result.

**Collaborative:** Research goals should be co-created with your team and stakeholders. Don't create them in isolation! You need to make sure that you have buy-in on everything you're setting out to do.

**Aim to have 3–5 research goals per project.**

Now that we've gone over the key characteristics of effective research goals, let's look at the goal-writing structure that you'll need to clearly articulate what you hope to achieve. I like to use the "3 Ws" for this — "who," "what" and "why."

**Who do you plan to research?** Who are your users?

**What do you want to understand by the end of your research project?** What type of insight are you looking for?

**Why is this understanding important to the overall project goals?** How will the information be used? What outcome are you hoping to achieve from this insight?

Below is a template you can use to incorporate each of these elements. Feel free to use it as an AI prompt to help you write your goals.

### Effective Research Goal Template:

Identify **WHAT** (type of insight) that/about **WHO** (users) in order to **WHY** purpose/outcome).

### Filled in Example:

Identify key rental and property criteria that renters care about, in order to improve their online housing search experience.

Sometimes, the easiest way to understand what not to do is to see it written down or visualised. I've come across so many "bad" goals that I feel like the comparison will be the most helpful in demonstrating what a good goal looks like.

Use the Effective Research Goals colour-coding to see if you can identify the "who," "why" and "what" within each of these good and bad research goal examples. Note how clear or unclear the examples are.

### Bad Examples:

Each of the sentences below is missing some part(s) of the requirements for an effective research goal.

**Example A. Determine the target demographic.** This statement is really vague. We don't know what the demographic is for, who is in the target demographic or why we want this information.

**Example B. Find out what needs exist related to refinancing a mortgage.** Here, we're only talking about the "what"— we've said nothing about who the user is, and there's no reason given for why we're trying to understand this.

**Example C. Understand user challenges related to shopping online.** This one's a little bit more specific than the example above, but not quite there yet. We've technically provided a "what" and a "who," but the term "user" is not specific enough (for example, they could be "DIY home owners") and we still haven't said "why."

**Good Examples:**

In comparison, see how these examples have each of the "3 Ws," and how much clearer the research goals are for stakeholders and team members to understand.

**Example D.** Identify the criteria first-time home buyers look for when comparing mortgages in order to create an experience that will empower them to make better financial decisions.

**Example E.** Understand the tools and services first-time home buyers are currently using to carry out their house hunt in order to find areas of improvement for the Mortgage Investment Online Tool.

**Example F.** Gain insight into the end-to-end process of purchasing a home (including first-time home buyer pain points and challenges) in order to streamline their home-buying experience.

The first step in your collaborative goal setting is to collect information from your stakeholders on their goals. You can do this at the kick-off meeting or in a discovery workshop during project initiation with key stakeholders and team members. These sessions are the perfect opportunities to ask your stakeholders about what they're hoping to learn from the research and what success looks like to them.

Afterwards, you'll need to synthesise what you hear from your stakeholders into a cohesive set of research goals following the "5 Cs" and "3 Ws." Then, finally, you should validate those goals with them, to triple-check that you're on the same page.

# Develop Research Themes and Questions

Next, you'll want to develop a set of research themes and questions to include in your research plan. These will act as the foundation of your interview or field guides and questionnaires.

- **Research themes** are high-level areas of study related to your research goals.
- **Research questions** are the questions you're looking to answer through the research.

Research questions aren't intended to be used as interview questions for your participants per se, although they might be similar. Instead, they provide a line of inquiry for your research that you can use to align the project team and ensure the type of information you plan to collect is in line with their expectations.

You'll start by generating a list of questions. Brainstorm questions with your stakeholders and your project team during an informal weekly check-in, then group those questions into research themes.

Some examples of high-level themes that are common in research projects are: user background and characteristics, technology and tools, "day-in-the-life," journeys or workflows and key motivations and pain points. These themes and questions will go directly into your research plan, which is why it's so important to create them in collaboration with stakeholders.

As you can imagine, there might be many questions within each of these themes that would be helpful to understand when conducting research to redesign a product or service. The number of themes and questions you settle on will be similar to your number of research goals: about 3–5 themes, and 3–5 questions within each theme (but you can include more if needed).

To demonstrate this, here are two examples of common research questions grouped by theme.

### Theme: User Background/Characteristics

These questions are usually asked when you're developing personas:

- What are their responsibilities?
- What are their main characteristics?
- What needs and wants do they have?
- What are their goals and motivations?
- How does this information differ with other roles or service groups?

### Theme: Day-in-the-Life Journey

These questions are usually asked when developing journey maps:

- What are their main tasks and activities? (Examples: attending meetings, project work, travelling, emailing, administration, etc.)
- How much time do they spend on each of these tasks and activities?
- Who do they interact with on a daily basis?
- What are the most common pain points and inefficiencies they experience as they go about their day and complete different activities?

Of course, you would never ask a participant, "What are your main characteristics?" or "What are your activities?" These questions are too general, and your participant wouldn't be able to answer them with the level of detail needed. But, asking yourself and your research team these questions will help you find different ways to probe and get this information from your participants in an organised, comprehensive way.

**Action Advice:**

Someone reading your research questions should be able to look at your insights report after your research is completed and decide whether you've provided the answers. These answers should help them as they move toward improving their product or service and realising their project goals.

# CHOOSE RESEARCH METHODS

The next step is to decide on the best research methods for your project. It's such a pivotal decision, and it will generally be based on timelines, budget, and — you guessed it — your research goals.

## DATA TRIANGULATION

Remember the golden rule of design research: you should mix methods every time. If you mix your methods effectively, you will achieve data triangulation. This will help you find insights that are truly robust… robust enough that executives will be able to base major business decisions on them.

Data triangulation is the gathering (and validating) of research findings from multiple sources and research methods.

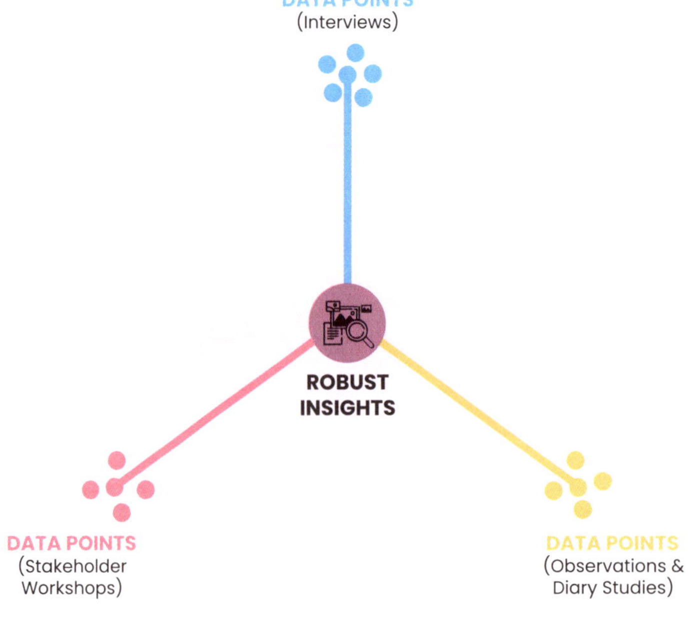

When you use a combination of research methods, like interviews, observations and workshops, you can rest assured that your data accurately reflects the reality of the users' experiences (without having to talk to hundreds of users).

This works because you'll see and hear the same things from different sources (participants), in different settings across different methods. Repeating data points and thoughts indicate that your data isn't being skewed by accidental bias or a non-representative participant or event, allowing those common insights to take on a new power.

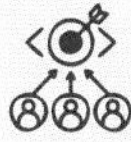

**Alignment Advice:**

Explaining the concept of data triangulation to your stakeholders will help show your expertise and reinforce the power of the qualitative research you're conducting, so they know the insights are real, actionable and not just "fluff."

I once had an executive look at an insights report and ask me, "How do I know these insights don't reflect the opinions of just one person? Should we be placing this much importance on a quote from some random participant?" At face value, they had trouble trusting that the insights we provided accurately represented the needs of the broader participant group. To be fair, this was because they were used to dealing strictly with analytics and quantitative numbers when it came to research.

In situations like these (which are very common), I'm able to gain buy-in through an explanation of both data triangulation and data saturation. (See chapter 7 for more on the latter.) When executives express doubt about my insights, I'll say something like: "That's a great question and one I receive often. We can be sure that these insights apply to many users thanks to a practice called 'data triangulation.' Because we've heard similar thoughts and ideas across our interviews, observations and workshops from various users, we can gather that a lot of users are dealing with this same pain point."

C-suite executives and VPs mostly care about hard numbers. The idea of qualitative research can feel "wishy-washy" to them. It's often tough for them to imagine making business decisions based on the thoughts and feelings of a few users. BUT, the amazing thing about design research (and qualitative research) is that it can actually empower revenue-generating strategy even at enterprise level organisations.

To unlock this power, you need to make stakeholder management part of your job, and work to educate your stakeholders about the value of the insights you'll uncover. Take advantage of presentations and weekly check-in meetings where you're reviewing research findings or discussing research plans, and include a slide explaining data triangulation and its importance. Bring it up often.

You can access and download this modifiable slide at the link to resources at the end of this chapter.

## KEY RESEARCH METHODS

There are a lot of different research methods out there, and they all have different advantages. In this section, I'll cover the six most commonly used ones. While these methods are probably very familiar to you, it's not always clear which methods are the best strategic choice for each situation, or which is the best way to combine them for real-world impact

So, here's a high-level look at each, to help you choose which ones are best for your project. I've dedicated full chapters to the four most complex and impactful methods: interviews, observations, diary studies and workshops.

Before, I explain each one, I've provided coloured symbols to represent each design research facet introduced in chapter 4, so that you can see which facets apply to each research method. (See the legend in chapter 4 for reference.)

### In-Depth Interviews 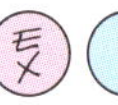 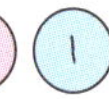 

In-depth interviews (described in chapter 8) are useful in helping you understand user needs, pain points and motivations, simply by asking them. They're also great opportunities to learn the "why" behind these details and facts. As the interview goes on, you can drill down deeper with probing questions to find out the reasons why they do or don't like something, why it's not working for them, why it's important to them and why they deal with it the way they do.

### Observations    

Also called "contextual inquiry," "field study" or "shadowing," observations (described in chapter 9) are best for uncovering unspoken needs and actions users might have trouble articulating or remembering in an interview. You also get to see what a user's surroundings look like, what kind of interruptions they experience, who they interact with, and many other factors that might affect their behaviour.

### Diary Studies    

Diary studies (described in chapter 10) help with tracking interactions over time and understanding recurring patterns in user behaviour, with the added context of photo and/or video evidence. You get to capture a user's unfiltered perspectives, as they reflect on and take note of their own actions, thoughts, feelings, etc. and send that information back to you, the researcher. The patterns you find in recurring data points can also help you predict future user behaviours.

### Workshops      

Workshops (described in chapter 11), whether they're conducted with project stakeholders or with users, can be a rich source of information, letting you take in multiple perspectives in a short period of time. They're great for learning more about your users and their experiences, brainstorming ideas for solutions, validating your findings, prototyping, and getting feedback from users.

### Surveys    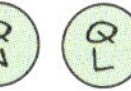

Surveys can be both qualitative and quantitative. They tend to be more cost-effective to set up than a lot of other methods, and the data can also be more straight-forward to analyse, depending on how you've formulated your questions. They're easy to implement if you already have an established list of customers you want to reach.

### Desk Research   

Desk research is best used for gaining a very broad understanding of the current state of an experience, and identifying gaps in existing information. It's great for when you're working within lower budgets and tighter timelines. If you have access to reliable documentation and previous research reports, you can absorb a lot of information in much less time compared to primary research methods.

It also allows you to create context for your primary research, with jumping-off points that can help you probe deeper into your areas of study, especially in cases where you know very little about the users or industry you're going to be researching.

Surveys and desk research should never be used alone in design research. Surveys can tell you some basic information about what your users' behaviours, actions and feelings are, but they'll never give you a full understanding of the "why" or "how" behind these factors. That's why they should always be used to support another research method, like interviews or observations.

Similarly, desk research should always be combined with primary research methods, because otherwise, you'll be relying too much on someone else's information that they captured in a different context. Not all of this information will be relevant or useful to your specific project, and you may end up making decisions based on assumptions instead of facts.

## COMBINING RESEARCH METHODS

You should aim to conduct at least two forms of primary research in all of your design research projects. (That's how you get truly meaningful insights — it's not a coincidence that this book focuses on primary research methods!)

As you start thinking about which methods to combine for your project, remember that your decision should be based on your overall purpose and goals. I've created a chart that can help you quickly identify which research method you should use, and for what purpose:

| Research Purpose | Project Stage/ Design Phase | Research Method(s) |
| --- | --- | --- |
| Understand project context, industry trends, align on goals, high-level processes, etc. | Project Initiation | Desk research, one-on-one stakeholder interviews, discovery workshops |
| Understand behaviours (how a user goes about a task or interacts with a product or service) | Discovery | Observations or diary study |
| Understand perceptions, expectations, overall satisfaction, etc. | Discovery | Interviews, surveys |
| Understand unspoken needs and pain points | Discovery | Observations |
| Understand user characteristics and background (great for creating personas) | Discovery | Interviews, surveys |
| Understand current-state journey or process *at a high level* | Discovery | Interviews, workshops |
| Understand current-state journey or process *in detail* | Discovery | Observations, diary study |
| Understand challenges, needs, desires and motivations | Discovery | Interviews, observations, surveys, workshops |
| Validate or prioritise findings and solutions (to ensure accuracy in the data, and that the design problem is addressed) | Define<br>Prototype & Test | Workshops |
| Generate ideas and solutions | Define<br>Design | Workshops |

To help make it tangible, I've included samples of common methodology combinations based on different research purposes and deliverables, to help you visualise your data triangulation plan.

### Sample Method Combo 1:

**Purpose of research:** Understand the end-to-end experience of users as they go about accomplishing a particular task/goal

**Project deliverables:** Journey map, personas and research report

**Proposed methods:**

- In-depth interviews: To understand user needs, pain points and characteristics, as well as identify key tasks and areas of friction
- Observations: A few days of onsite observations or job shadowing to ensure you get the detailed, step-by-step actions users take in their journey, and identify latent needs that could lead to big opportunities for improvement or innovation
- Validation/feedback workshops: Conducted with a subset of users to ensure research findings are accurate and that pain points are prioritised

### Sample Method Combo 2:

**Purpose of research:** Understand who your users are (when little is known about the target audience)

**Project deliverables:** User personas and research report

**Proposed methods:**

- Desk research: To gain meaningful context and insights related to the area of study and to inform the line of questioning for surveys
- Surveys: To gain a high-level understanding of who the users are, their characteristics and demographic information, and their biggest areas of frustration related to their experience with the organisation, product(s) or service(s), and to recruit participants for interviews
- In-depth interviews: To dive deeper into users' motivations, the tools they use, the activities they do and the pain points they encounter, in order to build out meaningful user personas

# DEVELOP A RESEARCH PLAN

I've run enough design research projects to confirm that creating a detailed research plan is almost always a great idea. It acts as a single source of truth that your team and stakeholders can refer to at any time when they have questions about what you're researching, why and how you'll do it. This is the type of document that actually sets you apart as a leader.

Surprisingly, so few people ever bother to do this step! They think it's enough to talk about the research in meetings and capture meeting notes in an email. The thing is, people will forget what you talked about, or struggle to find your emails, and the things that might be obvious to you (because you live and breathe this stuff) are not always so obvious to stakeholders. Don't assume that they know what's involved in your research, or that they're going to pour over every detail just because you distributed the notes.

To make your research plan, you'll be assembling and listing all of the decisions you made throughout your work in this chapter, in chapters 5 and 7, and in the specific research method chapters relevant to your project.

Here's a checklist to help you remember each element of your research plan:

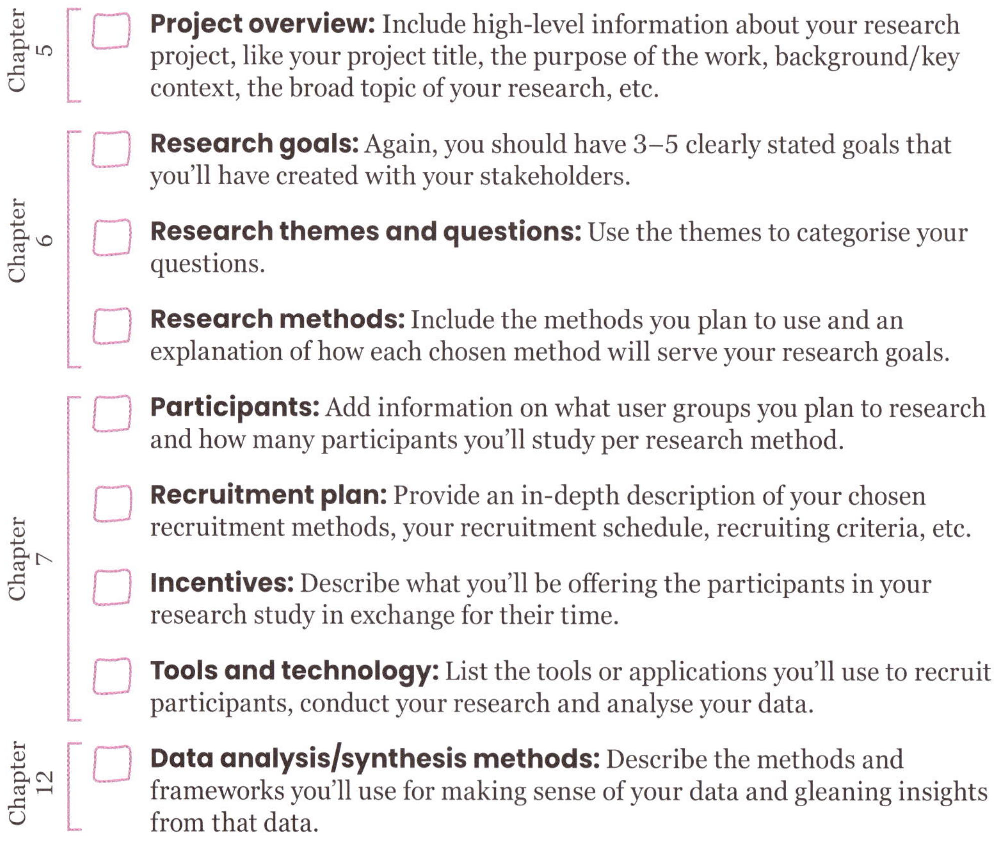

Chapter 5

- [ ] **Project overview:** Include high-level information about your research project, like your project title, the purpose of the work, background/key context, the broad topic of your research, etc.

Chapter 6

- [ ] **Research goals:** Again, you should have 3–5 clearly stated goals that you'll have created with your stakeholders.
- [ ] **Research themes and questions:** Use the themes to categorise your questions.
- [ ] **Research methods:** Include the methods you plan to use and an explanation of how each chosen method will serve your research goals.

Chapter 7

- [ ] **Participants:** Add information on what user groups you plan to research and how many participants you'll study per research method.
- [ ] **Recruitment plan:** Provide an in-depth description of your chosen recruitment methods, your recruitment schedule, recruiting criteria, etc.
- [ ] **Incentives:** Describe what you'll be offering the participants in your research study in exchange for their time.
- [ ] **Tools and technology:** List the tools or applications you'll use to recruit participants, conduct your research and analyse your data.

Chapter 12

- [ ] **Data analysis/synthesis methods:** Describe the methods and frameworks you'll use for making sense of your data and gleaning insights from that data.

- [ ] **Data privacy and storage:** Indicate how you'll be storing your participants' data and what methods, tools or best practices you'll implement to maintain their privacy. Online
- [ ] **Project schedule:** Include all deadlines and major milestones, and do your best to build in some leeway. Chapter 5
- [ ] **Deliverables:** List all of the design artefacts you plan to create and send as part of your final deliverables, including your insights report. Chapter 13

Again, your project team and stakeholders must review your research plan, give you feedback and work with you to approve it before the research starts. Going forward, this plan can become a living document that you'll adjust if and when anything changes.

# Conclusion

Thorough research planning will help you account for all of the logistical details of your research, keep your project on track and, most importantly, establish alignment with your stakeholders.

As you get into the actual research, not everything will go as planned. But the process of creating the initial plan will build trust and an open channel of regular communication between your stakeholders and the research team. That trust will make pivoting more smooth and less stressful for everyone involved. Your hard work in the planning process should establish you as a reliable leader for your team and a strong advocate for your research.

**Online Resources:**

Access a collection of practical, hands-on resources I've created specifically for your research planning at **designresearchmastery.com.**

What you'll find:

- DRM Research Planning Checklist & Workbook
- Data Triangulation & Saturation Slides
- DRM 50+ Methods & Tools

# * Key Takeaways:

1. **Research planning is crucial for project success.** It will help you run projects smoothly, gain insights that are highly relevant to your stakeholders' overarching goals, and inspire confidence.

2. **Effective research goals are carefully crafted, in collaboration with stakeholders.** They should never be created in a vacuum. Don't forget the 5 Cs of Effective Research Goals: comprehensive, clear, concise, constructive and collaborative. Your goals should also contain the 3 Ws: "who," "what" and "why" you're conducting research.

3. **Establishing research themes and questions will make the process of developing interview protocols or observation guides so much easier.** Your research questions won't be the same as your participant interview questions, but they'll act as a guide and line of questioning to inform your interview protocols.

4. **Data triangulation is an important way to ensure that your insights are accurate.** Combining research methods can help to rule out bias and non-representative data. I recommend using at least three methods for any design research project (two of which should be primary research). Data triangulation can also act as a major selling point to stakeholders: you can explain how it works, and show them why your qualitative insights aren't wishy-washy or anecdotal like some might think.

5. **Generally, there are six most common design research methods that you'll choose from based on the purpose of your research.** Those methods are: desk research, surveys, in-depth interviews, observations, diary studies and workshops. Use a combination of these methods to drill down into your area of study. (I won't cover desk research or surveys in depth in this book, but you can reference chapters 8–11 to learn more about each of the other four methods.)

6. **Drafting a formal research plan can help you stay on track through complex projects.** Your plan should include your established research goals, themes and questions, your research methods of choice and other key logistics including your project schedule, research tools and participant recruitment plan (which I'll cover in the next chapter).

# 7 RESEARCH PLANNING

## Defining and Recruiting Users

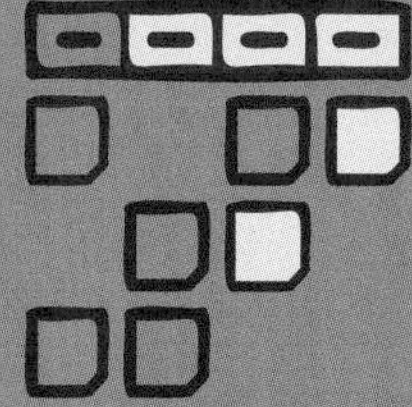

"No matter how good the team or how efficient the methodology, if we're not solving the right problem, the project fails."
— Woody Williams

# Introduction

User recruitment is a make-or-break part of research planning. If you don't do it right, you could lose stakeholder trust and set your project back by weeks, or even months... and doing it right is tough for a few reasons.

For me, recruiting users has always been one of the most annoying parts of the research process. If you're lucky, you get to enlist the help of a participant recruitment firm or use subscription-based research platforms with built in audiences to recruit from, which makes this part much easier. However, I've rarely been able to use these firms, mostly because of the client's budget, or in some cases, because the topics were so niche that using a firm or tool didn't make sense. This has often left me chasing people around and following up numerous times to get a participant booked.

If you're in the same scenario, you'll need to understand how to actually recruit the right people yourself, and make sure you get a diverse enough sample of people, while also having enough of the same types of people to see patterns in the data. It's a tricky balancing act, and there are a lot of logistics to keep track of. That's why the majority of the research tools and guides I've created over the years are focused around participant recruitment. I've been using them for some time, not only to keep myself and my teams on track, but to help with communicating progress updates to stakeholders. I've packed as much of this information as possible into this chapter and the related online resources I'll link you out to. By the end, you'll be in a better position to ensure the quality and usefulness of your research by recruiting the right people in the right amount, on schedule.

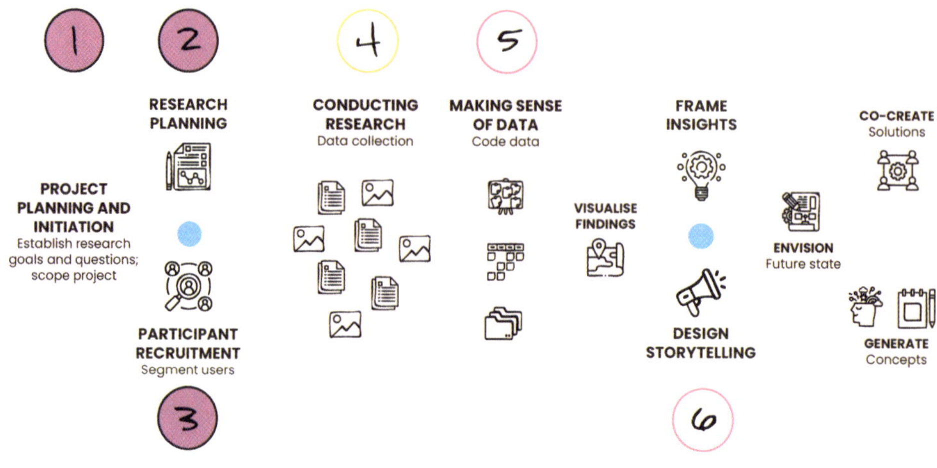


Referencing the Design Research Triple Diamond above, you can see that user recruitment should be done as part of your research planning.

# Determine User Groups

Identifying your user groups will help you narrow down your research participant criteria. A common mistake I see people making as they set out to identify and recruit participants for design research is they confuse "target audience" and "user groups". So, before we dive in, let's level-set on what user groups actually are, because they can be different from your "target audience."

**User groups** represent different types of users that access and interact with your product or service. Within each of these groups, people will have similar characteristics, including their motivations, habits, challenges, etc. Marketing teams tend to define target audiences through characteristics like age, location, and gender, which are less heavily weighted when defining user groups. These factors are still important to consider and will play a part – but user groups get a bit more nuanced, and place special emphasis on user goals and behaviours.

When you conduct research, you typically recruit a prescribed number of users from each user group as representative samples. Generally, most products or services will have 4–6 user groups. Some products and services may have more or less, but this range is generally a good guideline for scoping your project and ensuring that your research plan and timeline remain manageable.

For example, let's pretend you're doing research to improve the design of a grocery delivery app, so that people want to use it more frequently. The user groups for the app might look like the ones in the following chart.

| | User Group 1 | User Group 2 | User Group 3 | User Group 4 |
|---|---|---|---|---|
| Grocery ordering frequency | 1–2 times per week | 1–2 times per month | 1–2 times per month | Once every few months |
| Age range | 40–49 | 30–39 | 50–59 | 20–29 |
| Family size | 4–6 | 2–3 | 2–3 | 1 |
| Transportation | Car | Car | Walk | Bus |

You can see in the chart that age and location still factor in, but ordering frequency, family size and transportation are included as more nuanced characteristics that are highly relevant to users' grocery ordering behaviour.

Most of the time, you'll have a good idea of who the user groups are at the start of your research project, because it's likely that customer segments or target audiences were pre-defined by the organisation (and you can use them as a guide to building your user groups). Just make sure that you're not blindly mapping out your user groups one-to-one with these segments.

Now, if you don't have this context, you'll need to do some upfront work to define the user groups in collaboration with your stakeholders. To help, I've broken down your next steps into three scenarios.

**When user groups are *known*, and stakeholder priorities are *defined*:** Meet with stakeholders and ask them who they think the main users are. You should come prepared to the meeting with ideas about who they might be and what criteria you might use to recruit them. Spend at least 15 minutes workshopping these ideas with your stakeholders, and ask questions like, "Who are the different types of people that use your product or service?" and "What makes these types of people different?" You should also prompt your stakeholders with questions about age, goals, behaviours, pain points, and other relevant characteristics etc. For example, on a project about home buyers, you might ask them about the types of mortgages available, and if that could play a role in defining the user groups.

The goal of this meeting is to walk away with the high-level criteria, and a general idea of which user groups they want to prioritise in the research. From there, you can use your recruiting criteria spreadsheet to get more specific. (There'll be more on this spreadsheet later in this chapter.)

**When user groups are *known*, but stakeholder priorities are *undefined*:** Dig into the data and come up with data-based suggestions. Quantitative data (from analytics or marketing surveys) can be a great resource for helping stakeholders prioritise which user groups are most important or relevant to the project. Once you have some solid ideas for user group prioritisation, you can engage your stakeholders in a meeting like the one I described above, to validate your ideas and agree on how to move forward.

For example, from digging through existing data, you might find out that the vast majority of users are on mobile devices or come from a certain region. Depending on your organisation's goals, you might use this information to prioritise the majority of users, or you might suggest prioritising underserved user groups, and finding out what products and services they need.

**When user groups are *unknown*, and priorities are *undefined*:** I recommend doing some preliminary research to gain more context about the users and problem space. You could conduct stakeholder or subject matter expert (SME) interviews, discovery workshops, a survey or desk research. As you do this, you'll get clearer on what your user groups look like and which ones you and your stakeholders want to study.

The **2x2 User Group Matrix** is a great framework for brainstorming and organising users into groups. Here's how to build one:

- Draw X and Y axes
- Pick two scales to compare your users against
- Plot your users on the matrix
- Name your quadrants (which become your user groups)

For example, you might decide to compare users based on how many touchpoints they typically have with customer support, as well as their levels of tech-savvyness.

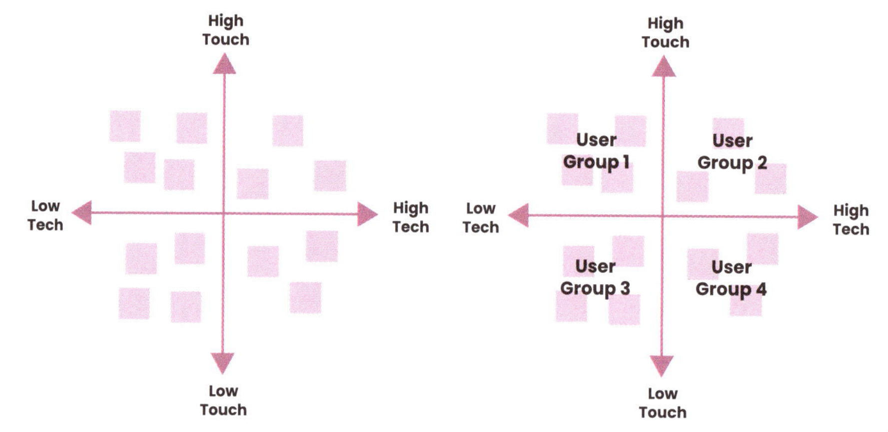

# Choose the Recruiting Criteria

Once you've defined your user groups and their main differentiating characteristics, you'll need to create more detailed recruiting criteria that will support you in identifying participants for your research. **Recruiting criteria** are parameters used to ensure that you're researching a mix of the right people who accurately reflect the diverse needs and perspectives of your users. **You should aim to have about 5–8 criteria per project, with subcategories.** To make this more clear, I'll walk you through some examples.

| **User/Participant Example** | **Recruiting Criteria**<br>(With Specified Subcategories) |
|---|---|
| **Users of a grocery shopping app:**<br>These criteria and subcategories come from the hypothetical example I mentioned earlier in this chapter. In this example, it might be interesting to contrast the experiences of users who have young families vs. those who live alone, or in a couple. Each would have different needs, expectations, and reasons for using the app. | **Grocery shopping frequency:** 1–2 times per week, 1–2 times per month, Once every few months<br>**Age range:** 20–29, 30–39, 40–49, 50–59, 60+<br>**Location type:** Metro, suburban, rural<br>**Family size:** 1, 2–3, 4–6<br>**Transportation:** Car, bus, bike, walking |
| **Adult learners:**<br>I led a project that focused on understanding adult learning barriers and needs as they incorporated their studies into their day-to-day lives. These learners' experiences differed based on things like the type of learning centre they went to, their learning level, how far they lived from school, etc. | **Age range:** 20–29, 30–39, 40–49, 50+<br>**Location type:** Metro, suburban, rural<br>**Learning level:** I, II, III<br>**Purpose for learning:** GED, upskilling, trade certificate or licence, ESL Certificate<br>**Institution:** Adult high school, college, community learning centre |
| **Mortgage and home buyers:**<br>In this study (referenced in some research goal examples in chapter 6), I wanted a balance of data between people who were buying their first homes, buying second homes, looking into investment properties or downsizing. These factors could easily influence the types of tools and advice they seek when making decisions about their future home purchases. | **Age range:** 20–29, 30–39, 40–49, 50+<br>**Location type:** Metro, suburban, rural<br>**Purpose for buying home:** First-time family home purchase, relocating, investment property, downsizing<br>**Budget:** <$250k, $251k–$500k, $501k–$1M, $1M+<br>**Mortgage lender:** Top-five bank, credit union, mortgage broker, other |

**Alignment Advice:**

The best way to ensure you're recruiting the right users? Collaborate with your stakeholders in forming your recruiting criteria. Getting everyone on the same page is crucial to getting it right. You need to avoid misunderstanding your stakeholders' needs in the first place and spending time and resources on data that they didn't actually ask for. You also need to avoid zooming out too far (looking at how users interact with the business as a whole, rather than the specific product or service you're working on), or getting led on a tangent (prioritising certain criteria purely because they interest you and your team the most).

Recruiting users is an involved, high-effort and high-investment process, and you don't want to lose stakeholder trust by creating surprises. Even if you're positive that the criteria you've selected is 100% relevant to your project, and your stakeholders were deeply involved in defining user groups at the start, your stakeholders still need to sign off. Ensure that you also update them regularly throughout the recruiting process to keep them in the loop.

To turn criteria into a useful tool for recruiting participants, I developed a **recruitment criteria spreadsheet**. This spreadsheet includes a template for criteria that you can use to segment your audience into different user groups, and determine and track the number of participants you want to study from each group.

Let's look closer at the home buyer example I mentioned earlier. In this study, we recruited a total of 20 people. So, for each criteria that we wanted to consider, like location, we broke it down into subcategories (metro, suburban and rural). And then, for each subcategory, we decided how many participants we wanted to study (e.g. 7 users located in rural areas). The total number of participants for that criteria (location) equalled 20: 7 from rural areas, 6 from a metro and 7 from the suburbs. I filled this spreadsheet ahead of a meeting with stakeholders, and then walked them through it on the call, adjusting the numbers where it made sense. From there, we used this to start the recruiting process.

**Total Number of Participants You Plans To Recruit:** 20

| **Criteria 1: Age Range** | **# of Participants** (That match criteria) |
|---|---|
| 20-29 | 5 |
| 30-39 | 5 |
| 40-49 | 5 |
| 50+ | 5 |
| **Criteria 2: Location** | **# of Participants** (That match criteria) |
| Urban/metro | 6 |
| Suburban | 7 |
| Rural | 7 |
| **Criteria 3: Home Buying Experience/Purpose** | **# of Participants** (That match criteria) |
| First-time family home buyers | 5 |
| Second house purchase (selling family home) | 5 |
| Investment property | 5 |
| Downsizing | 5 |
| **Criteria 4: Budget** | **# of Participants** (That match criteria) |
| Less than $250,000 | 5 |
| $251k-$500k | 5 |
| $51k-$1M | 5 |
| More than $1M | 5 |
| **Criteria 5: Preferred Mortgage Lender** | **# of Participants** (That match criteria) |
| Top five Bank | 6 |
| Credit union | 6 |
| Mortgage broker | 6 |
| Other | 4 |

(**Note:** You can access this spreadsheet in the online resources, which are linked at the end of this chapter.)

# Choose the Number of Participants

As you know, in design research, we're primarily dealing with qualitative research. With qualitative research, you don't need as many participants as you might think. This is because the focus is on the content of the data itself, rather than statistical averages, and because you will reach a point of data saturation. Your stakeholders might not necessarily get this at first, but this section should help you explain it to them with confidence and clarity.

**Data saturation** refers to the point during research when no new insights or information is provided by new data sources, i.e. participants. As you continue to ask the same questions to new participants or observe new participants perform the same tasks, you'll stop seeing or hearing about new perspectives, behaviours and challenges.

Below is a graph to illustrate how data saturation works. As the amount of data increases, the amount of new, valuable insights tapers off. At first, you'll receive all kinds of useful data that's relevant to your project, and then you'll hit a plateau where doing more of the same research with the same participants is no longer worth the time and money.

This is something that happens in all research projects, but when it happens will depend on the research methods you're using and what you're studying. In usability testing, it's commonly thought that it's a waste of resources to test more than five users total at each iteration of a design. Of course, with an exploratory research method like in-depth interviews, researchers are trying to glean a fuller and more complex set of findings, so they need about five users per user group depending on the research method.

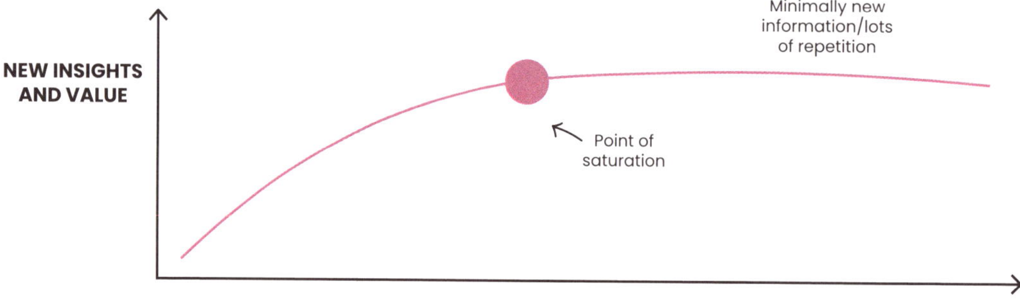


### Action Advice:

Data saturation is an important term for helping stakeholders buy into smaller participant sample sizes.

I've mentioned a few times that stakeholders, executives and other decision makers are generally more comfortable with qualitative research, where participant numbers are in the hundreds, and every statistic has been reinforced by those numbers. So, they might be surprised when you suggest conducting observations with a few participants from one user group, instead of 50 or 100. And they might start to worry that your data will be anecdotal, and not representative of your user groups.

That's where data saturation comes in. Explain it to your stakeholders as early on as you can — if you're presenting a slide deck to them, insert a slide dedicated to data saturation, as well as data triangulation (which we covered in chapter 6). Once they understand these concepts, and once you can prove that they work, your stakeholders will see that you're being smart about their resources and that you're not asking them to fund a bunch of research for the sake of itself. You're helping them be more strategic and only research the needed amount of participants.

In the chart below, I cover the typical amounts of participants you should study per user group for each of the research methods covered in this book. You should strike a balance so that you're able to identify patterns in the data without going beyond the saturation point.

| Research Method | Number of Participants |
|---|---|
| In-depth interviews | 6–8 per user group<br>(If you have 4–6 user groups, then you'll likely talk to 24–36 participants total) |
| Observations | 3–4 per user group<br>(This will add up to 12–20 participants total between two researchers) |
| Survey | 100+ total respondents* |
| Workshop | 8–15 participants per workshop |
| Diary study | 4–6 per user group |

*For surveys, you won't reach statistical relevance at 100 respondents, but the data you get will be more relevant from a qualitative perspective because of your mixed method approach.

(**Note:** You can use the same participants for multiple different research methods — they don't have to be fresh participants each time! In fact, it's recommended to have overlap. For example, you can and should interview at least some of the same people you're observing.)

# Choose a Recruiting Method

Once you've narrowed down your recruiting criteria and how many people you need, you'll need to figure out how you will actually find these people. This is the most daunting part. To help you, I've outlined nine of the most common methods for recruiting participants on the next two pages. I've ranked the difficulty level of all of these from "easy" to "hard," so that you can gauge what methods will work best for your team and timeline.

| Recruiting Method | Description | Difficulty Level |
|---|---|---|
| Previous participants | • Involves contacting people who've participated in a similar study by the same organisation | Easy |
| Contacting "good" or known customers | • Recruiting users or customers who frequently contact you, are early adopters and/or always purchase new products<br>• A great way to get started for organisations that are less comfortable with research<br>(**This method is not recommended to be used as the only method, because it can cause bias in your research**, if your known customers all love your products/services.) | Easy |
| Paying a recruiting firm | • A good option if your time/resources are limited, or if you aren't sure how to find participants<br>• The cost is a higher barrier to entry, and choosing the right firm can be tough<br>• It's recommended to ask around for referrals | Easy |
| Subscription-based research platform | • A fast option if your company can afford the subscription cost (or cost per participant)<br>• Good if you are recruiting members of the general public or topic isn't super niche<br>• Not great if your topic area requires users with a very specific background | Easy |
| Existing lists | • Applies to organisations that have customer lists they're allowed to share and contact for research purposes (e.g. newsletter signup lists or customer contact lists) | Medium |
| Leveraging partner organisations and community hubs | • Especially helpful in the public sector, where organisations that are in contact with applicable citizens can recruit on your behalf | Medium |

| Recruiting Method | Description | Difficulty Level |
|---|---|---|
| Customer support agents or sales representatives | • Support agents or sales reps who are talking to customers every day can be a useful recruitment avenue<br>(**Take extra care in preparing phone scripts so they know exactly what to say and do.** More on scripts and screeners for recruitment later in this chapter.) | Medium |
| Real-time recruiting | • Involves setting up a public space and approaching people in person to sign up as participants<br>• Difficulty level will depend on your tolerance for frequent rejections | Hard |
| Social media | • Users are found by posting on social media and using crowdsourcing tools and forums<br>• Success will depend on the reach and number of shares<br>• Can provide a wide variety of participants<br>**(I don't recommend this method because it opens your project up to impostor participants!)** | Hard |

(**Note**: Incentives, which are usually provided in the form of a \$50–\$150 gift card, are highly recommended to help facilitate your recruitment process, reduce the likelihood of no-shows and ensure a positive experience for your participants. The incentives you choose need to be appropriate for the people you're recruiting, address ethical concerns, and you need to be clear with participants upfront about how much, when and the type of incentive they'll receive. There's an online resource on incentive examples and related tips linked at the end of this chapter.)

### Design Research in Reality: *Impostor Participants*

When it comes to recruiting participants, don't believe everything you hear! This is a funny story I wanted to share with you. There was a project my team was working on that involved recruiting high school teachers from across a Canadian province in order to do some validation research of a teacher portal.

There wasn't enough budget to use an external recruiting firm, and the client didn't have any connections to local schools that we could reach out to. We also didn't have a lot of time for this project. So, we decided to use our own connections and also utilise social media (Facebook and LinkedIn) as well as public forums to recruit participants. We were smug and thought, "How hard could it be to find teachers? It's a pretty common job." Well, the joke was on us.

We did all the right things — we put together the recruiting scripts, the screeners, etc., and went through the process of finding people by putting out posts on these different channels, explaining what we were looking for and why. We even had people fill out a pretty detailed screener. If they matched the criteria we were looking for, then we contacted them and booked them in for some usability testing sessions. After the first three sessions, the team quickly realised they were NOT talking to Canadian teachers. The "participants" were impostors who had used fake information to fill out the screener, and had shared our call for participants with a whole network of people who scam these types of research studies to get access to the incentive.

In the end, we had to let our client know what had happened, and make up for the lost participants by working a few longer days and getting in touch with schools to help us. It delayed the project by about a week. At least we didn't pay the incentive to the impostor participants, because they weren't able to provide a verified school email address (a would-be screening factor we thought of after the fact)... but to be honest, we were a little embarrassed that we fell for it. That was the first and last time something like that happened to us, but I've definitely heard about it happening to others.

**The Lesson:** Build in extra time for recruiting the "right" participants. Push for it, even if your stakeholders are demanding that you go quicker, so that you can gather participants the right way, without being tempted to take any potentially sketchy shortcuts. Speaking of potential shortcuts, be very wary when using public forums or social media, and think of fail-safe screening criteria to help you verify that your participants are legitimate (like the verified school email address, which we only thought of after the snafu), so you can avoid paying incentives to scammers. Don't underestimate impostors, because they're getting smarter all of the time, and so are the AI tools that they can use to craft fake but real-sounding answers to your questions.

## Recruiting and Screening Materials

Users aren't always interested in talking to you, or they can be hard to get a hold of. You might have trouble finding or scheduling enough users to participate within a certain timeframe, or you might have a series of no-shows for your research sessions, etc. If you recruit the wrong users for your research, your data will be wrong, too. BUT, when you have the proper tools to recruit users successfully, you'll be amazed at how things come together. For one thing, creating official recruiting and screening materials will help you divide up the work, if you have team members or options for support. For another, these documents will keep you organised, focused and efficient, and you'll be able to easily review your progress.

## RECRUITING SCRIPT

Once you've decided who and how to recruit, it's time to prepare your **recruiting script**. A recruiting script is a template for explaining the nature of your study to potential participants. It provides background on your project so that users can determine if they have an interest in participating, and so they have a general idea of what they'd need to do.

Recruiting scripts should include:

- **The purpose of the research:** Provide a high-level overview of why you are doing the research and what it is about
- **Who you are:** What your role is in the project
- **What the participant will be asked to do:** Are they answering interview questions, filling out a diary study, etc.
- **How long will the research activity be**
- **When the research will be conducted**
- **Any incentive details**
- **Potential next steps:** For example, you might plan to schedule a screening call or send them a screening survey

I've put together a resource that includes copy-and-paste recruiting scripts — see the link at the end of this chapter.

## SCREENING QUESTIONNAIRE AND TRACKER

As participants express interest in the study, you'll need to screen them using a **screening questionnaire**. Screening is an important step that ensures your potential participants match your recruiting criteria. This process lets you confirm that you're conducting research with the right people. It also helps you figure out how many potential participants line up with your criteria for your different user groups, so you're getting a good balance of data.

If you or your organisation already know your users fairly well, screening won't necessarily be needed. But, **if you don't know your users well, screening is absolutely crucial**. Make sure to leave time for it in your recruiting schedule. This step is often skipped or overlooked – don't do that to yourself!

To start with, you should build a screening questionnaire with at least 5–10 questions specifically designed to determine if your potential participants meet your criteria.

Remember that as you're recruiting participants for research, you'll need to have a plan in place for gaining their consent, and securely storing and protecting their data. Being an ethical researcher means ensuring that all consent is informed consent. (Again, see the online resources listed at the end of this chapter. There's a sample screening questionnaire and a helpful guides to participant consent, data storage and data privacy.)

As you recruit participants, you should track them using a **participant tracker spreadsheet**. Build it using the same criteria from your criteria spreadsheet, and mark down how many screened people meet each of the different criteria. This process will help you ensure that you study a diverse group of people, and that you get enough data from each subcategory of users within each of your criteria. Getting this representative data will help you find patterns within and across your different user groups.

Here's an example of a participant tracker that we used when we were recruiting participants for that study on home buyers I mentioned earlier. It's also listed in this chapter's online resources.

| 2 | Participant | 20-29 | 30-39 | 40-49 | 50+ | Urban | Suburban | Rural | First-Time Home Buyer | 2nd Home | Investment Property |
|---|---|---|---|---|---|---|---|---|---|---|---|
| 3 | P1 | X | | | | X | | | | X | |
| 4 | P2 | X | | | | | X | | | | X |
| 5 | P3 | | | X | | | X | | X | | |
| 6 | P4 | X | | | | | | X | | | |
| 7 | P5 | X | | | | | X | | | | |
| 8 | P6 | X | | | | | X | | X | | |
| 9 | P7 | | X | | | | X | | X | | |
| 10 | P8 | | X | | | | | X | | | |
| 11 | P9 | | | X | | X | | | | | |
| 12 | P10 | | | X | | | | X | | | |
| 13 | P11 | | | X | | X | | | | | |
| 14 | P12 | | | | X | | X | | | | |
| 15 | P13 | | X | | | | X | | | | |
| 16 | P14 | | X | | | | | | | | |
| 17 | P15 | | | | X | X | | | | | |
| 18 | P16 | | | | X | X | | | | | |
| 19 | P17 | | | | X | | | X | | | |
| 20 | P18 | | | X | | X | | X | | | |
| 21 | P19 | | X | | | X | | | | | |
| 22 | P20 | | | | X | | | X | | | |
| 23 | TOTAL | 5 | 5 | 5 | 5 | 7 | 7 | 6 | 3 | 1 | 1 |

## RECRUITING GUIDE

If you have others helping you recruit participants, whether it's a partner organisation, support agents, sales reps or other project team members, you need to make sure that they're properly prepared. Consider creating a **recruiting guide** with clear instructions and distributing it to your team. This can reduce the chances of error and help you avoid repeating yourself if someone misses the training call or forgets a step.

You should also package up all of the recruiting scripts, your recruiting criteria spreadsheet, recruiting screeners, consent forms and any other required documents you've put together and send them ahead of time, so that the people helping you can review them and ask any clarifying questions.

Next, hold a training call to clarify the recruiting process and review any dos and don'ts. (This is especially important if your team isn't made up of experienced researchers, or if you're studying vulnerable populations.)

**You should always plan back-ups!** Sometimes, the first recruiting method you try doesn't pan out, and you need to be resilient. Don't be afraid to get creative, especially if you're on a tight timeline.

Here are some measures that can help avoid panic:

- Recruit back-up participants in case some of your participants end up being no-shows.
- Prepare alternate recruiting methods in case your primary method doesn't work.
- Be ready to enlist additional support if your recruitment team becomes overwhelmed, falls behind, or becomes unavailable.

Once you've completed your recruitment planning and you've identified the "right" users for your research, you can start scheduling participants. How you do that will vary based on the methods you're using. I've provided my best scheduling tips specific to conducting interviews in the next chapter, since interviews require the most hands-on and fast-paced scheduling.

# Conclusion

Your participants are the heart of your entire research project. True human-centred design puts real human users into focus and solves for their needs, in order to get the results that your stakeholders are after. If you get this key ingredient right (you recruit the right participants and you have balanced, unbiased representation of your user groups), your insights will illuminate the experience of the right users, and your project will create real impact for your organisation.

**Online Resources:**

Before you move on to the research methods (chapters 8–11), you might want to explore the many recruiting resources I've referenced throughout this chapter at **designresearchmastery.com.**

What you'll find:

- Recruiting Criteria Spreadsheet & Template
- DRM Recruiting Workbook
- 5 Copy-and-Paste Recruiting Scripts
- DRM Participant Tracker
- DRM Sample Screening Questionnaire
- Data Triangulation & Saturation Slides
- Participant Consent Types & Samples
- Participant Privacy & Data Storage
- Participant Incentives Guide

## * Key Takeaways:

1. **Develop your recruiting criteria thoughtfully, using the frameworks and background context and resources available to you.** This includes preliminary interviews with users, desk research and frameworks like the 2x2 User Group Matrix.

2. **Use data saturation guidelines to decide how many users you're recruiting from each user group.** This will vary depending on the research methods you've selected. I've included some typical ranges for key methods earlier in this chapter.

3. **Develop clear, well-worded recruiting scripts, screeners and screening protocols**. The questions you ask and the context you provide can make a huge difference in the success of this step.

4. **Give careful consideration to your recruiting methods and who you choose to help with recruitment.** Avoid recruiting participants from a pool of loyal customers who know the company well, because your research data is more likely to be biased in favour of the product or service in question. Prepare your recruitment team to do their best work, and be ready to pivot if your first attempts at recruitment don't succeed.

5. **Track your screened participants diligently, to ensure you recruit the right number of participants per set of criteria.** If you aren't able to divide the criteria evenly across the number of participants, ensure that your participant selection reflects your stakeholders' priorities, so that you get enough data from the most crucial user groups.

# 8 IN-DEPTH INTERVIEWS

"The important thing is not to stop questioning."
— Albert Einstein

# Introduction

All of the quotes that open these chapters are meaningful to me, but this one is special. My dad is a physicist and his idol is Albert Einstein. Growing up, we had this quote hanging above our front door. I saw it everyday for the better part of 20 years. I didn't realise how significant it would become in my career — I now lead a company where we literally get paid to ask questions. I also love this quote because it's a reminder to challenge the status quo, which requires constant questioning and learning. After all, challenging the status quo is a necessary part of driving impactful change to a product or service. And interviewing is a perfect first step.

Too often in UX and service design, we're asked to design based on assumptions, with very little research (if any) to use as a starting point. The truth that you gain through interviews is powerful because it comes from directly asking users about their own experiences. In-depth interviews in particular get their name because they enable researchers to understand these experiences on a deeper level. They give you the opportunity to ask targeted follow-up questions and guide interviewees further down interesting and relevant trains of thought. This helps with unpacking the "why" behind their thoughts and feelings and the motivations behind their interactions with a product or service. Inside that "why" is where you're ultimately going to uncover golden opportunities to improve that product or service and create real impact for your organisation.

In this chapter, I won't be taking you through the "basics" of interviews. I'll take you through the insider tips and tricks I've collected from my long career of both triumphs and lessons in coaxing meaningful answers out of interviewed participants, and managing stakeholder needs and expectations throughout the process.

This is the first of the design research methods that I'll go through in this book, kicking us off into the fourth stage of the Six-Stage DRM Process: actually conducting the research with your participants (primarily users) and collecting your data.

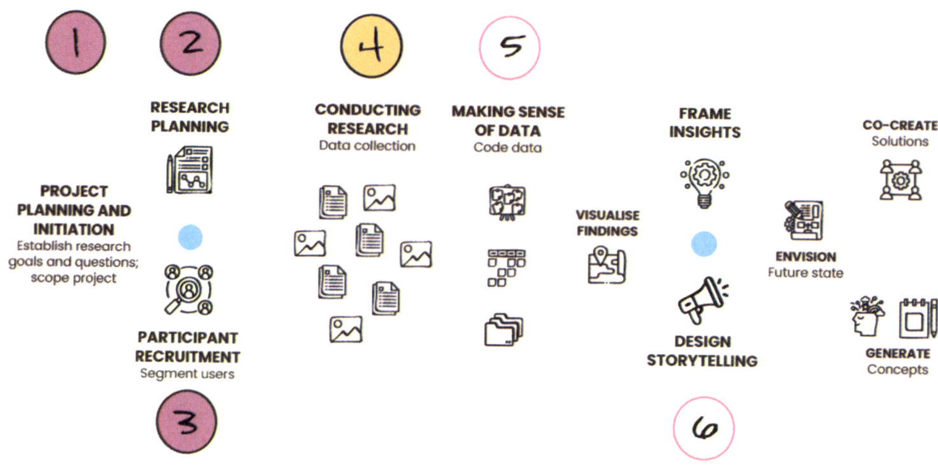


## KEY BENEFITS OF IN-DEPTH INTERVIEWS

Interviews are the most accessible form of research and the one most commonly used in design research projects because they're:

- **Straightforward to organise and conduct** (Compared to many other methods)
- **Adaptable to remote research** (Virtual interviews are just as effective)
- **Easier to document and analyse** (They can be recorded and transcribed, and you can follow a set order of questions, making it simpler to find patterns in the data)
- **Easier to cross-reference in synthesis** (There's less room for subjective interpretation between the data and the resulting insights)
- **Effective in understanding user needs, goals, pain points, and motivations**

Having said all of that, mastering the art of **in-depth interviews** — typically one-on-one, semi-structured, and at least 60 minutes long — can take years of on-the-job practice and learning about what not to do (so you don't get led down tangents, waste your time or introduce bias), and what to do (so you can uncover the most important information and probe strategically on your feet within a limited time frame). My goal is to help you conduct the most effective interviews possible so that you can yield robust data and gain actionable insights, proving to your stakeholders the unmistakable value of going "straight to the source" for user data.

# Interview Planning

There's a lot to think about when you're setting up interviews, and that strategic thinking is the "secret sauce" for truly successful design research. It'll make the difference between an insights report that just repeats things that your stakeholders already know, and one that rocks their world with new perspectives and useful suggestions they hadn't imagined.

Regardless of what you're studying, you'll have the same decisions to make as part of your interview planning. Running through this list and choosing mindfully will ensure that your interviews not only run smoothly, but yield useful data that will move the project forward toward your goals.

## CHOOSE THE PARTICIPANTS

Who you talk to will change the questions you ask, and how you ask them. You will need different kinds of participants to provide you with different sorts of information related to your study.

There are three main types of participants that you might interview throughout the course of your project: stakeholders, subject matter experts (SMEs) and users.

**Stakeholders:** Stakeholder interviews can be very helpful during your project initiation, before you've conducted any research with real users. You can use these opportunities to foster trust and ask stakeholders for more background on the overall project, including business objectives, broader project goals, their perspective on the current state of the product or service, and what related challenges or goals they're responsible for. (See also chapter 5 for more on project initiation.)

Interviews should always be one-on-one. Why? Because having two interviewees attend at the same time can:

- Create bias/influencing the other person's opinions, thoughts or judgements
- Make it harder to keep the interview on track and on time
- Hinder participants from opening up and feeling comfortable expressing themselves

In very rare cases, I'll make an exception if I'm interviewing stakeholders and they're short for time. But I NEVER do this with users.

For example, if you're interviewing two stakeholders at the same time, and one of them is the other's supervisor, there might be a pressure to agree with the supervisor's ideas instead of giving candid and genuine answers. This is why I generally won't support this dynamic. I'll typically give stakeholders the three reasons above as an explanation when they ask.

**Subject matter experts (SMEs):** SMEs have preexisting knowledge and expertise about the topic or system you're researching. These interviews are most often conducted during your project ramp-up. SMEs can help you to quickly immerse yourself in the area of study and identify trends, themes or areas for further consideration. You can also tap them to help you plan your interview questions, clear up any confusion or contradictions that arise during your interviews and validate emerging findings.

**Users:** Invariably, users are the "meat and potatoes" of your research project — they're the main event and the people you'll spend the most time seeking to understand during the "discover" phase. In-depth interviews will help you empathise with them, understand what drives them, and what's working or what's not when it comes to the product or service you are hoping to improve or digitise. Recruiting the right users (which I covered in chapter 7) will be critical to ensuring you collect the right data, but to get the most out of your user interviews, you'll also need to have stellar planning and listening skills, among other high-impact skills which I'll cover later in this chapter.

## CHOOSE THE ATTENDEE ROLES AND RESPONSIBILITIES

As you plan your interviews, you'll also need to make sure that all team roles and responsibilities are clearly articulated ahead of time, to avoid confusing participants. You'll need to determine who will be conducting the interview — you or another researcher — and who might be joining as a silent observer (not ideal, but some stakeholders might insist), and who'll be taking notes (optional, but helpful).

Everyone should be briefed on proper interview etiquette in advance. During interviews, everyone except the interviewer and interviewee should remain on mute, with cameras off. Silent observers and any human notetakers should be introduced at the beginning of the call, and invited to unmute at the end of the call to ask any additional questions they might have.

Stakeholders will sometimes want to sit in your user interviews. To avoid bias, I strongly recommend that you steer them away from this as much as possible.

It's happened to me more than once that a very spirited (read: micromanaging) stakeholder or product owner (PO) asked to sit in on interviews, and I made the regrettable decision of saying "yes" against my better judgement. Way more regrettable was the fact that I didn't think to do some quick expectation setting ahead of the interviews they'd be joining. Midway through the first interview, they started piping up with random leading questions that would 1) completely surprise the participant, because they were mid-thought and not expecting a new voice to pipe in, and 2) derail the line of questioning so that I didn't have time to ask everything I needed to. This made half of the interview useless from an analysis standpoint.

If you're interviewing a user and a stakeholder wants to sit in, the user could be thrown off, lose their train of thought, or censor their own honest feedback about a product or service to avoid tension. This is a huge issue because the users' honest answers are so crucial to understanding what is really going wrong with their experience, and it could prevent you from uncovering the insights and opportunities that will make a big difference to the product or service you are working on.

As long as you're tactful and you explain the risk of bias, your stakeholders will hopefully understand. Remind them that you'll share snippets of the interview transcripts and provide updates as you go. And if they do insist on sitting in, provide them a copy of your interview protocol and brief them on the required etiquette, to avoid experiencing the same thing that I mentioned above.

(**Note**: I'll bring this up again in chapter 9, because the presence of stakeholders can be equally or especially problematic with observations.)

## CHOOSE THE DURATION AND FORMAT

The length of your interviews will depend on your participants' availability, as well as how much information or how many questions you have. Your stakeholders might have less time free in their schedules compared to some of your users. But if your users are lawyers, for example, they might not want you to take away from their billable time, unless the end solution will be quite impactful to their day-to-day.

Interviews are typically 30–90 minutes, with most being around 60 minutes long. A good rule of thumb to remember: **for a 60-minute interview, aim for about 20–30 main questions**, plus your sub-questions, also called "interview probes." (There'll be more on interview probes later on in this chapter.)

Next, you'll need to figure out what interview format you're going with. This might differ depending on the type of participants or the user groups you're interviewing. In general, you have three options: remote via web conferencing (most common), remote over-the-phone, and in-person. When choosing a format, you should consider your participants' situation first, and not just whatever will fit best into your own established routines. Make sure to assess your interviewees' level of tech savvy-ness, their access to tech and their geographic location.

Depending on the demographics of your participants, some might not have easy access to wifi, a computer, or a smartphone, or they might not be able to find a private or quiet space during working hours. Or, they might have access to all of these things, but they might not feel very comfortable with using web conferencing tools. Whatever their situation is, prioritise making your interviewees comfortable, and do what you can to prevent lost time due to technical difficulties.

## CHOOSE THE TECH

The technology you use will obviously depend on the format of interview that works best for your participants. I've deliberately excluded the names of the tools and tech that I use, because things in the digital world evolve quickly, and there are new tools emerging everyday.

Use the ones that make the most sense for you, and consider the following categories when choosing your tech.

- **Scheduling:** I recommend using a calendar syncing tool that will help you avoid sending back-and-forth emails to discuss availability.
- **Conducting interviews:** Use a reliable web conferencing tool (if you're interviewing remotely).
- **Recording and transcription:** Obviously, if the interview is remote, then recording and transcribing will be easy. (Just make sure you get consent!) For in-person interviews, you'll need to use a reliable voice recording app on your phone

or bring a portable audio recording device with you. Then pick your tool or service for transcribing the audio files that you collect.

- **Data analysis:** Many tools can also help with identifying themes, organising your notes and pulling out early insights, on top of doing transcription.

Once you've given all of these key logistical decisions some thought, and you've chosen your participants and interview duration, you should get started putting together your interview questions.

# Developing Interview Questions

With your core planning decisions out of the way, the next critical step will be to create a list of questions to ask participants. I know this is a no-brainer, but asking good questions in a way that gets participants to open up and share meaningful responses — the kind that lead to valuable insights — all while meeting project objectives, is not as easy as you'd think.

Like most elements of your research planning, your interview questions should be developed in collaboration with your stakeholders. You'll want to brainstorm together while cross-referencing your original research goals and questions as a jumping-off point, to ensure that all of your questions are hyper-relevant to your area of study and the answers to those questions will help you in meeting your goals. Then, refine your list of questions by removing or consolidating duplicates, wordsmithing those remaining and formatting them cleanly.

Once you've got a solid list of questions, you'll need to organise and prioritise them. Chances are, you'll have more questions than you can feasibly ask in a 60-minute interview. Work with your stakeholders to find out which questions they care the most about and which ones are nice to have.

## QUESTION FORMATTING PITFALLS

You might relate to the feeling of watching an interview recording back and face-palming because you fumbled awkwardly, asked a useless question or accidentally led the participant down the wrong path. This section will help you systematically weed out bad questions that are a waste of time and should stay out of your interviews for good.

**Closed-ended questions:** Closed-ended questions assume simple one word (i.e. yes or no) or a few word responses. They can be necessary for gaining key background information (e.g., "How many years of experience do you have?"). But if you use them for the bulk of your questions, your interview and the resulting insights will be lacklustre. If you want good data that leads to great insights, your questions should mostly be open-ended.

| Closed-Ended Question | Open-Ended Question |
|---|---|
| • Gets finite responses<br>• Discourages free-flowing conversation | • Encourages the participant to share more about their experience<br>• Allows the researcher to learn information they're not expecting |
| Starts with:<br>"Are you...?" / "Do you...?" / "Would you...?" / When do you...?" | Starts with:<br>"How do you...?" / "How would you...?" / "Why do you...?" |
| Example:<br>"Do you order your groceries online?"<br>"Are you comfortable with using your smart phone to pay for parking?" | Example:<br>"How do you get your groceries?"<br>"How comfortable are you with using your smart phone to pay for parking?" |

**Leading questions:** Leading questions suggest or guide a participant to an answer, creating bias in your research. (You should always be wary of bias and actively avoid it.) When you're building rapport with someone, it's human nature to agree with what they say. That's why leading questions are such an easy mistake. If you suggest that a participant's commute is stressful ("How do you deal with the stress of traffic in your morning commute?"), they might try to find reasons why you're right ("Well, I guess it can be stressful sometimes, so listening to a podcast helps.")... when in reality, they might be pretty relaxed during their commute. You'll always want to catch leading questions and reframe them to neutral questions.

| Leading Question | Neutral Question |
|---|---|
| • Unintentionally guides participants to answer in a certain way<br>• Creates subconscious pressure for participants to agree<br>• Distracts participants from honest self-reflection | • Doesn't contain any modifiers, like "annoying," "easy," or "hectic"<br>• Invites the participant to reflect on their honest feelings and form their own opinion |
| Example:<br>How do you deal with the stress of traffic in your morning commute? | Example:<br>How do you feel about your morning commute? |

**Double-barreled questions:** Double-barreled questions combine two questions together in a way that confuses participants and results in incomplete or ambiguous answers. This ambiguity can also create confusion for you, the researcher — you might think that a certain statement answers one part of the question, when it really answers the other part.

Always make sure that the questions you ask in interviews are single-barrelled, meaning that they focus on a single topic or issue, and they seek one piece of information at a time. You can dig deeper with follow up questions and interview probes after you pose your main question.

| Double-Barrelled Question | Single-Barrelled Question |
| --- | --- |
| • Asks participants two questions at the same time, causing a confused/mixed response<br>• Creates ambiguity in the participant's answer<br>• Leaves lots of room for misinterpretation | • Asks questions to answer a single, simplified question<br>• Results in a clear answer from the participant<br>• Leaves little room for misinterpretation |
| Example:<br>How do you feel about your instructor's teaching techniques and is there anything that could make it better? | Example:<br>How do you feel about your instructor's teaching techniques?<br>Probing/follow up questions:<br>a. What do you like the most about the teaching techniques?<br>b. What do you dislike about them, if anything?<br>c. Is there anything you would do to improve your experience? |

## QUESTION TYPES AND SAMPLES

Now that you know what to look out for when phrasing your questions, there are a few common types of questions that will be useful at different points in your interview. You've probably asked these types of questions before, but being hyper-conscious of how they differ and their best use cases will make you a more strategic interviewer. Next, let's compare them and look at some examples.

| Question Type | Description/Purpose | Sample Questions |
|---|---|---|
| **Background** | This type of question is typically asked at the beginning of an interview, as a warm-up and to get to know your participant. Background questions help you build rapport with the participant.<br><br>**(Many of them will technically be closed-ended, and that's okay, since you're just warming up.)** | • What is your role at [company]?<br>• What are your main responsibilities day-to-day?<br>• How many years have you worked in [industry]? |
| **Day-in-the-life** | Also called a "journey question," this type is most useful when you're looking to understand a user or customer journey, and/or you're building journey maps as part of your final research deliverables. | • Can you describe a typical day-in-your-life from morning until evening?<br>• Can you tell me about the last time you did [task]? Please describe that process in as much detail as you can remember.<br>• How would you typically go about [activity]? What would you do beforehand? Is there anything you would do after?<br>• Can you walk me through the step-by-step process you take when you [activity]? |
| **Current experience** | A current experience question provides you with context for understanding the current state of the product or service. It's useful in identifying challenges and pain points. | • What, if anything, did you like most about your experience? ("If anything" gives the participant an out, to avoid a leading question.)<br>• What challenges, if any, did you face?<br>• What, if anything, could have been improved?<br>• What, if anything, did you like about your experience? |

| Question Type | Description/Purpose | Sample Questions |
|---|---|---|
| **Ideal experience** | Like it sounds, an ideal experience question invites participants to dream about an ideal scenario or future state of the product or service. This is useful for pulling potentially innovative solutions directly out of the minds of users. It helps participants think "outside the box" of what they assume as possible. | • In an ideal world, what would you want your experience to look like?<br>• If you could wave a magic wand, what are the top three things you would change about your experience?<br>**(The second question is my personal favourite, and can lead to ground-breaking ideas for high-impact product improvements or digital transformations.)** |
| **Rated scale** | Asked when wrapping up an interview, a rated scale question prompts participants to summarise their overall reaction to an experience with a product or service. | • How satisfied were you with your experience of the product or service? Please rate it on a scale of 1–5, where "1" is not at all satisfied and "5" is very satisfied.<br>**(Always follow this up by asking the reason why they provided that rating, to validate the response.)** |
| **Probe** | A probe (also called a "sub-question") is used for digging deeper into the response to an initial or "core" question, so that you can get enough detailed information from your participants.<br>(Asking this type of question is not needed if the participant is very forthcoming with details.) | **Core question:**<br>• Can you walk me through your step-by-step process for renting an apartment?<br>**Probes:**<br>• How do you filter for apartments that you might want to rent?<br>• What do you do when you've found an apartment you want to go see?<br>• How do you arrange to go see the apartment?<br>• What challenges, if any, did you encounter in that process? |

## BUILDING AN INTERVIEW PROTOCOL

Once the logistics are out of the way, you can develop your interview questions and build them into an **interview protocol**. Sometimes called an "interview guide" or a "discussion guide," it outlines the scripts and standard questions you'll ask/read to participants, allowing you to follow a smooth flow. Using a protocol as your guide will ensure that you make the most of each interview. Interviews go by quickly, and it is easy to lose control of the session and run out of time, or forget to ask about key areas.

Interview protocols ensure that you stay on track and remember to ask all of your questions. It'll also help you maintain consistency in your data collection. Asking the same questions to all participants within a user group ensures that you'll uncover repeating themes. If your questions are all generally asked in the same order too, it'll be much easier to analyse the data and find patterns later on. It's important to **create a separate interview protocol for each of your user groups**, otherwise it can get complicated to remember which questions to ask and which to skip as you move through each interview. (You should print out your interview protocol for reference or create a digital copy and have it open on your screen during each interview.)

In general, interviews should be semi-structured, meaning you'll have consistent, prepared sets of questions, while still allowing room for the participant to bring up ideas or topics you might not have thought to ask about. Think of your interview protocol as a story, with a beginning, middle and an end. Let's break down these different parts in an interview below. Time estimates are based on a 60-minute interview. (As you put together your protocol, feel free to use the Sample Interview Script & Protocol listed in the resources at the end of this chapter.)

### BEGINNING: Introduction (2–5 minutes)

The introduction of your protocol is where you're warming up and hopefully setting the participant at ease. Make sure to be prepared, be on time and project a friendly demeanour.

The introduction section of your protocol should include:

- **A welcome script:** This includes a brief introduction of yourself (your role and who hired you) and any other attendees sitting in, as well as a description of the purpose of the interview (including who the interview is being conducted for), and a very brief explanation of the research project.
- **An oral consent statement:** This depends on how you've decided to handle consent. (Refer to the online resources listed in chapter 7 for the different forms of participant consent.)
- **An interviewer checklist** for your use only, so that you can avoid skipping any steps.

  - [ ] Cover the points in your welcome script

- [ ] Read the oral consent statement (if applicable)
- [ ] Ask permission to record (if you plan on doing so)
- [ ] Remind attendees of the length of the interview
- [ ] Ask the participant if they have any questions before starting
- [ ] Press record!

You should include a big "PRESS RECORD" reminder in red text at the end of your introduction script and before your questions. I can't tell you the number of times I forgot to press record in an interview... and how many times since that big red press record reminder has saved me from losing quotes and or forgetting great ideas that were mentioned.

### MIDDLE: Interview questions (40–50 minutes)

Your questions are the heart of your interview protocol. You should focus the majority of your time on preparing excellent questions and putting them in the most optimal order.

Make sure to:

- **Categorise and order your questions in a logical, practical, and natural way.**
- **Ensure that your priority questions are marked/highlighted**, so you can skip lower-priority questions if needed on the fly.
- **Ask easier, lighter background questions first**, to warm up the participant, build rapport, and to qualify potential follow-up questions.

As you progress through the interview, you can ask questions that are more specific, complex and/or sensitive.

 **Action Advice:**

As I've mentioned, **it's very important that your interview has a natural flow**. I can't stress this enough. Over the years, I've reviewed a lot of interview protocols, and the most frequent problem I've noticed is when interviews feel awkward or stilted, because they're missing this flow.

Order your questions in a way that reflects the chronological order of steps that your participant follows when interacting with the product or service. This will help them remember their user or customer journeys more easily and accurately.

Also, don't jump back and forth between different topics. Avoiding this will create smoother opportunities for probing deeper into your participant's responses. And you'll make the resulting data so much easier to cross-reference later on when you're in the analysis stage, because responses will be organised per question.

At the end of the day, you want your interview data to lead to actionable, relevant insights. That means doing everything you can to get accurate and meaningful data out of your interviewees.

### END: Conclusion (5–10 minutes)

At the end of the interview, you'll still have a few details to sort out. Follow this list to wrap up your interview properly:

- **Ask about the participant's overall satisfaction and ideas for the future.** Consider using rated scales to ask them about their satisfaction level, as well as ideal experience questions. (See the question types and samples listed earlier in this chapter.)
- **Ask any other attendees if they had additional questions for the participants.**
- **If you're providing an incentive, explain when and how they'll receive it.** Don't forget to also confirm their contact information.
- **Explain the next steps in your research.** This explanation is optional, but it can be nice to let them know what part the interview will play in the bigger picture; you can outline the next stage of the research, or let them know if/when they can expect a future update.
- **Ask the participant if they have any questions or additional thoughts that you didn't cover.** Make sure to ask your participants if you discussed everything in your questions or if they have anything else they want to bring up.
- **Thank the participant for their time.**

**Alignment Advice:**

Remember that gaining alignment with stakeholders is key to earning and keeping their trust as you plan and conduct your research. You shouldn't work in a vacuum. Once you've created a draft protocol mirroring the structure above, share it with your project and stakeholder team to get feedback and then, refine the questions and protocol. This is a crucial step! It's so important to ensure that your stakeholders have all seen and reviewed your interview questions beforehand. You need to make sure you're collecting information that they care about and that align with your research goals and project goals.

You might think that all this checking in (that I refer to many times throughout this book) will exhaust or annoy your stakeholders, but it's better to overshare and involve them more rather than less. Let them decide when/if they want to review something but at least you've given them the chance to participate.

## Interview Scheduling

Once you have your planning out of the way and you've used the tips from chapter 7 to recruit the "right participants," it's time to get things underway with scheduling. Over the course of my career, I've scheduled and conducted a lot of interviews, and I've learned a few things to help you avoid tech problems, participant no-shows and worst of all cognitive fatigue. Interview days require a lot of focus and they can be very tiring. After a certain number of interviews in a day, your brain will get "full" and you'll stop retaining information from your sessions. The interviews will start to blend together in your mind, and that can impact your ability to make sense of the data later on. You need to mind your energy and processing limits.

So, to prevent this and more, I've translated my lessons into an **interview scheduling checklist** that my teams live by:

- [ ] **Block out your calendar during the week(s) when you're conducting interviews.** Don't commit to doing a bunch of other tasks. (I can't tell you the number of times I forgot to block off slots in my calendar for appointments!)
- [ ] **Set a maximum of three interviews per day (four, if absolutely necessary).**
- [ ] **Ideally allow 15–30 minutes between booking.** This will give you time to update your notes and prepare for the next interview. It will also speed up your data analysis after the fact.
- [ ] **Ensure that your scheduling tool is integrated with your web-conferencing software and is properly synced to your calendar.**
- [ ] **Test the scheduling link before you send it out.**
- [ ] **Plan back-ups.** This is a great way to mitigate risk in your interview planning. There are two types of back-ups that can help you when and if things go a bit sideways: technology back-ups, in case your web conferencing tool bugs out or

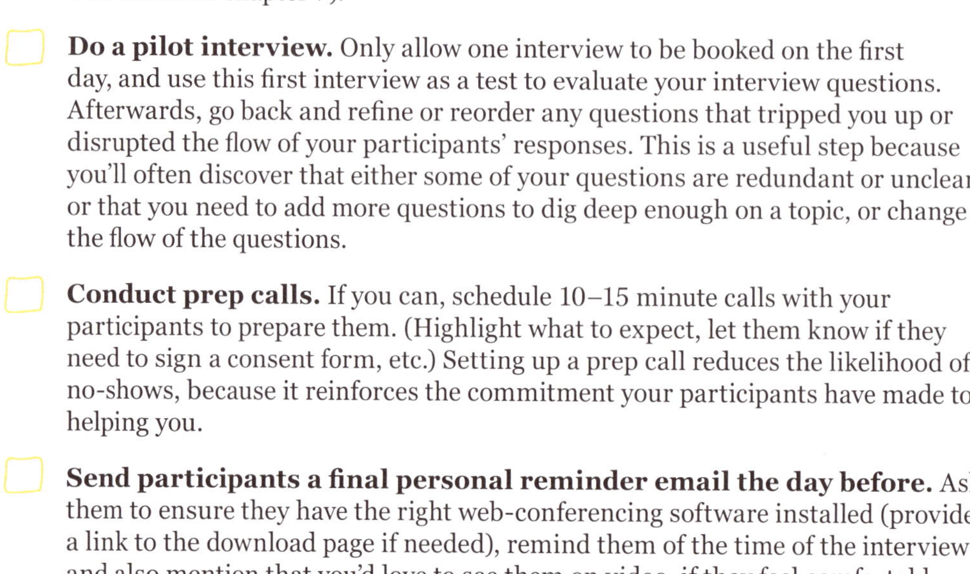

someone's wifi drops; and participant back-ups, in case of no-shows (which I mentioned in chapter 7).

- [ ] **Do a pilot interview.** Only allow one interview to be booked on the first day, and use this first interview as a test to evaluate your interview questions. Afterwards, go back and refine or reorder any questions that tripped you up or disrupted the flow of your participants' responses. This is a useful step because you'll often discover that either some of your questions are redundant or unclear, or that you need to add more questions to dig deep enough on a topic, or change the flow of the questions.

- [ ] **Conduct prep calls.** If you can, schedule 10–15 minute calls with your participants to prepare them. (Highlight what to expect, let them know if they need to sign a consent form, etc.) Setting up a prep call reduces the likelihood of no-shows, because it reinforces the commitment your participants have made to helping you.

- [ ] **Send participants a final personal reminder email the day before.** Ask them to ensure they have the right web-conferencing software installed (provide a link to the download page if needed), remind them of the time of the interview and also mention that you'd love to see them on video, if they feel comfortable putting their camera on.

These guidelines will help you maintain your sanity, ensure that you retain key information (making data analysis more approachable), and save you a lot of scheduling mishaps.

**Always keep stakeholders looped in throughout your interview planning as well as the interview process.** This is important for quelling any fears that they have about the process — they'll want to know you've got it handled and that everything's moving ahead smoothly. They'll also want to know about anything preventing or delaying next steps, and what you're doing to address these issues.

You'll see additional advice in the same vein throughout the method chapters in this book. This is because status updates are one of the most pivotal steps you can take to (Say it with me!) build trust with your stakeholders. Also, the ways you do this will change slightly depending on which method you're using, because of variations in timing, length, stakeholder interest and effort, etc.

As your interviews progress, send a status update email to your stakeholders, and include details like:

- **The type of users interviewed**
- **The number of interviews conducted**
- **The number of interviews left to conduct**
- **Updated timeline info** (if the timeline has changed — and if it hasn't, confirm that everything's on track)
- **A quick update on high-level findings** (if appropriate)

- **Blockers/issues** (identifying any current or upcoming issues, what you're doing about them, and what you might need support with, if applicable)

Here's a sample email I've used to provide a mid-interview update to a client:

### Example: Interview Progress Update

Hi [First Name]

I wanted to give you a quick update on the interviews so far. All of the calls have gone well and participants seem happy to share their feedback with us!

**Interview totals:**

- **Interviews completed:** 6 (4 recipients, 2 payers)
- **No-shows:** 0
- **Interviews to be conducted:** 6 (all scheduled for next week)
- **Interviews to be scheduled:** 4 have yet to be scheduled

High-level thoughts on the first interviews:

- There is some confusion around timing of things (i.e. when they would be processed, how long would it take to enrol, when they would receive enrolment forms etc.) and setting expectations early in the enrolment process.
- Participants said they would trust the technology if it was available and they think that would be a much better route than making a phone call.
- We also heard from participants that this new tool could help educate beneficiaries on possible enforcement actions and with submitting successful applications.

**Project Schedule:** Green. We are on schedule, interviews should wrap up by June 29th.

**Blockers/Issues:**

- There are 4 participants who haven't scheduled interviews yet. We will email them again to remind them to schedule. We have recruited additional back-ups and if we don't hear from these four by EOW, we'll move to the back-ups.
    - **Possible schedule impact:** If none of participants schedule soon, worst case scenario an additional week may be added to the schedule.

Let me know if you have any questions or concerns.

Thanks!

(**Note:** You should also provide a round-up of these details in your formal project status report. See chapter 5 for more on effective status reporting through a project.)

## Skills for Conducting In-Depth Interviews

Whether you're bringing on other researchers to take on some of your interviews or you're working on mastering your own craft, these skills are important to learn and perfect. They'll help you conduct eye-opening interviews with deeply valuable findings.

### DIGGING DEEPER

This skill is about flexing your curiosity muscle. Approach every interview with a genuine desire to understand "why" and get to the root cause of things. As I mentioned earlier in this chapter, preparing probes in your protocol is a great way to ensure that you ask all the questions you need and dig deeper into a response. You should also be ready to make up some of your sub-questions on the fly. If the participant starts to hint at an interesting and relevant viewpoint, take a moment to ask them to elaborate through questions like "Can you tell me more about that?" or "Oh that's interesting, why do you think that happened?" and "Can you explain that in more detail so I really understand?"

 **Action Advice:**

When you're probing in interviews with users, you should always be focused on finding problems and needs. Specifically, you should be doing whatever you can to identify and understand the challenges that users are having with the product or service in question, and what they need in order to have a more successful experience.

You should be attuned to your overarching research goals in everything you do, from the beginning of a research project, to the end. Remember that design research is conducted for the purpose of design. You're trying to collect information that will inform a better product or service.

If one of your goals is to create a customer journey map about the experience of filing a small claim, you'll need to be asking questions about the user's process and their step-by-step tasks. However, you might want to avoid asking details unrelated to the "journey," like the background reasons for starting a legal dispute in the first place. You can see how that might open up a can of worms that would be hard to close the lid on. Basically, if you try to cover too many aspects of an experience, you might run out of time, and miss the details that will allow you to properly map the user journey.

## ACTIVE LISTENING

Also called "listening openly," this is hands-down the best skill that an interviewer can develop. To listen actively, you should make a habit of repeating key points back to the participant. This shows them that you're actually listening and it will make them feel more comfortable and confident. If you're looking to probe deeper into one of their responses or ideas, start by re-stating their initial answer as a jumping-off point. For example, you could say, "I heard you say your biggest challenges are [X, Y, Z]. Is there anything else?" Just be careful that you don't get so chatty that you're interrupting your participant or adding your own anecdotes. Your interview should feel like a conversation, but it's not meant to be an equal exchange. Resist the urge to bring in your own experiences.

## BUILDING EMPATHY AND RAPPORT

Learning to build rapport with a user is one of the most pivotal skills to cultivate as an interviewer. Let's look at how you can do this with your interviewees.

First off, you should always be warm and considerate in your pre-interview communication. Your first impression starts with your recruitment outreach, and you can start to establish a working relationship as you send through emails to schedule interview sessions, get contact information for incentives, etc.

When you're in the interview, use a soft, inquisitive and understanding voice, and validate your participant's feelings. You want to give the impression that you don't have an opinion on the product or service, but you're curious about their thoughts and welcome their ideas. If you sense strong emotions like frustration in their tone of voice or body language, acknowledge those emotions and let them know that you understand their perspective. You can say something like, "It sounds like that was very frustrating," or even a simple, "I understand." This will reassure them and encourage them to keep sharing.

It can also be helpful to remind participants of your motivation, and affirm that the participant's feedback is useful and relevant. Emphasise that your priority is to learn about them, understand their needs, and gain perspectives on how the product or service in question could be improved. After all, you're not putting them on the spot to assess their knowledge and/or speaking skills. I say things like, "Thank you, that's very interesting," or, "I've heard that before — you're not the only one!" Being an interviewee can be a vulnerable and strange experience. These affirmations will help ease any insecurity they're feeling.

## BEING FLEXIBLE

As I've said before, flow is so important in your interviews, and some flexibility is needed to achieve it. This might mean adjusting the order of your interview protocol slightly as you go along. If a participant starts talking about a topic that you planned to cover later on in the interview, don't interrupt them or make them wait for those questions to come up later. You should pivot, flip to the appropriate page of questions, and make yourself a note to come back to the rest. The interview will feel more organic and conversational, and your participant will be able to maintain their train of thought.

You might also need to improvise by omitting or adding questions in the moment based on their relevance or lack thereof. For example, if you ask a question on a topic that your participant already brought up earlier, you could end up wasting time, and it might seem to them like you weren't listening. On the other hand, it's a good idea to practice phrasing off-the-cuff questions in a smooth and neutral way, in case you want to probe deeper on an interesting point.

A great interviewer knows which questions are the biggest priorities, how much time they can afford to spend on an unexpected topic, and when the participant is getting uncomfortable and needs a change in topic.

## NAVIGATING PERSONALITIES

As you plan your interviews, it's good to keep in mind that your participants are going to come in all forms. They might be chatty or talkative, going overboard with their answers... or they might be shy, bored or quiet, and not be very forthcoming. You might get some participants who are raving fans of the product or service you're studying, and/or some angry critics who've had very bad experiences with it, or who really don't like the organisation. You'll also get people who are neutral, and have no strong feelings either way.

Each of these traits bring different positives and negatives that you should be prepared for as you plan your interviews. On the next page, I've listed out the pros and cons for the most common personality traits I've encountered and tips on how to manoeuvre each one.

| Personality Trait | Pros | Cons | Tips |
|---|---|---|---|
| Talkative | • Easy to get answers from<br>• Will answer questions without you asking<br>• Will readily provide details | • Can easily go off-topic<br>• Difficult to rein back into the interview | • Brush up on your facilitation skills<br>• Stay mindful of the time<br>• Recover quickly and tactfully from tangents |
| Quiet or Bored | • Interviews will be efficient (you'll get through all of your interview questions) | • It can be difficult to pull answers out of them<br>• They're less inclined to provide details | • Push through with probing questions<br>• Prepare extra back-up questions |
| Angry | • Will provide valuable details on pain points and challenges<br>• Will remember an experience more clearly because of their strong emotions | • Can easily go off-topic<br>• Difficult to rein back into the interview<br>• Might sometimes redirect anger toward the interviewer | • Hold and demonstrate empathy for the participant with active listening<br>• Spend some extra energy building rapport and trust<br>• Brush up on your facilitation and diplomacy skills<br>• Stay mindful of the time |
| Raving Fan | • Easy to talk to and very willing to answer questions<br>• Will provide lots of positive feedback on what's working well | • Might not provide feedback on pain points or challenges<br>• Might not reveal opportunities to improve the current experience | • Intentionally probe deeper into challenges<br>• Encourage them to imagine what they would change about the experience |

## FACILITATING WITH TACT

Good facilitation will also allow you to get through all of your questions in the allotted time without sacrificing conversation flow or diminishing the rapport you've built, no matter what kind of participant personality you're dealing with. This means guiding your participants efficiently and with tact. **Carefully pick your moments to cut in and reroute tangents.** If your participant starts talking about something that's not relevant to the study, don't interrupt them, but use the soonest pause to gently reel them back in.

Also: **Don't reject any of your participants' ideas.** If they're going off-topic, you can say something like, "That's very interesting. Staying mindful of the time, there are a few more questions about [topic] that I'd like to ask you about."

### SITTING WITH DISCOMFORT

Often, participants need to think about a question before they can answer. Waiting in silence after asking a question can feel awkward, but it's a necessary awkwardness. Try to embrace it, and remember that your participant isn't thinking about whether or not the conversation is awkward — they're thinking about the question you just asked them. I like to count to 10 in my head to give them time to jog their memory, especially if you're asking about an experience that they haven't gone through very recently, or that they haven't reflected on before.

In some cases, if you sense that your participant needs it, you might actually want to suggest a small pause. Mentioning that you need a few seconds to catch up on your note-taking can help relieve any pressure for them to respond right away.

## Conclusion

Conducting effective in-depth interviews is an art. It's a delicate balance of active listening, probing into the subject matter you're most curious about, managing your time, creating a logical and natural flow, and gaining an understanding of your participants' motivations, needs and challenges. If that seems like a lot, try to focus on improving one aspect of your interviews at a time, and give yourself lots of leeway to plan your interviews thoroughly. This effort is invaluable — you'll start to see big improvements in the quality of your data and in your insight-gathering process.

**Online Resources:**

The resources at **designresearchmastery.com** are designed to help you formulate your questions and assemble all needed materials ahead of your interviews.

What you'll find:

- Sample Interview Script & Protocol
- Participant Consent Types & Samples
- 50 Ready-to-Use Interview Questions
- DRM Interview Planning Workbook

## Key Takeaways:

1. **In-depth interviews are the most used method in design research because they're a direct line to the interviewee's perspective**. In-depth interviews are also:
    - Straightforward to organise and conduct
    - Adaptable to remote or in-person scenarios
    - Easier to document, analyse and cross-reference in synthesis
2. **Your in-depth interviews should always be conducted one-on-one.** This will help save your participants from being overly self-conscious or from being influenced by other attendees.
3. **When developing your interview questions, avoid making them closed-ended, leading or double-barrelled.** It's all too easy to introduce bias this way. Your questions should never guide participants to answer in a certain way, confuse them about what answer you're looking for, or come from potentially false assumptions.
4. **Always build your interview protocols with a beginning, middle and end.** Maintaining a logical order to your questions is crucial for optimising your interview time, getting the information you need to achieve your research goals, and keeping your participant in an engaged state.
5. **To conduct effective, stand-out interviews that deliver "aha" moments, you'll need to develop and hone your skills in these key areas:**
    a. Digging deeper
    b. Active listening
    c. Building empathy and rapport
    d. Being flexible
    e. Navigating personalities
    f. Facilitating with tact
    g. Sitting with discomfort

# OBSERVATIONS

"To acquire knowledge, one must study; but to acquire wisdom, one must observe."
— Marilyn vos Savant

# Introduction

In product development, there tend to be two camps: One that thinks we should leave users out of the conversation when it comes to innovation, pushing to skip research altogether, because they think users will give you "dud" ideas. The other (the camp that readers of this book will belong to) sees research as a way to discover a user's unspoken pain points and needs. And these hidden pieces of truth can help us identify new and brilliant solutions.

Unspoken or "latent" needs are needs that users aren't aware of, so they won't be able to flag them to you in an interview, workshop or diary study when you ask them. That's why I love observations — there's no research method that is better at helping you actually grasp what users really go through. You can't understand how busy it is for a doctor when they're doing their rounds unless you see it live for yourself. You can't understand how draining it is for patients to go on dialysis unless you see it, or how hard it is for their families. You can't understand how absolutely frustrating it is for brokers to switch between 10 different underwriting and estimating tools while being told off on a call with a customer.

With proper observation methodology and a trained eye, you can gain all of this context, and uncover huge opportunities for product, service and feature innovations and improvements — ones that can even disrupt the market or dramatically improve people's lives. This is where observational research can help you make a big impact. In the end, it's not the user's job to come up with the brilliant idea and "aha" solution — it's actually our job as practitioners of human-centred design. Of course, before we can come up with the "aha" solution, we have to fully understand what needs and pain points we're solving for.

This chapter will guide you through everything you need to conduct observations effectively and gain truly actionable insights from your work. These insights will be crucial in helping your stakeholders achieve their goals, and see huge value in the research.

## KEY BENEFITS OF OBSERVATIONS

Observations are a great way to get a clear and accurate picture of how and why participants behave and interact with a product or service. They're great if you're hoping to understand information like:

- **The step-by-step tasks a user performs** to accomplish a goal
- **A user's reactions and behaviours** during these interactions
- **How long it takes a user to perform each task**
- **The pain points that a user encounters** while performing their tasks
- **Their environment,** including how it looks, sounds, and feels and how it might impact their experience or their ability to complete their tasks
- **The people they interact with** as they work on their tasks and how they interact with those people
- **The tools (technological or otherwise) that they use** to accomplish their goals

Unlike any other form of research, observations allow you to be "in the thick of it" with a participant as they go about their day or interact with a product or service. You get to experience the world as they do. This can help you better understand the broader context of a user's day-to-day life, notice details that others miss, and build more empathy for users. Everyone has obstacles and pain points that they run into, and you get to see not only what those are, but how your participant navigates and overcomes them in real time. You'll gain a greater appreciation for their challenges. You'll live and breathe their experience, and you'll fundamentally "get it."

As a result, the insights that you gain will be more insightful, and more convincing. It'll be easier to tell a compelling story and bring up real life examples on the fly when stakeholders inevitably question you during your presentation of the insights. You'll also think of better suggestions for your action plans in your final report. This will all help you convince stakeholders to act on your recommendations, because it'll be clear that those recommendations come from a source of valuable knowledge that your stakeholders didn't previously have.

## OBSERVATION TYPES

There are three common ways to conduct observations: Contextual inquiry, fly-on-the-wall, and shadowing. In my experience, **shadowing is the most common type** of observation, because it can be adapted to the widest range of settings and processes.

One of the struggles I've often faced in the design research space is the confusion and overlap that can happen in our research lingo — we're not always on the same page about the names of our approaches or observation "types," the distinctions between them, and, most crucially, the advantages of each. So, before I move on, let's clarify things with a quick comparison.

| | Contextual Inquiry | Fly-on-the-Wall | Shadowing |
|---|---|---|---|
| |  |  |  |
| **The researcher's approach** | **Active**<br>The researcher asks questions about how and why the participant is doing something. | **Passive**<br>The researcher watches and listens to how people act and behave from an appropriate distance, without drawing any attention to themselves. | **Active and Passive**<br>The researcher follows a participant around as they perform activities. They can ask questions during a quiet moment, but they shouldn't disrupt the participant. |
| **Where it's used** | **Work and office environments** | **Public areas where there's no expectation of privacy**<br>Some examples include libraries, food courts, stores, parks, etc. | **Any environment, as long as the participant consents** |
| **The advantage it offers** | **An understanding of the participant's situation from their perspective**<br>This includes how they see their environment, the steps involved in their task sequences and the tools they use. | **Less chances for participant subject bias**<br>This style of observation is covert, which means the participant is generally unaware of being observed and might act more naturally.<br>**No consent or recruitment is needed**<br>This makes it very quick to set up and conduct observations. | **The opportunity to observe participants' behaviour during both longer and less conscious tasks**<br>The participant experiences fewer interruptions, and the researcher can observe closely without needing to be covert. |

Fly-on-the wall research can also be paired with guerrilla research and user intercepts. While I don't focus on these methods as part of this book, I encourage you to look into them, because they're quick and cost-effective, perfect for scenarios where you aren't given a lot of time to plan and execute. **Guerrilla research** essentially is the practice of approaching people live, in real-world environments, and asking them about their experience with the product or service. User intercepts involve approaching users of digital products specifically, and can be conducted in person or through a digital tool that intercepts users with an in-app message or notification.

As I mentioned in chapter 3, "starting small" is a smart strategy when you're working with an organisation that doesn't believe in the value of design yet. In-person user intercepts and guerilla research are very accessible ways to interview and observe people, and get useful insights into their experience. Of course, they can only happen if you're studying a product or service that's interacted with in a public setting. For example, you might be working with a clothing retailer who wants to understand the customer's in-store experience, or a government authority interested in studying the experience of users getting their passports at a passport office.

# Observation Planning

If you've ever felt completely overwhelmed when planning for observations, you are not alone! They can be a bit of a logistical nightmare. There are so many details to get right. You want to have everything go smoothly and get the information you need, but every environment is different and it's hard to know what to expect before you get there.

After a decade of doing observation days, I realised that there were a few key planning decisions that could make my life a whole lot easier, if those decisions were made thoughtfully. That's why I wrote this section: to help keep you organised, based on what I've learned.

(**Note:** These tips are most relevant to shadowing, but they can also be helpful for the other observation types.)

## CHOOSE THE LOCATION AND DURATION

Your first step will be to decide how many locations you'll visit and how many observation days you'll need. I usually decide this based on how much time I have for the whole project (8 weeks, 12 weeks, etc.) and how many potential participants or organisations/partners are willing to participate. I also factor in the amount of information we need to gather about an experience, and how much that experience could differ from location to location. If you know the experiences will be relatively similar, it may be sufficient to only do a couple of days of observation. But, if you suspect the experiences will vary greatly, and there's a lot of data you need to gather and understand, then you might need additional days.

Five days (spread across multiple locations) is usually the ideal span of time for observations, but if you have less time, you can still make the most of it by prioritising certain locations, user groups and tasks that you and your stakeholders have deemed most important. I've also done longer stints of observations on projects. One involved three or four weeks of shadowing across Canada, with one week spent in each city. The information we had to understand was so complex and so different from one location to another, that trying to zip across the country with only one day per location wouldn't have given us the information we needed.

### Design Research in Reality: *Physician's Journey For Better Patient Outcomes*

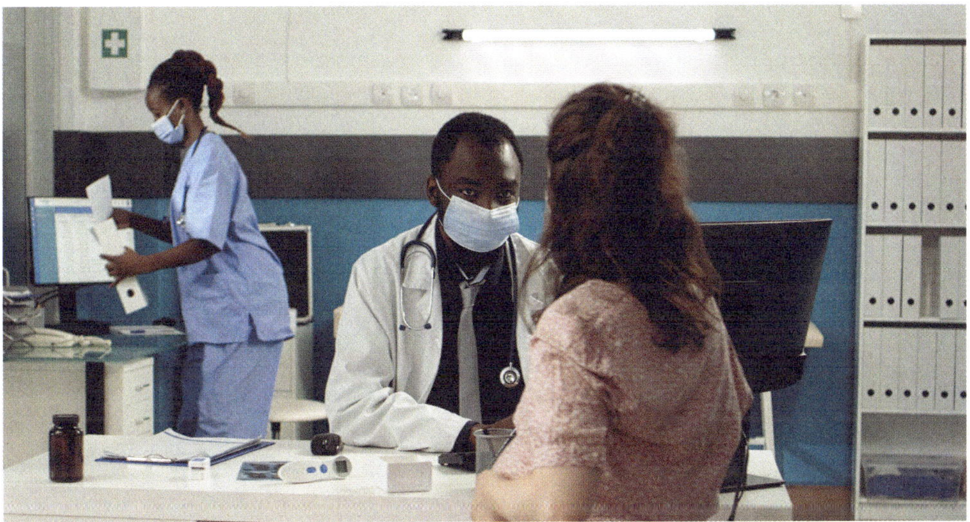

A few years ago, I conducted a large-scale research study with the purpose of improving an electronic health record (EHR) used by physicians across the US. The research involved a series of on-site observations and in-depth interviews conducted with medical practitioners who were implementing this EHR system, in order to understand how their workflows were affected, including their biggest challenges with the new system, and to identify possible areas for improvement. They hoped that improvement of this system would allow them to respond more effectively to patients' needs.

The research planning followed all the steps I've mentioned in this book. I developed a project schedule, research plan, recruiting criteria, interview protocols, observation field kits, and I organised and scheduled participants. I created email and phone scripts for recruiting, screening questionnaires, and many other materials. The on-site observations were conducted at five different clinics/offices across the Midwest and Southwest United States, where we flew and drove between locations.

Myself and another researcher shadowed physicians, nurse practitioners and medical assistants as well as front and back office staff at each practice. We also conducted in-depth interviews with 25+ physicians and medical professionals before the observations. These interviews helped us get a strong sense of the challenges and their motivations, while the observations allowed us to clarify and validate that knowledge. From this data, I developed customer journey maps that depicted end-to-end clinical workflows to identify process inefficiencies and points of friction which would ultimately inform product improvements for the EHR. I also created user personas that reflected the needs, pain points, motivations and characteristics of the physicians.

Along the way, something even more interesting emerged. Beyond fixing the redundant and painful workflows that physicians and their staff were facing, our research sparked new ideas for improving patient outcomes.

During the observations, we also spoke with and observed patients and caregivers, to learn more about their experiences with chronic disease. It turned out that they could have poor health outcomes, often fatal, because the medical interventions received at the hospital, in-office and/or at the clinic by different practitioners would conflict or interact. That wasn't any human's fault — it was happening because the medical information about their separate treatments were documented in different systems and, of course, these systems didn't talk to each other. (While this isn't a common challenge for the average "healthy" person, it's unfortunately a reality and danger for patients suffering from chronic disease.) This caused additional stress for caregivers who were doing their best to track these details without any medical training.

To reduce this stress on caregivers, our action plan recommended a new patient portal that would give patients and their caregivers access to their personal diet requirements, prescribed medications, dosages, scheduled treatments and patient history.

Our action plan also highlighted the need for an EHR that was easier to understand, and integrated with other healthcare tools. That way, if a patient had an unexpected hospital visit and was later checking in with their doctor, there would be a single source of truth for patient information. Their regular doctor would have all of the necessary context when prescribing follow-up treatments, and no conflicts would occur.

I told this story in the final insights report using anecdotes, quotes and images of real-life patients and doctors, which brought a vivid realness and urgency to the recommendations. This is a great example of how beneficial and pivotal observations can be, and how investing time to do this work in person is incredibly worthwhile.

(See also chapter 13 for a section on action plans.)

## CHOOSE THE PARTICIPANTS

Next, you'll need to decide on the number of participants and the roles you'll shadow at each location. If you don't have a plan and you try to observe everything and everyone in general, you'll be spread thin and you'll struggle to get detailed, in-depth data for each task that you want to understand. Identifying patterns in your data later will also be harder.

In most cases, there will be multiple roles and/or user types for you to observe. They might perform different tasks and activities, and have different needs. For instance, in my story about observing at doctors' offices and clinics, there were several roles that we wanted to understand, including physicians, nurses, nurse practitioners, medical assistants and receptionists. They all had different duties and areas of expertise, and observing each one helped us see how they used the EHR at various points in their workflow.

While every project is different, I typically recommend conducting observations with **8-12 participants**, and dedicating a **minimum of 2 hours up to a full day per participant.** If you have multiple researchers attending, the number of participants can increase. Ultimately, the total number of participants you observe will be dictated by the number of days you have to conduct observations.

**Example:**

If you have two researchers and five full days of observations with a half-day dedicated to each participant, each researcher could probably observe 10 participants, for a total of 20 participants. (2 researchers x 5 days x 2 participants per day = 20 participants)

These numbers aren't set in stone, and if you're only aiming to observe each participant for an hour or two, your number of participants will go up. Just make sure you spend enough time with the "right" people (your top-priority participants) to get the information you need. Some participants will be crucial for you to observe, while others will be categorised as "nice to have." Work with your stakeholders or your client to prioritise the participant types/roles that are most needed for the research.

Ask yourself:

- **Which participants are most important to observe, and how much time do you need with them?**
- **Which participants could be observed for a shorter time if needed?**

Figure out these priorities before the observation day, so that if you end up with more or less time, you can make quick decisions and smart compromises. Make sure that you review your participant priority list with any stakeholders or other researchers you're bringing along, to ensure you're all in agreement.

If you don't feel that having a stakeholder or client join you in observing is a good idea, trust your gut.

Enthusiastic clients, executives, product owners or business analysts might request to join your observation days. Sometimes, it might be a good thing. After all, they might already be familiar with the office, location and participants and if so, they'll be able to offer a bit of continuity for everyone involved. It can also help them to buy-in to the research as they will gain more empathy for the user by "walking a mile" in the user's shoes for a day. You might invite them to take notes, or assign them certain roles or participants to shadow for the day. Just be sure that you or another researcher will also be observing that role or participant at some point. Your stakeholder might not take the same type of notes that you will — either because they're less experienced at observing or because they're looking at situations through the lens of their own interests.

On the other hand, a stakeholder's presence could influence participants' behaviour negatively and create bias. On top of this, stakeholders are not usually trained researchers, and including them might mean you can't bring other researchers with you and you might miss out on key insights.

If you're feeling it could be problematic, when stakeholders ask, you can explain that while you love the idea, to avoid skewing the research, you recommend that they stay behind if they're comfortable doing so. Reassure them that you'll capture all of the information they need and that you'll work with them in advance to make sure everyone's aligned on what tasks you should observe. Then, after day one, report back via email to give them a summary of all the juicy information you observed. This will help them feel more confident in you, knowing that they're in safe hands with you, and so are their customers or users. (See more strategies for avoiding bias in the tips section in this chapter.)

## CHOOSE THE TASKS AND QUESTIONS

In chapter 6, we went through the process of setting clear, meaningful research goals so you can glean data and insights that are actionable. With these research goals top-of-mind, you should plan out what you want to observe well in advance, to avoid creeping out of scope.

A good way to do this is to create an **observation task list** that you'll bring with you on observation days, to remind you of what tasks you need to capture. Then, check off the list as you go along. This will help you keep track of what you've seen and haven't, so you can quickly adjust during an observation day as needed.

Follow these steps to get your priorities straightened out while staying within scope:

- **Brainstorm a list of tasks with your team and client/stakeholders.**
- **Group these tasks by participant role.** For example, in a clinic, group physician-related tasks together and nurse-related tasks together.
- **Prioritise and narrow your list of tasks.** Remember that you won't be able to observe everything!
- **Finalise your task list and add it to your field kit.** See the field kit section later in this chapter.

Below is an example of an **observation task list** I used in the adult learners study that I also mention in chapters 7 and 10. Our research involved both observations of educators and a diary study for the learners themselves.

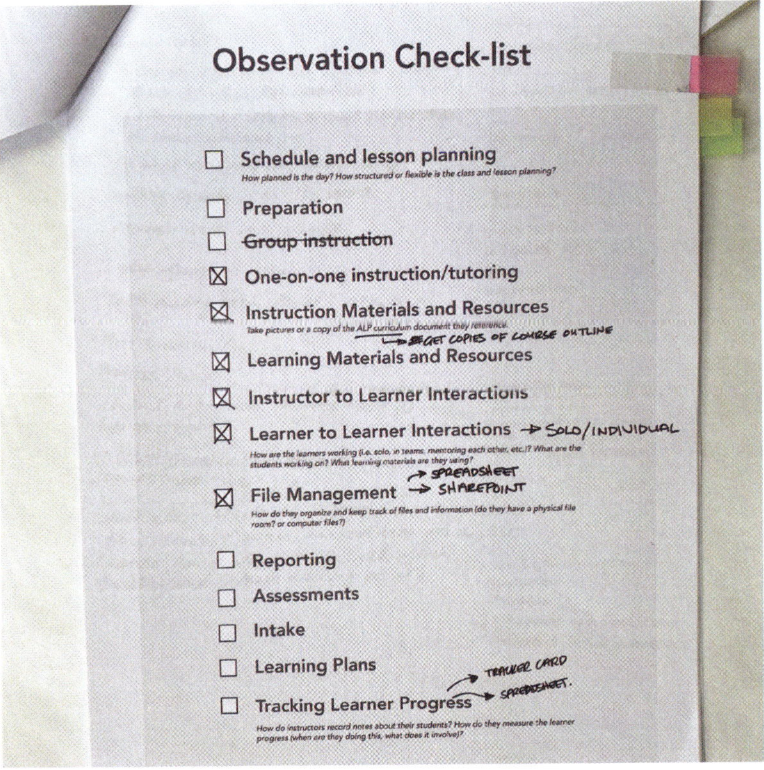

Observation Check-list

- [ ] Schedule and lesson planning
  How planned is the day? How structured or flexible is the class and lesson planning?
- [ ] Preparation
- [ ] ~~Group instruction~~
- [x] One-on-one instruction/tutoring
- [x] Instruction Materials and Resources
  Take pictures or a copy of the ALP curriculum document they reference.
  → GET COPIES OF COURSE OUTLINE
- [x] Learning Materials and Resources
- [x] Instructor to Learner Interactions
- [x] Learner to Learner Interactions → SOLO/INDIVIDUAL
  How are the learners working (i.e. solo, in teams, mentoring each other, etc.)? What are the students working on? What learning materials are they using?
- [x] File Management → SPREADSHEET → SHAREPOINT
  How do they organize and keep track of files and information (do they have a physical file room? or computer files?)
- [ ] Reporting
- [ ] Assessments
- [ ] Intake
- [ ] Learning Plans
- [ ] Tracking Learner Progress → TRACKER CARD → SPREADSHEET.
  How do instructors record notes about their students? How do they measure the learner progress (when are they doing this, what does it involve)?

Once you've done this, you'll need to **start thinking about pre-observation and post-observation interviews.** Even though observation isn't centred around asking interview-style questions, it can still be helpful to develop some questions ahead of time. You may or may not get the opportunity to ask these questions (a 30-minute window is ideal at the start and end of the day), but you should be prepared just in case.

Pre-observation questions are usually background questions you ask at the beginning of the day, asked with the aim to learn a bit more about the participant and provide context in preparation for your observation day. Post-observation questions are usually focused on learning more about a user task flow, or about any pain points and challenges they have. They're also great for clarifying anything you witnessed during the day that didn't make sense to you.

**Alignment Advice:**

You shouldn't develop your task list in isolation. You absolutely MUST do this collaboratively with your clients or stakeholders, for two reasons. For one, you'll want to access their subject matter expertise to understand what tasks and activities your participants do. And for another, you'll need to align on which tasks to prioritise for your observations.

It's important to remind stakeholders that you may not have enough time to observe everything, and that you can't control exactly what you will observe, because you are at the whim of what is going on during the participant's day. That being said, your list will help you stay on track. Assure your stakeholders that you'll observe as many of the tasks on the list as possible.

## CHOOSE THE TIMING OF ACTIVITIES

As part of your planning, you should build out an agenda for each day. You'll need to factor in the roles, participants and tasks you want to observe, and how much time you'll need for each. Your days will go smoother if you create a clear schedule that breaks this down.

A typical observation day might look something like this:

- **8:30 a.m.** Arrive at location, do introductions and go over logistics for the day
- **9:00 a.m.** Shadow front-desk staff
- **12:00 p.m.** Lunch break and informal Q&A with the staff
- **1:00 p.m.** Shadow back-office staff
- **3:30 p.m.** Conduct a post-observation interview with the manager
- **4:00 p.m.** Team debrief and wrap-up

You won't be able to get too specific before arriving, but a high-level schedule will help you and your team stay on track, and it will put the participants at ease. Professionalism is paramount on observation days, so make sure that your arrival time is achievable and not too tight — you REALLY don't want to be late.

# Logistics and Participant Prep

To run observation days smoothly, it's crucial that your participants are aware of your plan ahead of time. If those being observed know what to expect on the day of, they'll be more comfortable and will act more naturally. In this section, I've listed out some things you can do to set the right tone and help everyone come prepared.

## SEND A "CULTURAL PROBE"

**Cultural probes** are informal research artefacts that prompt users to do some solo reflection about their experience with a product or service. They're designed to "probe" or explore a more in-depth perspective on a user by triggering them to define the "cultural" context for their activities in a creative and personal way.

Prep this artefact by choosing a format and a guiding question (or set of questions) customised to the specific environment, project and user. Then, assign it to them as a piece of homework to complete and turn in by a set date/time. I've had great results with "A Day-in-the-Life" sheets, where the user notes their activities, feelings and needs at different points throughout the day. See an example of this type of worksheet below.

**A-DAY-IN-THE-LIFE** NAME:

| | MORNING | AFTERNOON | EVENING |
|---|---|---|---|
| THINGS I DO | | | |
| THINGS I FEEL | | | |
| THINGS I USE/NEED<br>SERVICES/DEVICES/APPS | | | |

Some other examples of cultural probes:

- Asking users to find a picture that represents how they feel on a daily basis about their work (like in the example coming up)
- Sending a postcard to users with probing questions on the back, to fill out and send in
- Prompting employees to create a map of workplace relationships

These self-reporting exercises can yield unexpected data that might inspire in-depth follow-up conversations with your users. If you plan to use a cultural probe, I recommend that you send it to participants about two weeks before your planned observation days and ask them to return it before you begin.

### Design Research in Reality: *Probe to Powerful Metaphor*

My team and I once gave this prompt to participants: “Send us a picture that represents how you feel about your job, and a brief explanation.”

One picture a user sent back to us showed a person sitting in a cockpit, looking at a huge control panel full of different buttons and knobs. The participant wasn’t a pilot, and their work had nothing to do with planes or operating heavy machinery. The image was a metaphor for their sense of overwhelm: they had way too many tasks to complete and decisions to make on a day-to-day basis.

The simple act of choosing an image let them express their pain points in an open and accessible way, and it let us start a productive conversation about potential solutions.

## PREPARE PARTICIPANTS AND SET EXPECTATIONS

I also suggest you create and send participants a "What to Expect" document. It's a simple one-pager that explains your research project to your observation participants, including what kind of research is being conducted and what your goals are. In it, you should describe what a typical observation day looks like. Outline what kind of facts you'll be recording, what the participants' roles in the process will be, etc. Remember, you're going into their workplace or their home, which can feel uneasy and unsettling for them. This document can help them feel more comfortable and ready for the day ahead. Send it along with the high-level agenda you created. (See the image below for an example.)

**THE GOAL**

The goal of this project is to gain an understanding of your characteristics, values, needs and goals as a [user type]. We would like to understand your primary interaction points as you go through your day; the steps and processes that you take, your pain/friction points and your goals. We will be using this research to improve the [experience of product/service].

**WHAT TO EXPECT**

**Pre-observation chat:** 15–30 min interview

Before you begin your day, our on-site team leader from [company] will ask you a few questions about your role, your main tasks and workflows, and your current use of different technologies. This will take approximately 15 to 30 minutes [and will involve one or two other researchers, who will act as silent observers.]

**Consent:**

With your consent and that of your office staff, and [other participants for whom consent is needed], our observations will be recorded (using notes, video and/or audio, and images) in order to facilitate data analysis and ensure no important details are left out. The team will bring consent forms for all participants with them for review and signature.

**Observations:** All day shadowing

Following that, as you go about your day, our team members will be silently shadowing you and your staff, taking notes and photos of what they observe. They are particularly interested in how you go about completing your tasks, the people with whom you're interacting and the operational challenges that you may face during your day.

We hope to be as unobtrusive as possible in order to allow you to continue your daily tasks as you would normally. If at any time during the observations you would like to be alone, please advise our researchers and they will take a break.

**Midday check in:** 15 min (optional)

Halfway through the day, researchers will be asking a few questions when appropriate to ensure that they understand your workflow and to clarify any questions that come up throughout the morning.

**Post-Observation Questions:** 15–30 min interview

Once you have completed your regular tasks and have a chance to debrief with our staff, our on-site leader will ask you some follow-up questions regarding our team's immediate observations. This will take approximately 15 to 30 minutes.

## CONFIRM TRAVEL AND LOGISTICS

Finally, there's some "boring stuff" that, while boring, is also important to confirm ahead of time with your main point of contact. This should include the dates, times and exact locations/addresses for your arrival, as well as the people who will be on site to greet you. Get their contact information, and make sure they have yours. This is especially needed if you're travelling far distances or in rural/remote areas where a car could break down. I've been on the road during a hurricane... in that circumstance, I needed to confirm with my point of contact that their location was still safe for us to get to! I've also had delayed flights and missed connections ahead of observation. Plan for the unexpected, and ensure that you have a phone number to call in case the same thing happens to you.

## Field Kit: An Essential Tool

Let me fill you in on one of my most favourite tools that I've ever created: **a field kit**. It's a printed booklet that includes your task list, agenda, interview questions to ask on-site and structured spaces for note-taking, all in one place. It helps you keep your observation days and participant notes organised.

I know the easiest thing to do is just bring a note pad and a pen to an observation day — or at least, it seems that way on the surface. I used to do that. But then, I quickly started missing things. I'd forget to write down something I'd observed, I'd forget which participant said or did what, or I'd forget to observe certain activities altogether, because the days were moving so quickly, and I had no reminders of what I needed to observe or take notes on. I'd find myself fiddling with papers, trying to locate my printed-out questions, becoming flustered and wasting the participants' precious time. By the end of the day, my notes would be practically illegible, and I'd spend more time trying to remember, decipher and organise them than I would actually analysing data. It just became a big mess. It's one thing to deal with if you're doing a single day of observations, but it's quite another if you're doing a full week.

Observation days move super fast, and they demand a lot of focused attention. You have to avoid disrupting the participant, switch between different people, follow the participant as they get up and move around, and catch all the details of the surrounding space and their interactions and behaviours in a completely new setting. For example, when I was shadowing those doctors during the EHR research project I mentioned earlier, I was moving in and out of patient rooms, watching while doctors documented notes on electronic health records, following them to their offices to finish documenting their patient visits, and then following them again as they walked to the front desk to mention something to a medical assistant, then walked back, etc.

You have to be right on their tail and not miss a beat. It's all harder than most people realise. If you're reshuffling your stack of notes and questions instead of concentrating on what your participant is doing, you might lose out on key insights. Remember, it's costing your company a lot of money to send you there, and it will be a big waste if you don't capture enough information.

That's why I ended up creating this field kit. (I'm also very into organisation, and I love creating tools for design and research.) Building it was a game-changer. I can't tell you how many clients have commented on how useful it was, or how many researchers would ask for the field kit template afterwards to use on their other projects.

This field kit can:

- **Act as a master checklist:** It can help you avoid missing crucial details, steps or questions.
- **Ensure consistency in your note-taking:** If you have multiple researchers doing observations at the same time, you can have everyone use the exact same field kit format, and breathe easy knowing that you're all capturing the same types of information.
- **Facilitate data analysis:** Observations are hectic enough without having to face a mess of unordered notes at the end of the day. When you use a field kit, your notetaking will be more structured, and it'll be easier to document repeating patterns.
- **Keep notes organised and separate:** Participants can start blurring together after a long and fast-paced day or week — it can be hard to remember who said or did what. Since you should have a general idea of how many participants you'll be observing before you arrive, I recommend printing out one field kit per participant so that your notes are organised, and so that you don't mix anyone up.

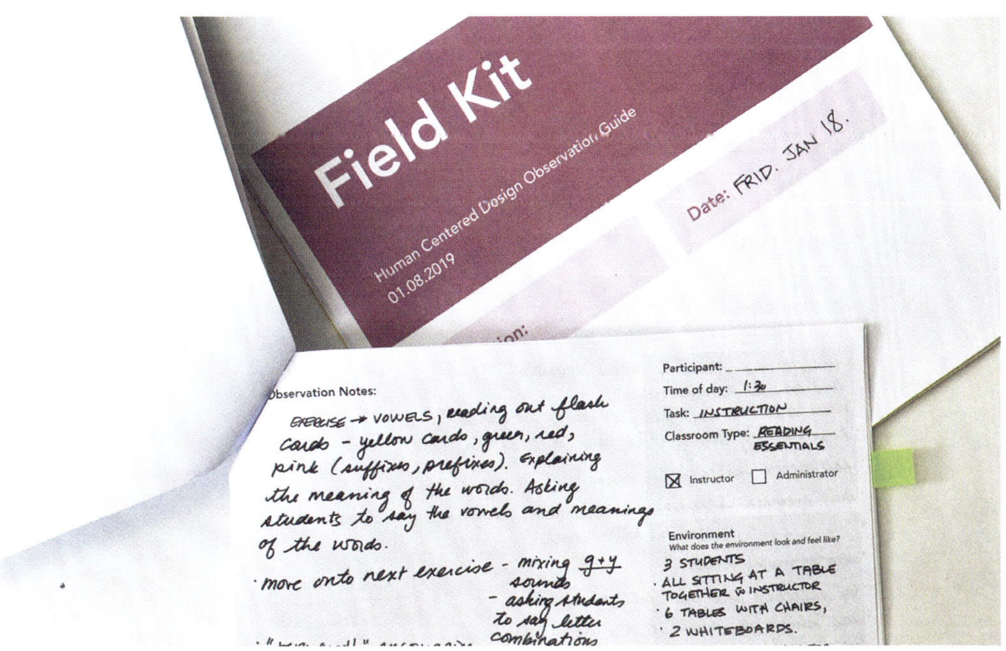

Your field kit should include the following sections:

1. Title page
2. Agenda/plan for the day
3. Introduction script
4. Observation checklist
5. Pre-observation interview questions (optional)
6. Midday check-in
7. Space for observation notes (and the AEIOU or POEMS framework – see the next section)
8. Post-observation interview questions (optional)
9. Additional blank pages for note taking

Bring clipboards, pens, and extra notepads with you. And be sure to print extra copies of field kits in case you end up observing more people than you expected.

Add post-it notes or colour-coded tabs to each of the sections of your field kit, so you can quickly flip to a section when you need it without fumbling around.

Go to the link at the end of this chapter for a sample field kit that you can use to build yours, as well as a "What to Bring" checklist, so you don't forget any essentials.

## FRAMEWORKS FOR OBSERVATION

Applying a framework to your observations (and to your field kit) can make the process of observing and documenting everything in real time much less chaotic. There are two main frameworks used for observational research: the AEIOU and the POEMS frameworks. They can serve as a reminder of all of the different details you should be taking notes on. Both are outlined below.

### THE AEIOU FRAMEWORK

The AEIOU framework was coined in the 1990s by industry leaders from the Doblin Group to help researchers remember the key elements that they should focus on during their observations.

**A — Activities:** The actions and activities that need to be performed for a participant to reach a certain goal (This includes the sequences of tasks and processes that participants perform)

**E — Environment:** The surroundings of your participants (Details should include what the atmosphere looks and feels like, and what other activities are going on in the area)

**I — Interactions:** The ways that participants are interacting with other elements in their environment as they work toward a certain goal (These elements can include both people and inanimate objects)

**O — Objects:** The artefacts, tools, technology and other physical details in the environment or that participants use to accomplish their activities (You should also note how these objects relate to the activities and interactions you're observing)

**U — Users:** The participant and other people who they interact with while accomplishing their goals (Note who they are, how they act, what their roles and responsibilities are and what kind of characteristics and motivations they have)

Here's an example of the AEIOU framework in action:

<table>
<tr><td rowspan="3">Activites</td><td>Participant:<br>Time of Day:</td></tr>
<tr><td>Environment<br>What does the environment look and feel like?</td></tr>
<tr><td>Object and Tools<br>What objects are the participants using? (includes devices and applications)</td></tr>
<tr><td>Users<br>Who are the other people in the environment? Include characteristics and motivations of the participants and others.</td><td>Interactions<br>Who and what is are participants interacting with?</td></tr>
</table>

This template is from my field kit. After a lot of trial and error, I realised that the "activities" section is where you'll do most of your note-taking. (I used to split the page equally between all the sections, but then I never had enough space to write down all the steps and things participants were doing.)

## THE POEMS FRAMEWORK

This framework (initially used by the Illinois Institute of Technology and IDEO) is also popular, and it provides a structure similar to the AEIOU framework. At my company, Outwitly, we use the AEIOU framework, but this one can be used instead if you prefer.

**P — People** (i.e. the "users")

**O — Objects**

**E — Environment**

**M — Messages** (i.e. "interactions;" relates to the communication between people, including their tone of voice and body language)

**S — Services** (i.e. "activities;" relates to the services being offered)

# Tips for Smooth Observation Days

## START THE DAY OFF RIGHT

As I emphasised in the logistics section earlier, another major part of building trust on an observation day is getting everybody on the same page about how the day will go. Plan a 15-minute meeting with your main point of contact, your research team and your participants at the beginning of the day. You should arrive early and hold this meeting first thing, before everyone starts working, so that you can introduce yourself and any other researchers you've brought with you. You should ask to meet everyone you might be observing that day. Your on-site point of contact may want to give you a quick tour of the location so that you can do this.

Then, revisit your high-level agenda with them for the day and make any needed tweaks. Divide up the observation tasks between you and any other researchers, so that you have all of your bases covered. Once you've done that, ask if anyone has questions for you. This will help relieve any apprehension they might have about the day, and they'll get more comfortable with you.

## READ THE ROOM AND ENVIRONMENT

As an observer, you should try to blend into your participant's environment. Being observed can feel really strange, so do everything you can to make them comfortable.

**Look into the dress code.** Think about what your participants will probably be wearing. If you're going into an office, will they be dressed casually? In business-formal? In uniforms? For one project, I actually wore a lab coat to avoid standing out in a clinical setting. If you're unsure what's best, you can always ask your client or your main point of contact for this information.

Beyond your outfit, you should also consider the socio-economic background of the people you're visiting or anyone else who will be around throughout the day, and be sensitive to that. If you're observing workers in an office that serves low-income families, for instance, getting decked out in expensive clothing, luxury handbags and jewellery could have a loud, alienating effect.

**Keep a minimal crew.** Don't flood a workspace with researchers. A smaller research team presence can help participants forget that they're being watched. Like I mentioned earlier in this chapter, you should also gently dissuade your stakeholders from sitting in on observations. The more people in the space, the more noticeable your presence is, and the more your participants will get that "watched" feeling.

**Don't interfere.** Even if you're using the contextual inquiry method, you want to avoid any interruptions that might speed up or slow down an activity, cause your participant to forget what they were doing, or otherwise sway them toward a specific action. As hard as it can be, you should resist talking for the majority of time you're observing someone. If you need clarification about anything, write your questions down and ask them later on during a break in the action.

**Know when/when not to ask.** There are good times to ask questions and there are bad times to ask questions. Even if you're conducting contextual inquiries, you should be sensitive to your participant's needs. If they're working on a really important, high-priority task, they're under a tight time crunch, or they're interacting with another person, give them some time. Reapproach them with your questions when the storm of activity slows down, and in the meantime, capture as many notes as you can.

**Match your participant's communication style.** When you're in conversation with your participants, focus on approachability, and address them the same way that they address you. Mirroring participants in this way can keep them relaxed, and it can also help you react to their answers in a neutral way, making you less likely to influence what they say next.

**Accommodate comfort levels.** If you notice that a participant's feeling uncomfortable in your presence, offer them a break from being observed. If you see that they're hesitant to complete a certain task or interact with a certain person in front of you, don't wait for them to say something. Give them an "out" with a line like, "Is it okay for me to join this part, or would you prefer if I came back in 10 minutes?" If needed, remove yourself from their space for a short time until they're ready to call you back in.

### Design Research in Reality: *First Impressions Matter*

During one series of observations, two things went wrong that became big lessons I'll never forget. Those lessons are now baked into all of our standard operating procedures for observations at my company.

The people attending the observation days were myself, another researcher and a client stakeholder. I had taken all the usual planning steps: printed field kits, organised the logistics, sent "What to Expect" documents, and so on. Everything was set to go perfectly well.

**The first mistake:** We arrived at the location on time, but we'd assumed that the receptionist would inform our main point of contact of our arrival when we presented ourselves at the front desk. In reality, the receptionist had let a different person in the office know that we'd be arriving, but that person had no background knowledge of who we were and didn't inform the correct person when we got there.

So, we sat waiting for 30 minutes, and then we were called out for arriving late. I let them know that we'd arrived and introduced ourselves on time, but there was no redoing our very underwhelming first impression.

**Lesson 1:** Always get the cell phone number of the person you will be meeting with when you arrive, and text them when you get there — even if reception has said they've passed the message on. Don't leave it in someone else's hands.

Speaking of first impressions, the fun didn't stop there. There was also the issue of what my team was wearing. I showed up wearing my typical business uniform (blazer, blouse, dress pants and close-toed shoes). And I assumed everyone else would dress the same. But, no. Work attire means different things to different people.

On one of the observation days, the other researcher wore jeans and a plaid button-up with a fedora, and the client stakeholder showed up wearing a short skirt and cowboy boots — fashionable, but not the attire that was expected of us. Our main point of contact interpreted the casual attire as a lack of respect for the setting, and called up the VP of our project to complain. Of course, she didn't realise that one of the "researchers" was actually from the client's side as well, and that added an extra layer of awkwardness that I had to explain and take responsibility for. In any case, as the project lead, I bore the brunt of it and thankfully, I was able to smooth everything over!

**Lesson 2:** Always, always, always check what the dress code is beforehand, make sure anyone joining the observation day is aware of it too, and remind them of the dress code once before they pack for the trip, and a second time the day before. Don't think that everyone joining you for the trip will automatically wear business attire. There are a lot of environments where anything goes, so it's easy for anyone to assume and make this "faux-pas."

## DOCUMENT EVERYTHING AND CAPTURE PROCESS

Take as many hand-written notes as you can in your field kit. Document every little thing you're observing, especially steps or actions they take to accomplish their tasks, even if they seem like mundane details — you never know what kind of patterns you'll notice later on when you're analysing the data. Something that seems small in the moment could end up playing a larger part in understanding a user's problems.

Take photos and record audio and video of the environment, tools, main processes, interactions, etc. that you're observing. Adding these details also paints a fuller picture of an experience for anybody reading your research later, which can help them develop empathy for the users involved.

You also need to make sure you're capturing the processes that are most important to your study.

**Write down the exact steps that a participant follows to complete each task.** You'll probably need to watch them go through the same process multiple times. Don't worry if some of your notes are repetitive or redundant — the goal is to understand that process inside and out, even if it takes some time.

**Capture pain points and areas of friction that you notice as you're observing.** These issues, along with all of the other steps you record, will inform the journey maps, process diagrams or service blueprints that you'll produce later on.

**Example:**

The business analyst you're observing is searching for information in a data management system. As soon as they get to this one point in their workflow, the tool crashes. They sigh and say, "This always happens." Then, you notice that to work around this issue, they open up another tool to search for the information instead. They turn to you and say, "We technically aren't supposed to use this other tool, but it's so much faster."

**Take notes on the timing of tasks when it applies to your research goals.** This will help you understand how your user spends their time in a day. Not only that, stats about task timing can also become metrics that your stakeholders can use as key performance indicators (KPIs). By measuring performance using these KPIs, they can understand how much faster a new product, tool or service works compared to the last version.

**Example:**

If you're observing support agents in a call centre, you should note down how long each call takes, how long customers are on hold, how long it takes the agent to document the case after or between calls, and the timing of any other tasks that call for efficiency.

Strike a balance between observing and documenting. When you're scrambling to write everything down, it's hard to be present in the moment and notice small details. It can help to take shorthand notes and use breaks to go back and fill out your notes in more detail. (This juggling act is definitely challenging, and it puts a lot of strain on your brain. Make sure to get a good sleep the night before, and trust that the more you practice, the easier it'll get.)

## EMBRACE FLEXIBILITY

Even at the best of times, observations can feel a little awkward or unnatural. You can work hard to plan everything out and get everyone aligned with your agenda, but things might still go sideways. You're always at the mercy of your participant and whatever comes up in their day.

Going with the flow and restrategising are important skills you'll need for mastering the observation process. It's okay if you can't observe every task that you set out to observe on a single day. Just do your best to capture as much as possible. If you have observation days left, revisit your plan going forward and try to make up for what you missed on another day.

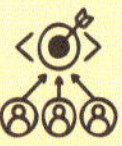

**Alignment Advice:**

I recommend skipping your scheduled team meeting with your stakeholders or client during an observation week, to avoid filling up all of your limited time. Observation days are intense. You and your research team will need time to decompress between each observation session, and you probably won't have the energy for those extra recurring meetings outside of the field trip.

You should also assure your stakeholders that you'll send them quick updates as the observation week goes on, so that they're looped into the process. These updates could take the form of early insights or just a few notes about how the research is going and what tasks you've been able to watch so far.

Schedule a meeting with your stakeholders for a few days later, so they can look forward to hearing more. This will help build stakeholder trust and it'll also get them excited to learn about your findings.

## PLAN TEAM DEBRIEFS

If you're conducting observations on a team with other researchers, plan a 30-minute debrief with them at the end of each observation day. You might be so fried after a day of observing that you might be tempted to just lay on the couch (or hotel bed), but this extra step can make the difference between a research project that meets minimum expectations, and one that uncovers innovative opportunities. Don't waste the opportunity to discuss what you learned, compare the participants and processes you were each observing and highlighting major similarities and differences in what you saw. This is your chance to make note of any unanswered questions you have left, flag any tasks you didn't get to observe yet, and start sketching out the processes you did observe.

You can even map out the journey of an individual participant to get everyone's wheels turning and to make sure you've captured your processes properly.

## TYPE UP YOUR NOTES ASAP

Because you're trying to document everything as you shadow a busy participant, most of the notes that you take during an observation day are scribbled, jumbled and even incomplete. You'll start writing down your train of thought, and then suddenly, there'll be an interruption, and you'll forget to finish your sentence before moving on to the next note. There might be a bunch of jargon that your participant uses, and you might write it down thinking you'll remember what it means, and then find a few days later that you've forgotten.

To make things worse, the more observation days you do, the more the days start to blend together in your memory. When you're looking back, you might mix up two participants in your mind, and your rough notes might start to confuse you.

The best way to avoid this: to type up your notes as soon as humanly possible, while they're still fresh in your mind. In an ideal world, you should block out some time at the end of your day, or the next morning. Fill in any half-written notes or incomplete sentences that might be unclear to you later on, and add any quotes that you can remember your participant saying. (If you don't remember the exact quote, you can paraphrase for now, and then check your recordings later.) I also like to colour-code the different types of pain points that I've marked down in the notes so it's easier to find them later.

## UPLOAD AND ORGANISE YOUR FILES

Organising your photo, video and audio files as you go along is also critical. It can be hard to remember which photo was taken during which task or process, and which person or location is in each recording. If you take pictures of locations with no people in them, those locations can also be tough to distinguish from each other.

At the end of each day, ensure that you upload all of the photos, videos and audio recordings you took to your shared drive or database. Give your files clear, consistent names, with participant IDs so you can keep track of what data came from which person, and make sure to clear enough space on your device for more photos and recordings. I've forgotten to do this before, and I ran out of space for more photos in the middle of an observation day. I had to stop, take out the SD card from my camera, upload the files onto my laptop, empty the card and put it back in, all while wasting valuable observation time. I'm telling you this now so you don't have to repeat my mistakes!

# Conclusion

Observation days are perfect opportunities to dig deeper into the daily lives of users and watch them experience pain points in real time. The more we understand users, the easier it gets to identify problems in a product or service, the sooner we can come to some enlightening conclusions and actionable insights.

If you plan out your observation days well, navigate day-of operations with finesse and finish strong, you'll build more trust with your stakeholders and set yourself up for project success in the next stage.

**Online Resources:**

When it comes to observations, there are lots of logistics and pieces of information to track. I've built the resources at **designresearchmastery.com** to help.

What you'll find:

- Observations "What to Bring" Checklist
- DRM Sample Field Kit

## Key Takeaways:

1. **Observation is an amazing design research method for capturing unspoken and latent participant needs and pain points.** They're also invaluable in helping you learn important context about a participant's environment, interactions and workarounds that you wouldn't otherwise learn through other research methods like interviews, surveys and diary studies.
2. **Planning and preparation is crucial for a successful observation day.** This involves working out all of the logistics well in advance of your field trip, including travel, building and printing field kits, creating consent forms and agendas, etc.
3. **Share your agenda and "What to Expect" document with participants ahead of time.** This will help you build trust with your participants, put them at ease and allow the day to go more smoothly.
4. **Take copious amounts of notes on the day using your field kit and the AEIOU or POEMS framework.** Place most of your focus on the step-by-step tasks the participants take as they go about their day, but make sure to note details about their environment, tools and the people they interact with.
5. **Stay organised: debrief with your team, clean up and file your notes as soon as possible after an observation day.** Otherwise, if you wait, the different observation days and participants will start to blend together and you'll forget which is which. As a result, data analysis and debriefing will be harder.
6. **Be courteous and considerate about your appearance and behaviour.** Know that you are entering the participants' world. They've graciously allowed you to be there, so make sure to dress appropriately, show up on time and accommodate them as much as you can.

# 10 DIARY STUDIES

"Somewhere, something incredible is waiting to be known."
— Carl Sagan

# Introduction

In chapter 9, I talked about how observations unlock latent user needs and challenges by observing a user's experience in context, including their surroundings, their interactions with people and tools, their moment-to-moment reactions, etc. Like with observations, diary studies can help you understand things that aren't going to be revealed in an interview. They give you a glimpse into someone's day-to-day life when no one else is around, and they can help you pick up on user needs and challenges that can only be fully understood if they're tracked over an extended period of time.

When you uncover these little mysteries, you can find amazing opportunities for innovation that competing organisations with lower design maturity might never find. That can spell real ROI and business impact, as well as increased buy-in for your research initiatives.

Of course, to pull these valuable findings from your diary study and turn them into actionable insights, you'll need to build a solid plan, conduct the research mindfully and exercise excellent follow-up skills, both with your stakeholders and your users. This chapter will walk you through all of the above, including a step-by-step process for conducting **the most effective and illuminating diary studies possible.**

## KEY BENEFITS OF DIARY STUDIES

Users participating in a **diary study** report on their experience over a long period of time, logging their day-to-day interactions with a product, service or organisation, as well as their thoughts, feelings and reactions. While they might be a lot of work put together, diary studies can bring in some very rich and robust data.

Diary studies can help you:

- **Gain deeper insights into user experiences,** by allowing you to understand user habits that reoccur, see how their behaviours change over time, and map out their journeys more accurately

- **Build more empathy for users**, because you can get a holistic picture of their day-to-day lives and the interactions and challenges that influence their experiences
- **Collect larger amounts of data faster**, through easily scalable digital studies with tools that prompt users to provide multiple data points across a timeframe, and that provide researchers with real-time updates
- **Study users who are less reachable**, either because they're located in remote areas where observations are less feasible, or because they're performing tasks where it's impractical to shadow them

**Alignment Advice:**

The reliability of your data is a major factor in achieving and maintaining stakeholder buy-in. As I've mentioned a few times in this book, one of the biggest issues with getting stakeholders on board is the false narrative about qualitative data being "fluffy" or anecdotal. Your job is to disprove this by ensuring that your data is representative of the user groups being studied.

When done right, diary studies are practically purpose-built for negating fluffy data. You can investigate whether or not an interaction changes based on the day of the week, time of day or other related factors, and you'll have more opportunities to validate findings and themes.

## DIARY STUDY TYPES AND PURPOSES

Diary studies can come in two different basic forms: **traditional** (i.e. analogue) using a physical journal and **digital**, using an online diary study tool, email or text. I've done it all, but I have to say that I love traditional studies, because they're tactile, and they're especially great for studying users who are less comfortable with technology. It's also fun to put together physical packages that your participants can get excited about.

At the same time, the digital format is great for sending prompts and notifications to keep participants accountable and on track with their tasks/answers. Some of my favourites even incorporate gamification to motivate participants with kudos and milestone notifications.

Because diary studies are a larger investment (in terms of time, incentives, materials and/or subscription costs), it's important to know exactly what you're trying to accomplish and whether a diary study is the right method for your project.

There are three main purposes you might have for conducting a diary study, laid out below. To illustrate each one, I've provided a real-life example from a design research project that I've personally led.

### Purpose: Understanding a Specific Activity

In this scenario, you're trying to understand how someone accomplishes a specific goal, such as studying the journey of someone buying their first car.

**Design Research in Reality: *Understanding the Adult Learning Experience***

**Diary study type:** Traditional (for accessibility reasons)

**Duration:** 2 weeks

**Number of entries:** 10 (on school days, over a 2-week period)

**Reason:** Understanding learning barriers for adult learners when attending school/ classes

**Description:** We conducted a diary study with adult learners to understand how they were feeling about their classwork and to get detailed information of the overall experience of using publicly offered adult learning programmes. We also needed to understand how their schooling fit (or didn't fit) into their day-to-day lives.

**Outcomes:** The study aimed to redesign adult learning programmes across a Canadian province in order to make the curriculum and programme delivery more consistent and also to ensure that they met the unique needs of adult learners, in order to give them the best chance for success. The diary study helped us to understand that adult learners have unique barriers such as childcare needs, difficulty finding transportation, and work commitments that make it more challenging to attend and succeed in their classes. Using this understanding, we were able to recommend flexible study arrangements and identify key success factors that could then be integrated into the curriculum and adult learning programming.

## Purpose: Understanding a General Activity

You might need to study how someone goes about regular daily activities, which could include multiple varying goals and tasks. This type of study investigates a broader experience or journey like grocery shopping and might not be tied to a specific product or service. Conducting diary studies for this purpose can inspire innovative development of new products or services.

### Design Research in Reality: *Understanding Grocery Shopping*

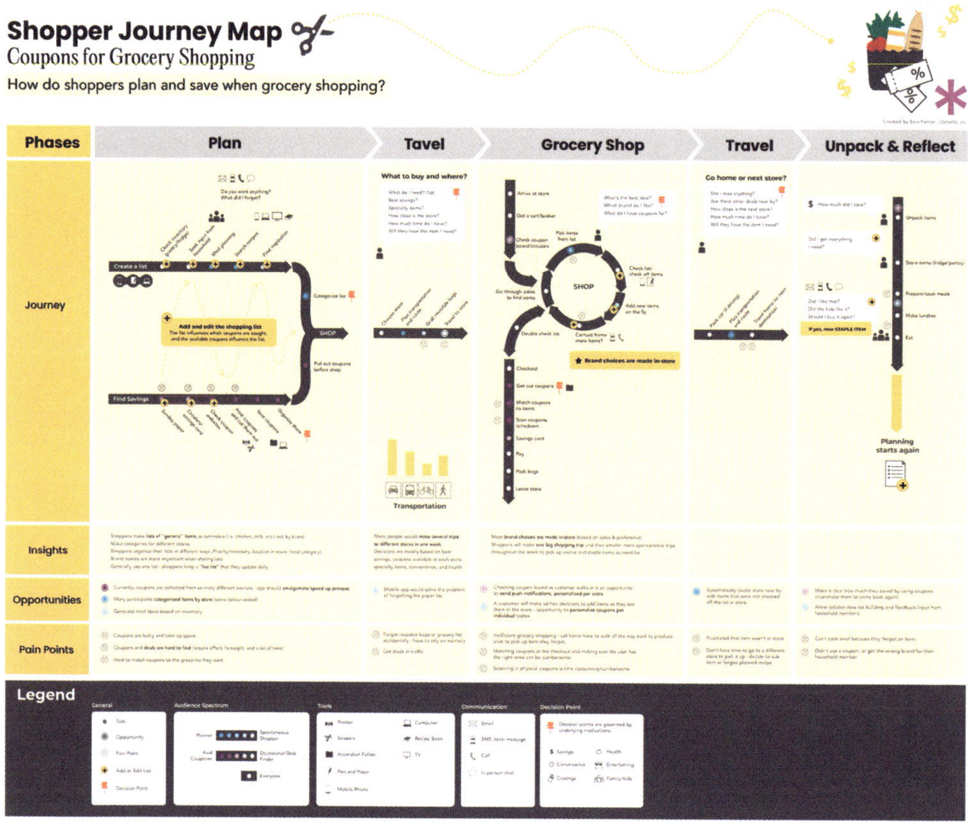

**Shopper Journey Map**
Coupons for Grocery Shopping
How do shoppers plan and save when grocery shopping?

Phases: Plan | Tavel | Grocery Shop | Travel | Unpack & Reflect

Journey
Insights
Opportunities
Pain Points
Legend

**Diary study type:** Digital

**Duration:** 4 weeks

**Number of entries:** 9–18 (depending on the total number of shopping trips)

**Reason:** Understanding the general activity of grocery shopping

**Description:** We embarked on a diary study with grocery shoppers to understand how they make grocery shopping lists as a family, how (and if) they use coupons, and how they shop. Participants reported their behaviour and reactions on 3–4 different shopping trips, as well as pre- and post-trip activities. They had questions to answer both before and after shopping.

The diary questions covered a broader range of individual user tasks and goals, including the use of coupons, navigating a store (any store), family meal-planning and list-making, unpacking groceries, etc.

**Outcome:** The insights from this diary study helped us identify key opportunities for integrating coupon-cutting into an MVP of a grocery shopping app.

### Purpose: Understanding an interaction (With a Product, Service or Website)

This is a very common purpose for diary studies, which involves investigating the experience of a company's existing offering, whether that's a product/app, a feature, a service, or a website in order to improve it.

**Design Research in Reality:** ***SaaS 30-Day Trial***

**Diary study type:** Digital

**Duration:** 4 weeks (approximately a month)

**Number of entries:** Up to 20

**Reason:** Understanding users' issues with the app and reasons why they were abandoning after the trial period

**Description:** We used a diary study to understand first-time users of a specific SaaS B2B application during their 30-day free trial. We needed to understand how users onboarded onto the app, what kind of support they needed, if any, what setup challenges they might be running into, and what factors led to subscription renewal vs abandonment. Then, we could investigate why many users abandoned the trial or didn't renew, and why the company was losing potential customers to competitors, in order to help them improve the trial experience and retain more customers.

**Outcomes:** Through the diary study, we uncovered the biggest challenges that users faced as they started using the trial, including long customer support calls, difficult data migration and a steep learning curve. This helped us provide design recommendations and improvements that ultimately increased customer retention.

(**Note:** Some users didn't stick around for the full trial, so we had less data for them. But, the diary study did encourage others to stick around longer, so we made sure to account for that fact in the findings to avoid bias. We mentioned that some people might have abandoned earlier if they hadn't been participating in the month-long study.)

# Diary Study Planning

Diary studies can feel like a big and complicated production, but by methodically breaking them down into individual steps, you can make your work more approachable (and potentially more effective).

Below is a diagram showing how I would typically structure an ideal diary study, followed by a broad overview of what's involved in each stage. This chapter will touch on each of these stages, with advice from my lived experience.

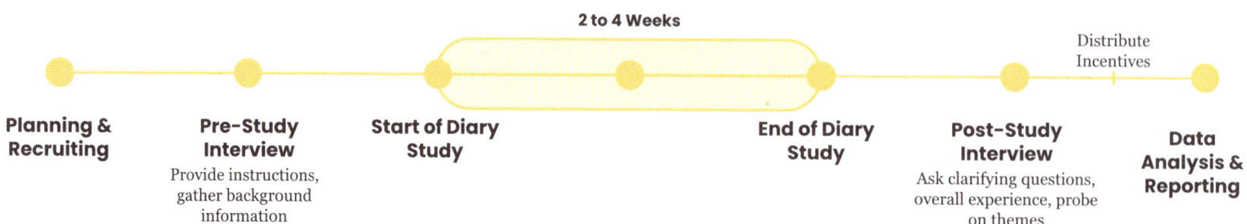


- **Planning and recruiting:** In this stage, you'll decide on key logistics for your diary study, recruit participants and then create the "diary" for your study. Do this at least 4–6 weeks before the study.

- **Pre-study interviews:** This is when you'll prepare the participants, gain some background information about them and clarify participation logistics. This typically takes 2–5 days; do this no more than a week before the study.
- **Start of diary study:** Once participants receive the diary study and start, you'll monitor activity, provide prompts, perform check-ins and send through incentive instalments, if applicable. This typically takes 2–4 weeks.
- **End of diary study:** Retrieve/access the studies, organise and categorise the data, and ensure that all are accounted for.
- **Post-study interviews:** This is your chance to gain clarity on the data, learn about your participants' overall feelings about the experience, probe further, envision an ideal future state and even gain feedback on the study. You'll generally do this over 2–5 days, no more than a week after the study.
- **Distribute incentives:** Finally, you'll send the final instalments or lump sums as thank-yous for participating.
- **Data analysis and reporting:** I'll cover this stage in chapter 12 and 13.

Once you've determined the key purpose and scope of your study, there are six key decisions to make that will guide you forward in your diary study planning. These are based on the questions I ask myself whenever I'm planning a diary study, once I have a clear idea of my research goals.

You'll need to choose your: **participants, format, trigger types, duration, incentive** and **tech**. Your goals, along with the needs of your participants, will inform the rest of the decisions to be made.

## CHOOSE THE PARTICIPANTS

Just like with other design research methods, the purpose of your diary study will determine who you select as your participants. As discussed in chapter 7, you'll target specific demographics, behaviours or traits, depending on what criteria are most relevant to your organisation's business goals. When you're defining the user groups for a diary study, you'll also need to give careful consideration to the following factors, as they'll influence whether you choose a traditional or digital diary study.

**Location:**
Are your users living locally, centrally, or in remote locations?

**Technology access:**
Are they able to access wifi and digital tools throughout their days/activities?

**Technology savvy-ness:**
How comfortable are they with using digital tools?

**Accessibility:**
Do they need accommodations or support for processing audio or visual information, or for using physical tools like keyboards, pens, cameras, etc.?

**Literacy/language:**
What's their level of proficiency in reading, writing and comprehension of the language(s) being used in the study?

## CHOOSE THE FORMAT

So, are you going with a digital diary study or a traditional one? This decision will dictate what kind of materials you need, how much assembling you'll need to do ahead of time and how much cost you'll incur putting together the diary study packages. To help you, I've created a comparison chart with some pros and cons.

| Advantage/ Disadvantage | Digital | Traditional |
|---|---|---|
| Efficiency | **Faster**<br>You can leverage online forms, apps and smartphones to set up studies and send/receive information quickly. | **Slower**<br>You'll need more time for set-up and follow-up, including assembling materials, delivering physical packages and arranging return postage. |
| Data acquisition | **Real-time**<br>Data can be received, analysed and reviewed by researchers as participants send in responses. | **Batch**<br>No data is seen or reviewed by the researcher until the diaries have been retrieved from the participants. |
| Researcher/ participant interaction | **Real-time**<br>Researchers can send instant notifications to participants, prompting or reminding them to complete logs. | **Offline**<br>Researchers will need to manually follow up with participants through email, phone or text; participants may or may not answer. |
| Accessibility and approachability | **Restrictive**<br>The study won't be as accessible to those without wifi, laptops, or smartphones, or to those less comfortable with technology. | **Inclusive**<br>More accessible; this form is good for anyone who is comfortable hand-writing entries and using a camera: it's also more approachable for those who are less tech-savvy. |
| Cost/affordability | **Costly Subscriptions**<br>There are ways to DIY a digital diary study through emails and messaging groups, but if you use a diary study app, you'll need to factor in the paid subscription. | **More Cost Effective**<br>Traditional diary studies can often be more cost effective if you're creating the diaries yourself and printing in black and white. The cost could increase depending on shipping/delivery. |

Even though you might notice more cons in the table for a traditional format, there's something so fun about a physical diary — it can be more engaging for your participants to complete, and more exciting to receive and analyse. There's a feeling of getting "closer" to the participant, because you're passing these tangible items back and forth, and the little booklets you put together provide a personalised, tactile experience they can really dive into.

I've gotten especially amazing feedback on my traditional diary studies, where clients have said how happy they were with the results. Participants of these studies have also responded to this format with glowing feedback — many said they had actually had fun filling out their answers; some talked about how they'd never had anyone really care about their experience before, and the diary study process helped them feel seen and heard.

## CHOOSE THE TYPE OF TRIGGERS

You'll also need to decide when and how participants will report on their activities, thoughts and feelings. In other words, you'll need to decide how your diary study triggers will work.

Your triggers will depend on what style of reporting will be best for your users and for your needs. There are three main categories of participant reporting for diary studies:

**"In-situ" reporting:** The diary study triggers participants to report on their experience in the moment while they're performing an activity. This style of reporting should only be used if it won't negatively impact the participant's day or disrupt the activity.

**Snippet reporting:** The diary study triggers participants to take brief notes or photos in the moment, and then elaborate on their answers later on when they have more time. This is the most common form of reporting, and I've definitely used it the most in my diary studies.

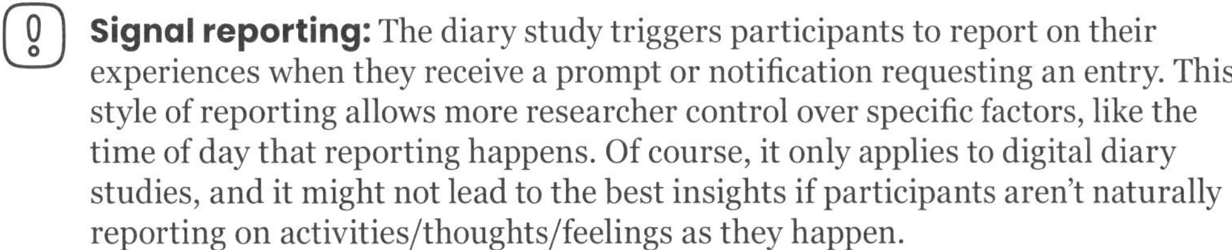

**Signal reporting:** The diary study triggers participants to report on their experiences when they receive a prompt or notification requesting an entry. This style of reporting allows more researcher control over specific factors, like the time of day that reporting happens. Of course, it only applies to digital diary studies, and it might not lead to the best insights if participants aren't naturally reporting on activities/thoughts/feelings as they happen.

**Action Advice:**

**Don't choose triggers or a triggering schedule that could alter participant behaviour.** This is an especially dangerous pitfall when you're conducting digital diary studies, because you can decide exactly when to trigger reporting.

Also, don't have your participants perform activities that they wouldn't normally do, or in a different order than they'd normally carry them out. Avoid asking them to do activities at uncharacteristic times, or times that are awkward or difficult for them.

For example, it would be disruptive to ask participants for in-situ reporting while in class, because they need to be paying attention to their lessons. It would make more sense to trigger reporting when they're at home or on their train commute.

Never forget: to ensure your data is unbiased and totally relevant to your users' experiences (and actionable as a result), you need your users to act and react as naturally as possible.

## CHOOSE THE DURATION

The duration of your diary study is a crucial thing to get right, because you need to make sure you get enough data — if the study is too short, you might not capture the full user journey and all of the scenarios users encounter. If it's too long, you risk losing participants and becoming overwhelmed with too much data in the analysis stage.

As I mentioned in the diary study process overview, a typical diary study will last around two to four weeks. Of course, the duration you choose will depend on the activities you're studying.

For example, if you're studying the activities of students going to class, you'll get data every day of the week Monday to Friday, so two weeks of data might be enough to catch them in different classes and see how they do their schoolwork at home. But, if you're studying grocery shoppers, they might only do one or two trips per week, so you will need a longer study to get the same amount of data points.

If your research time is limited to less than two weeks, you should opt for observations instead, since you won't be able to get enough data points for it to be worth your while.

## CHOOSE THE INCENTIVE

Incentivising participants is key to a successful diary study in my experience. This is because diary studies are more work for participants and longer than most other design research methods.

You might choose to provide a lump sum incentive, instalments, or a tiered system. I recommend tiered incentives, because in my experience, they can prevent problems with drop-offs towards the middle and end of a diary study. It might be a little more complicated to execute, but this structure will keep participants engaged for the entire duration of the study.

When you're deciding how much to offer for your incentives, you should:

- **Align the incentive amount with the level of effort required by participants.** The decisions you've made about the duration, triggers and format will inform your incentive choice, because these factors affect the amount of participant effort required... and you want your incentives to be fair.
- **Consider the level of interest your users will have in the area of study.** They might be willing to participate for less if they're passionate about it, or if they know that improving that experience would significantly impact their lives.
- **Consider the industry that users are operating within.** The circumstances of that industry might impact their availability, the time or energy they're willing to give, or their level of interest in the topic.
- **Compare with previous incentives you've used for other methods.** Use previous methods or studies as a jumping-off point to determine the best range, comparing the incentive value to the amount of time and effort required.

I personally recommend choosing an incentive in the $100–$300 range, depending on the factors above. (See the online resources listed at the end of this chapter for advice on incentive payment structures.)

## CHOOSE YOUR TECH

There's a quickly growing number of digital diary study tools, many or most of which are AI-driven. I encourage you to explore your options, but make sure you do a thorough pilot test with any new tech, and ensure you're using a platform that only grabs data from the real users that you recruited. (Some tools out there are built to collect data from fake AI personas as stand-ins.)

# Creating the "Diary" for Your Study

This section will cover all of the key elements that should be included in the actual "diary" that you'll be passing off to your participants, whether you're printing and assembling physical ones or setting things up in a diary study app. Like with your interview protocols in chapter 8, your diaries should have a distinct beginning, middle and end. This will help you ensure that you don't forget any action items and that your participants stay on track.

| Beginning | Middle | End |
|---|---|---|
| Welcome, initial questions, diary instructions | Activities, answering main questions, completing assignments | Wrap-up questions, thank-yous, next steps |

Now, let's get into some more details and steps involved in crafting your actual journal, a.k.a. the diary.

At the outset, your diary study should be organised in a way that makes a good first impression, sets your participants at ease and ensures that they have everything they need to complete the study properly.

As I've mentioned before, this method is a larger time investment for participants, so make sure that you're setting them up for success. You'll get better data if you're organised and your participants are confident about what they're supposed to do. At the **beginning** of the diary study, you'll want to do the following:

1. **Welcome the participant to the diary study:** You'll welcome them verbally in the pre-study interview, but it's also recommended to write a welcome greeting directly in the diary.

2. **Provide instructions outlining how to fill out the diary:** Include information about when to complete assignments, approximately how long each assignment will take, etc.

3. **Include introductory questions in the diary itself:** This is optional, but still recommended, especially if you didn't have time for a formal pre-study interview.

The **middle** section will make up the bulk of your diary study, where you'll gain findings directly related to the activities/interactions that you're studying. There are three main components that participants should log:

4. **Activities:** These will be activities that are naturally part of the experience you're studying, and should be performed at times of day that are natural for each participant. An example could be creating their grocery list or going grocery shopping.

5. **Assignments:** Assignments will involve performing an assigned, deliberate action and answering questions before and/or after that action. Examples of this could be recording their grocery list brainstorming process or taking a photo of their grocery haul.

6 **Questions:** Include the questions that participants should answer before or after different activities, or as part of additional assignments.

Below is an example sheet from the adult learner diary study that I mentioned earlier. You can see that I asked participants to take pictures of different items, and I also provided clear instructions below certain questions to ensure clarity:

**DAY 6**

**Take pictures of...**

- [ ] Your classwork or classroom activities
- [ ] Books, worksheets, notes, websites you use for your classwork
- [ ] Any classwork you did at home and your desk or work area at home
- [ ] Your classroom (if you go to class)

1. **What did you do today?**
   This should include what you did at home, at work, and in the classroom.

**If you DID NOT go to class or do classwork:** Please tell us what your day was like. Did you plan to go to class and were you not able to go? If so, what got in your way?

2. **What classes did you attend today or what classwork did you do today?**
   Please give detail, for example: "I went to Math class and worked on fractions" or "I worked on a novel study in English"

3. **What did you like the most and what did you like the least about your classwork?**

I liked...

I disliked...

4. **How did you feel about your classwork?**

**Why did you feel that way?**

Make sure you carry your diary study all the way through to the finish line — create a formal **end** to the study. You'll want to:

7 **Ask wrap-up questions:** At the end of the study, I like to ask a few higher-level questions about their overall experience and what could be done to improve it.

8 **Thank your participants for their time:** Diary studies are a big commitment not only for you, but for them, too.

9 **Provide clear instructions on next steps:** This might include how to complete and submit the diary study or any next steps about incentives.

Here's an example of a wrap-up section, from the same diary study about adult learners:

**WRAP UP**

**You're almost done! Please fill out these 5 questions on your last day.**

1. **What is you main learning goal?**
   Tell us why you decided to enroll in the programme. What are you hoping to achieve?

2. **Do you feel like you are making progress towards achieving your goal?**
   Tell us why or why not.

3. **What was the hardest thing you worked on in the last 10 days?**

4. **What were you most proud of in the last 10 days?**

5. **What could make your learning programme better?**

Once you've got your rough instructions and questions assembled into your diary structure, you can share drafts of your diary study with your stakeholders and project team to get their feedback. And if they want to co-create the diary study with you, all the better. Just remember that **all of your questions and assignments should relate directly to your main research questions and goals.**

The finalised diary study can be distributed to participants after they've been screened (as part of your recruiting process) and properly briefed in your pre-study interview. See the end of this chapter for a link to the diary study sample shown in the screengrabs above.

Ensure that you ask the same questions for each activity or assignment. This will help you to identify patterns during data analysis (because logs for repeated activities will be easy to cross-reference) and it will help the participant create a comfortable day-to-day routine (because they'll remember what to do more easily).

With the adult learning study shown in the example, I wanted to understand the students' experience of going to school over two weeks

— so I ensured that every day, they were asked to fill out the same set of questions and complete the same assignments. This allowed me to see how homework or class experience changed on a day-to-day basis. Had I asked them different questions each day, it would have been very hard to identify patterns in the data.

## Pre- and Post-Study Interviews

While there's an entire chapter in this book dedicated to conducting interviews (chapter 8), it's important to note some specific best practices and uses for interviews that are conducted before and after your diary studies, as part of your overall diary study methodology.

Both interviews should be about 30 minutes long — from my experience, that's the optimal amount of time for getting through everything. You'll also want to prepare interview protocols, scripts and consent forms. (And, like any interviews you conduct, they should ideally be recorded.)

Your **pre-study interviews** (sometimes called "briefing calls") will serve two main purposes:

1. **Preparing the participant:** To prepare the participant, you'll want to do your best to set expectations with them at the outset. For example, you may want to indicate how often they're expected to log information and when, how much detail you're looking for, and what kinds of photos or recordings you need. You can also use this to confirm the timeline and the date of a post-study interview, as well as clarify the incentive structure. Lastly, go over any required tools and tech, and give your participant an opportunity to ask clarifying questions.

2. **Gaining background information:** The pre-study interview is a great time to learn a bit more about your participants. Add in some background questions to learn about their experience, industry of work, roles and responsibilities or some general background questions about their life tailored to what you are researching. Their answers to these questions will provide meaningful context that can help you interpret their diary study responses and categorise participants into user groups and create personas later on.

Your **post-study interviews** (also called "debriefing calls") are great opportunities to feed your analysis with even more context and food for thought, validate the themes you've been finding so far, and tie the study up in a neat bow. I like to use this time to clarify anything I didn't understand about their responses to the diary study and to expand on any areas that need more detail. I'll typically ask them more questions about their overall experience with the product, service or activity being studied (especially any major likes or dislikes), and about how they think their experience could be improved, including any ideal future states they can imagine.

If there's time, it's also useful to probe further on emerging research themes and validate your findings with them, or get feedback on the diary study experience itself. Basically, this is your chance to clear up ambiguities, dive deeper into any areas that still feel a bit mysterious to you, and ensure that participants have a positive experience with the research study.

# Tips for Robust Diary Studies

The most effective diary studies strike a balance of efficiency, consistency and thoroughness, so that you can gain the most robust data possible, while keeping your stakeholders happy and your participants engaged.

The tips below are designed to help you achieve this, while avoiding common challenges that I and many others have run into. In fact, all of these tips come from experiences that I've learned the hard way. Hopefully, they'll help you achieve your goals faster and with more ease.

## MOTIVATE PARTICIPANTS

Again, diary studies are long and take a lot of sustained effort from participants. It's easy for them to get off-track, forget to log their activities, or be tempted to give up on the study altogether.

I've had participants flat-out ghost me — at the beginning, they often seem really engaged, and you think they'll be good to do the whole thing, and then at some point, they just stop filling things out or stop responding. Other times, I've had participants just do the bare minimum in order to get their incentive, with vague one-line responses, and photos that are unusable and don't really show you much.

You'll almost always have at least one participant who does this. It's annoying, but don't let it be discouraging. In the end, you'll usually end up with some solid participants who make up for the ones that either stopped midway through or did a careless or half-baked job.

Just keep doing everything you can to sustain the other participants' engagement. Incentive instalments can help — and so can staying in touch. (See the next page.)

## PROVIDE CLEAR INSTRUCTIONS

It's crucial that participants understand exactly what's expected of them — what activities to log, when to log them, what photos or videos to take, etc. The last thing you want is to receive submissions at the end of a long period only to find that some guideline was misunderstood or forgotten, and the data isn't relevant or complete.

Include stand-alone instructions in the diary package or in-app, and provide an example of a completed entry (or, better yet, record a video to show them how the diary study works).

## STAY IN TOUCH

This strategy is fundamental for keeping your participants accountable and helping them remember to complete their logs and assignments. Make sure participants have a readily available point of contact for questions, check in with participants regularly about their progress, and send in-app prompts and reminders for when entries are due or overdue.

**Alignment Advice:**

Remember that your users aren't the only ones you should be checking in with you during your diary study. **You should also be giving your stakeholders regular updates throughout the diary study to let them know how progress is going.** Diary studies take a while, and they can be a major investment, so you want to reassure your stakeholders as the days go by, and as incremental incentive payments go out, that you have everything under control. They'll want to know that the participants are doing what they're supposed to be doing, and that you're uncovering exciting information about the user experience.

(See chapter 5 for more on stakeholder management throughout research project execution.)

## ACKNOWLEDGE FEEDBACK

Besides keeping participants motivated, acknowledging feedback regularly and in a friendly way can help participants feel appreciated. It sends the message that their opinions are valued and that someone (you) is going to actually spend time pouring over the work they're doing. Acknowledge log entries as they come in, thank participants for continuing to enter their information, and respond in a personal way. If a participant mentions in their feedback that they had a terrible day full of inconveniences, make sure to respond to those personal details first — e.g., "I'm sorry to hear you've had a bad day."

## PROCESS DATA IN REAL TIME

I've definitely drowned in diary study data before. Especially if your diary study ranges past two weeks or you have a lot of participants, you're going to have a ton of data points to analyse, and that can be really overwhelming.

The analysis paralysis of previous years might be less of a pain point now with AI-assisted analysis tools, but chances are, you'll still have huge heaps of data from so many individual diary entries to track and review, and you might still find yourself getting stuck on small details when you're correcting errors or refining themes from the AI output. Also: not all of the data from a diary study will be relevant and useful, so it will ultimately be up to you to decide which pieces make sense to analyse and which makes sense to leave out.

In the case of digital diary studies, a good tip for reducing overwhelm is to organise and analyse data as it comes in, rather than waiting until the end of the study, when the amount of data will bog you down. Doing this might also help you find early themes/patterns to validate or investigate further in your post-study interviews. (I'll talk more about analysis in chapter 12.)

Follow these tips and your diary studies will go more smoothly, your data will be more detailed, and you'll be able to definitively prove the value of this incredibly useful method to your stakeholders.

# Conclusion

When you set up participants for success, ask them the right (stakeholder-approved, goal-serving) questions, and keep them motivated throughout a diary study, you're laying the foundation for something powerful. The resulting insights will have the potential to fuel innovation, improve the lives of users and even foster success for your organisation.

**Online Resources:**

If you go to **designresearchmastery.com** you can get free copies of my favourite diary study tools that I've built over the years.

What you'll find:

- Diary Study Sample
- DRM Diary Study Checklist & Workbook
- Participant Incentives Guide

## * Key Takeaways:

1. **One of the most unique benefits of diary studies is the ability to understand how user perceptions and behaviours change over time.** Diary studies also help you to understand user habits that reoccur, build more empathy for your users, map out their journeys more accurately, collect larger amounts of data faster, and even study users who are less reachable.

2. **There are three different diary study purposes for understanding user behaviour:** you might be looking to study general activities, specific activities, or products/services/websites. Your specific purpose will affect how you build your diary study (what tasks you observe, what questions you ask, what secondary research you conduct, etc.)

3. **While digital diary studies are way more common than traditional ones, the latter can provide wider accessibility.** Yes, diary studies allow for real-time data access, more participant motivational opportunities and more efficient analysis. On the other hand, you never know what circumstances your participants might be in, and whether they're tech-savvy or even have easy access to digital technology or wifi.

4. **Choosing the right types of triggers and triggering schedule will help your participants act as naturally as possible throughout the study.** This involves assessing which type of participant reporting will fit best with the experience you're studying:

    - **"In-situ" reporting** — Participants report on their experience while it's happening
    - **Snippet reporting** — Participants take brief notes during an experience and elaborate on them afterwards
    - **Signal reporting** — Participants report on their experiences only when prompted

5. **Pre- and post-study interviews are highly recommended as part of your diary study methodology.** Conducting interviews prior to your study can help you sort out any logistical questions your participants might have and give you some background information on them. Interviews after a diary study provide you a chance to gain clarity on the data, probe deeper on certain themes and even get feedback on the study.

6. **It's critical that you maintain participants' motivation and ensure that they stick around for the duration of your study.** This is a unique challenge with diary studies, since they require more long-term effort from your participants. You'll want to think about the right incentive structure, focus on staying in close touch, and consider strategies like using gamification to keep them engaged and reporting regularly.

# WORKSHOPS

Conversation doesn't just reshuffle the cards: it creates new cards.
— Theodore Zeldin

# Introduction

Design practitioners love workshops, with good reason! This method can help with gathering input quickly, making it a cost-effective way to explore and validate ideas. In-person workshops cost more, but are still very worth it. There's nothing quite like the in-person synergy that's created when you and your participants are all in a room together. I recommend conducting at least one in-person workshop per project, if you can swing it.

Beyond gathering data you need, workshops have the power to completely re-engineer your relationship with clients and stakeholders in particular, as you demonstrate empathy for their perspectives, invite their input, showcase your facilitation skills and craft amazing, inspiring experiences for them. The collaborative spirit in workshops — where every perspective is treated as valuable — can also cultivate game-changing levels of trust, creativity and enthusiasm.

There are so many different types of workshops and workshop exercises that entire books are dedicated to them. Instead of repeating the same information, this chapter will highlight the key workshop types and related tips that will create the biggest impact in your design research projects. Depending on your project's budget and timeline, you might only get to conduct one or two workshops. Regardless, the tips that follow will help you command any workshop with expert flair and establish yourself as a strategic and reliable design leader. If your participants have a great time and the ideas that emerge are highly useful, you might end up inspiring your stakeholders, creating more opportunities for workshops in the future.

# Key Workshops in Design Research

These workshops and approaches can help you quickly gain context, so that you can plan your research with the current state, stakeholder goals and anticipated risks in mind. They're great opportunities to collaborate and ideate solutions or iterate on versions of deliverables. Last (but definitely not least), they generate excitement, ownership and buy-in among your attendees.

There are three types of workshops that I've used most often in my design research projects: **discovery, co-design and validation workshops.** Each has a different purpose and is conducted at a different time in your project. All of them will help you coax both divergent and convergent thinking out of your participants, produce great ideas and gain clearer direction for meeting your project goals. I find that workshop outcomes vary based on the participant list, which is why I've broken them down into stakeholder-focused and user-focused categories.

Before I move on — remember those facets of design research that I talked about in chapter 4? Workshops are always considered primary research, qualitative, and participatory. What differs is whether they're **exploratory, generative or evaluative** in nature. I'll indicate which workshop types fall into each of these categories, to help you determine when to use them in your project.

## DISCOVERY WORKSHOPS 

The first type of workshop you might hold in your research project is often called a "discovery workshop." Discovery workshops are rooted in exploration. They can be leveraged to set up background context and gather preliminary data to kick-start your research planning. What data you collect and how you use that data will depend on where exactly you're at in your project timeline, and who you decide to invite.

### Discovery Workshops With Stakeholders

The discovery workshops you hold with stakeholders are generally conducted as part of project initiation, to help you get off on the right foot and uncover how much is known about the area(s) of study. All of this context will inform your research and your research plan, so you can ensure that the data you collect is relevant to the business, and that the resulting insights are actionable. Often, stakeholders don't have time for these workshops — but they're a very welcome bonus when you get to conduct them.

**You can use discovery workshops with stakeholders to align your stakeholders and gather key business requirements.** They're great for breaking the ice and establishing a strong collaborative working relationship between the project team and management. You can take the opportunity to pull out stakeholder hopes and fears about the project, which can inform your risk mitigation strategy. (If needed, see the chapter 5 section on risk management.) Discovery workshops can also be used for identifying the key project drivers and business goals that will inform your research goals. You and your stakeholders might use this time to align on your research priorities, i.e. which processes, pain points and user groups to study, if these haven't been called out already.

This type of workshop can also help you to **inform research planning**. For example, you can get your stakeholders' help in understanding the use cases that should be focused on in the research and designed for. To help you orient and plan your research, you could also identify gaps and unknowns about the current user experience, so that you know which gaps your research will need to fill.

Depending on your stakeholders' familiarity with their users and how much time you have for your workshop, you might also dig a little bit deeper, and actually define user groups, do some empathy mapping to understand the users better, build out a service blueprint for a key process, or create a journey map depicting a known current-state user journey. **Any deliverables you create together at this stage will be based only on assumptions about your users** and their experiences — but you can use these assumptions as a jumping-off point for the questions in your interview protocols, diary study packages, observation field kits, etc.

Here are some examples from a discovery workshop I conducted to understand more about key user groups in one of my past projects.

*Empathy map created in a discovery workshop:*

*Proto-persona created in a discovery workshop:*

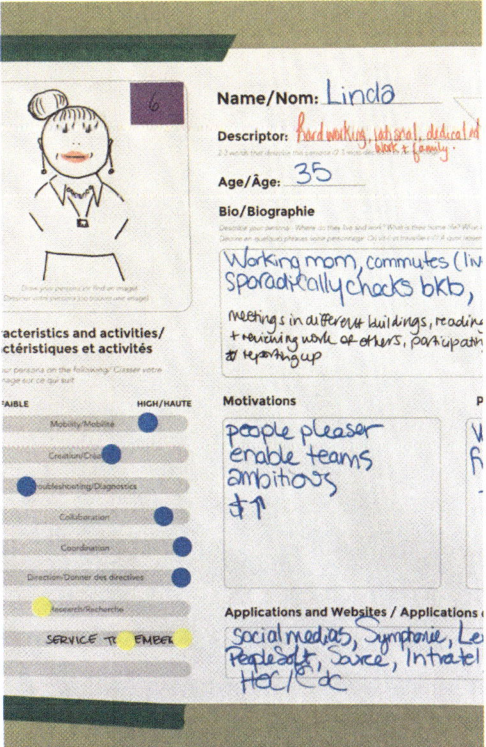

### Discovery Workshops With Users

If you have the opportunity to hold discovery workshops with users, you should do so right before or in parallel with your other core research methods, like interviews, observations and diary studies. Discovery workshops with users allow you to understand their backgrounds, points of view and motivations/goals. They can help with understanding the current state of a product or service from your users' perspectives, including the pain points they encounter while accomplishing certain tasks and which pain points are impacting their experience the most.

As design researchers, we often have to skip this workshop due to budget constraints. However, if you can gain buy-in for them, discovery workshops with users can bring a lot of value to your research. They can help you triangulate your data, allowing you to hear from multiple participant viewpoints in the same session. You can also gain a lot of information from a lot of people in a short period of time.

Like with your stakeholder discovery workshops, you might have your participants map out one of their journeys or create empathy maps, build a rough service blueprint of a process, use affinity mapping to categorise their ideas or pain points, etc. (See chapter 12 for more on affinity mapping in a data analysis context.)

## CO-DESIGN WORKSHOPS 

Co-design workshops are useful as you move into the "define" and "design" phases of the design process, where you're translating information into action. They're also highly versatile! They invite others to actively participate in the co-creation of deliverables, solutions and early concepts, or the prioritisation of key project tasks. You won't be able to tackle all of these purposes in one workshop, so you'll need to decide what's most crucial to your project.

### Co-Design Workshops With Stakeholders

The purposes you aim for when you're conducting co-design workshops with stakeholders will be a little different than those you conduct with users, because your stakeholders (as I've said many times now) are NOT your users. They'll be working purely from their assumptions about the user. That being said, their understanding of the business context can be incredibly valuable.

You can use co-design workshops with stakeholders for **brainstorming opportunities and solutions to inform your design recommendations and action plan.** In these workshops, stakeholders can offer their perspectives on how to prioritise the key pain points identified in the research, and weigh in on which should be addressed first in the product or service. Or, you might ask them to help to conceptualise and envision an ideal future state in the form of a future-state journey map or service blueprint.

A fun idea is to come prepared with opportunity cards pulled from the research as well as synthesised findings, and ask stakeholders to work in groups to develop and ideate on possible fixes/solutions. Then, have each team present what they came up with to the larger group, and have participants dot vote on their favourite solutions. The point here is not to develop fully-formed solutions to the problems you uncovered, but to inspire and prioritise key solutions that could be elaborated on in the future or that could become part of your action plan.

The beauty of involving stakeholders in this way is that they fundamentally understand what will work in their organisation and what opportunities can and should be implemented. Ultimately, they're the most informed about the product, the business goals and the resources that are available. Not to mention, it gets them excited about taking action after the fact! This increases your chances of making a real impact.

### Co-Design Workshops With Users

Involving users in designing solutions is highly beneficial because you're getting ideas and information "straight from the source." Because they're the people who will directly interact with the product or service being studied they will naturally have a stake in the results of the overall project. This makes them reliable in determining if a design recommendation or concept will actually solve for their needs.

If you didn't get a chance to hold a discovery workshop with your users and you have the time, you might want to use a co-design workshop (or create a hybrid workshop) to help you understand a bit more about your users, their pain points and the problem area, while also co-creating solutions.

You can use co-design workshops with users to quickly conceptualise real-life solutions to their problems and the pain points pulled from your research. Users are an amazing source of creativity, and when you bring them together to solve issues that directly affect them, the synergies created by having all of their minds working together in a structured way are truly invaluable. You'll see ideas and concepts that you might never have thought of emerge from the workshop, and then you can use these ideas as design recommendations, or as part of your action plan in your report.

## VALIDATION WORKSHOPS 

Validation workshops are collaborative sessions conducted with the purpose of reviewing (and validating) research and design deliverables in order to get feedback. They give participants the opportunity to discuss, mark up and even make edits to your artefacts, key findings and insights, concepts, design recommendations and anything else you want their opinion on. The exercises and participants you choose will depend on what deliverables you're creating and where there might be gaps in your research that need clarification.

### Validation Workshops With Stakeholders

Validation workshops are great opportunities for gaining stakeholder feedback on rough drafts of your design deliverables, including your insights reporting, design recommendations and/or action plans. As you conduct your research, you can ask stakeholders to weigh in on which uncovered opportunities are the most interesting and useful to them. This can give you direction for further research and for prioritisation of insights and findings going into your final reporting.

If you've further along in your research project and you're moving into the design phase, you can use a validation workshop to align your stakeholders and the project team on an early design direction or, you can ask for validation of existing design concepts to ensure that they satisfy stakeholder needs.

### Validation Workshops With Users

By the time you've created deliverables and insights from the research, you might be pretty familiar with the needs, challenges and pain points of your users, but you'll never know them as well as your users do. So, it's always valuable to get confirmation that you're on the right track with your data analysis, synthesis, design storytelling and recommendations.

*Journey map reviewed by users in a validation workshop:*

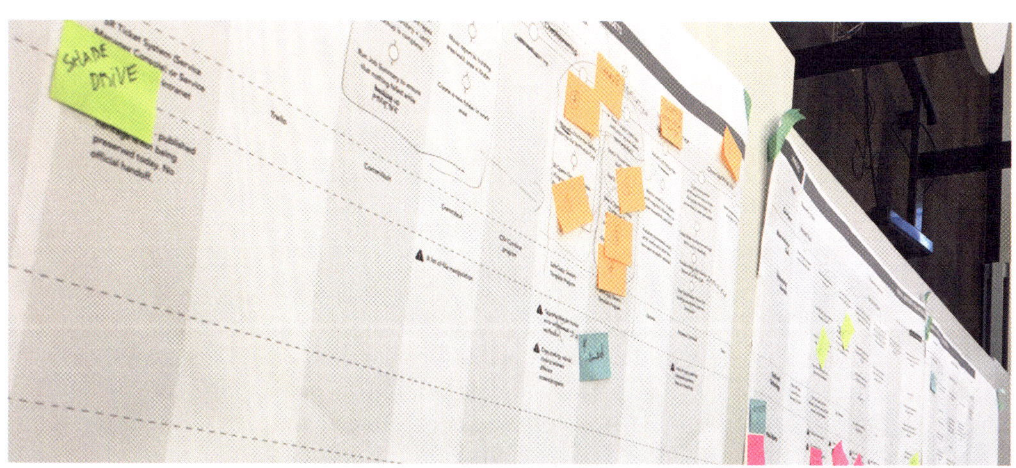

In a validation workshop with users, you can ask for feedback on emerging findings from your research to make sure they are reflective of the thoughts, feelings and experiences of your users, or you can ask for direct feedback on design artefacts (including journey maps, service blueprints, personas, etc.) to ensure that they're accurate. As you begin designing and prototyping, you can also use this type of workshop to get feedback on real designs (like wireframes or service prototypes) through activities like rapid prototyping.

**Action Advice:**

Warning: feedback (or validation) workshops are not opportunities to alter research findings. Be very careful about what kind of feedback you accept and apply to your deliverables. It's fine to slightly soften negative feedback and adjust wording when raw findings sound overly harsh... but fundamentally changing or omitting relevant findings is unethical, whether it's because of stakeholder fears, company politics or any other reason.

Also, I've often found that painful truths are the most valuable. If there's a fundamental issue with a product and you allow it to be ignored, then you've lost the point of the research. Your organisation won't get the same ROI from making surface changes as they would from examining the root cause of an issue and uncovering opportunities for major impact.

That's why you need to build stakeholder trust throughout the research process — so that when you get to this stage, they're open to accepting change, assuming that you frame that potential change in a tactful and strategic way. (See chapter 3's sections on using diplomacy, using language to your advantage, handling stakeholder objections and fears, and connecting your research to ROI.)

# WORKSHOP USE CASES IN CONTEXT

Now that I've taken you through the high-impact workshop types that I use the most often, I want to give you some realistic examples of how and when you might actually include them in your research project. As I noted above, and as you've probably come to realise in your own projects, you don't typically have an endless budget to conduct tons of research and workshops – so you have to be strategic and make them count. Here are two real-life scenarios that show you how you might incorporate workshops into your research project according to the Six-Stage DRM Process, based on time and budget.

| **DRM Process Stage** | **Scenario 1** (Bigger Budget/More Time) | **Scenario 2** (Smaller Budget/Less Time) |
|---|---|---|
| Project initiation | • Hold a kick-off meeting.<br>• **Conduct a discovery workshop with stakeholders** to understand and align on goals, identify key user groups, understand the biggest pain points that impact the business, etc. | • Hold a kick-off meeting. |
| Research planning | • Conduct and finalise research planning/recruiting. | • Conduct and finalise research planning/recruiting. |
| Conduct research | • Conduct user research (e.g. interviews and observations).<br>• **Include a discovery workshop with users** in conjunction with your other primary research methods, to understand who they are, their pain points, their journeys, etc | • Conduct user research (e.g. interviews and observations). |
| Make sense of the data | • Analyse and synthesise the data.<br>• Create design artefact drafts.<br>• **Conduct a validation workshop with users** to ensure that you've accurately depicted user journeys, processes and related pain points, and to ensure that nothing's been missed. | • Analyse and synthesise the data.<br>• **Conduct a co-design "hybrid" workshop with users.** Use your learnings from the research to discuss and prioritise pain points with users and build design artefacts or design solutions in the same workshop. |
| Design storytelling | • Finalise your design artefacts and insights report.<br>• Formally present these deliverables to your stakeholders. | • Create design artefacts, and an action plan based on data from the workshop.<br>• **Conduct a 2-hour feedback session with stakeholders** to review design artefacts and ensure that recommendations solve for business needs.<br>• Incorporate the stakeholder feedback, and finalise artefacts and report. |

# Workshop Planning

Building creative, productive and enjoyable workshops calls for finesse. You can conduct a great workshop that excites and aligns participants and delivers value, or you can conduct a workshop that's clumsy, useless and a waste of time. In order to avoid the latter, you actually need to engage in some (you guessed it, and at this point, I'm sure you're not surprised)... planning!

The decisions in this section will help you assemble logistics faster, prepare for the unexpected, and make more space in your brain for creatively curating exercises that best fit your needs and your participants.

## CHOOSE THE PURPOSE AND PARTICIPANTS

This step might seem obvious... but the truth is, poorly-crafted workshops happen all of the time, and they don't result in constructive conversations or actions. Get crystal-clear about *why* you're getting people together and *what* you need to get out of it. Once you know the purpose of your workshop, and you've set objectives for the session and validated them with your stakeholders, deciding on the right participants will be easier. It's important to be discerning about who you bring together, to limit the potential for bias and ensure great synergy. (See more on recruiting in chapter 7.)

When you invite your participants, be sure to craft a clear, concise invitation email script, detailing what the workshop is about and what purpose it's serving, what kind of exercises to expect during the workshop, and any other logistics, including proposed date(s), time(s), duration and tech requirements. Remember that every touchpoint you have with your participants contributes to the overall experience, and should be handled with care.

**Alignment Advice:**

The effort you put into choosing your workshop participants can make a huge difference in reducing the chance of bias, producing high-value ideas and creating alignment across your project teams. This is especially true when you're inviting staff and stakeholders to participate, because the internal dynamics of their departments and teams can make or break the synergy.

When possible (and if it makes sense), mix cross-functional teams and different levels. Consider separating people from the teams they work with every day, to encourage connections and new ideas between different departments. Combine junior and senior personnel into groups together, so they can benefit from each other's perspectives when coming up with solutions.

...BUT, if you're mixing different levels, you should also be VERY mindful of power imbalances. These might exist between managers and individual contributors, or with stakeholders that report to other stakeholders. Participants are much more likely to be self-conscious and censor their contributions if they're forced to brainstorm alongside their direct supervisor, client, or the person who signs their paycheques. Do your homework to find out what dynamics exist and avoid putting anyone in this situation.

I also recommend thinking about personality types of the participants, if you have that luxury and you know the stakeholders well. Workshops conducted with nay-sayers can be more difficult, so choosing people who have influence and are open-minded generally creates the best environment for creativity and innovation.

## CHOOSE THE FORMAT AND DURATION

Will the workshop be remote or in-person? Your answer to this question will affect its duration. For remote workshops, aim to limit each session to two hours — four hours maximum, if absolutely necessary. Trust me, it's much harder to keep virtual participants engaged any longer than that. For in-person workshops, you have more freedom to plan longer workshops. Doing full-day workshops (with breaks) is an amazing opportunity for extended collaboration. However, I do NOT recommend doing half remote, half in-person workshops. Adjusting workflows gets complicated fast, and you run the risk of losing your virtual participants.

## CHOOSE THE CORE EXERCISES AND AGENDA

In order to deliver the best possible workshop, you'll need to choreograph your workshop activities carefully and gracefully. A detailed agenda based around your core exercises will be instrumental. You should create and keep two versions of your agenda: a facilitator's agenda, with any scripts and reminders you might need for keeping things running smoothly; and a simplified, high-level agenda outlining key activities that you'll send out to participants.

(**Note:** I also have an entire section coming up that's dedicated to tips on great workshop facilitation.)

## CHOOSE THE HANDOUTS AND HOMEWORK

Prep, print and/or assemble any necessary documents or frameworks that your participants will need to complete your exercises. They can be an amazing tool (especially for in-person workshops) to help participants in following activity steps and crystalising their thoughts and ideas. In addition to handouts, consider preparing some pre-work for your participants that could help get them thinking ahead of time. Is there any homework that you want to assign in advance, like the cultural probes I outlined in chapter 9. Is there a messaging channel you want to create in advance to introduce yourself and create engagement ahead of time?

In a similar "cultural probe" exercise to the one I shared in chapter 9, I once asked participants to send me pictures that represented how they felt about the challenges of youth education. At the start of the workshop, we had each participant take one minute to describe the image they brought and how it related to the problem at hand. It was really engaging and set the day up for lots of creative thinking and shared experiences.

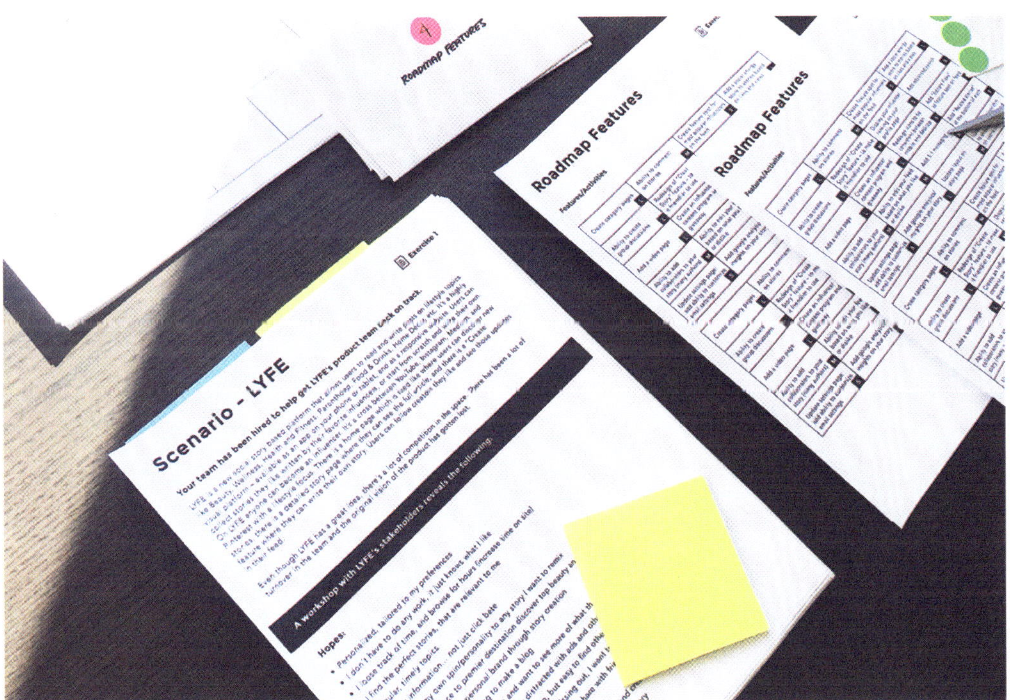


# Tips for Workshop Flow

The exercises you pick for your workshops will be very specific to your project and goals, but every workshop you conduct should have a strong flow that encourages calm collaboration and care-free creativity. The upcoming tips should help you weave those exercises together in an optimal and natural way.

## SET UP AN OPTIMAL WORKSHOP "ENVIRONMENT"

This is an especially important factor for in-person workshops. Take time to think about the overall experience, because the tone you set can have a real impact on collaboration. For remote workshops, spend a few extra minutes carefully editing your virtual boards so that they're visually appealing, clearly labelled, and curated to follow the flow of your exercises, so your participants don't get lost. Find a playlist with some non-intrusive background music (like lo-fi) to help set participants at ease. Take advantage of any music options you might have in your workshopping tool. For in-person workshops, I recommend finding a beautiful, well-lit space — windows are a "must"— to get participants into an engaged, inspired mindset. On your tables, lay out colourful markers, post-it notes, or any other fun materials you might need, and some printed agendas, if you haven't already emailed one out. And don't skimp on water, food and coffee!

## PLAN A CLEAR STRUCTURE

Every exercise you conduct should have a phase of divergent thinking (opening) and convergent thinking (closing), and your participants should always have a clear idea of what they're doing now, what they're doing next, and how it all ties together. (This point comes from *Gamestorming: A Playbook for Innovators, Rulebreakers, and Changemakers* — I highly recommend this book to anyone wanting to improve their facilitation skills.)

Give your participants time to warm up their creative minds, and "open"/brainstorm as many ideas as possible. Then, give them the opportunity to make sense of those ideas (in the middle of the exercise) by grouping or discussing them with their peers. Finally, each exercise should have a closing activity, even if it's small and brief. You might summarise the key themes or takeaways of the last activity, or work on prioritising the ideas that emerged. This should set you up for your next exercise.

**Example:**

You might decide to conduct a "hopes and fears" exercise, where participants write down their top three hopes and fears about the project. After all of the ideas are presented and on the board as sticky notes, you can ask participants to group them into themes through affinity mapping, and close the exercise by prioritising the grouped hopes and fears with dot voting. (I'm a big fan of closing out a workshop this way.)

## DEVELOP SMOOTH TRANSITIONS

As much as possible, curate your exercises so that they connect in logical sequences. You can use the outcomes of the previous exercise to inform the inputs of the next exercise.

**Example:**

Using the previous example, you might follow the hopes and fears exercise with an alignment exercise where you ask participants to crystallise the top hopes into a set of goals and success metrics for the project. Then, going into the next exercise you could discuss and prioritise risks and mitigation strategies based on the fears that emerged.

This strategy will create a sense of unified purpose among your participants, and it will ensure each exercise is valuable. It also keeps you accountable to only adding exercises that will yield useful information.

## REVEAL STEPS GRADUALLY

Control the flow of information and instructions to your participants, to avoid overwhelming or confusing them. A lot of newer facilitators will present all the steps of an exercise at once, and explain all of them in quick succession before sending their participants off to get started. This is a quick way to get inundated with questions: "What are we supposed to do?" "How does the last step work again?" etc. ... or, worst case, your participants don't ask any questions, and they complete the steps improperly, making your workshop extra chaotic.

Remember that participant attention spans can be pretty short in workshop settings. Do yourself (and them) a favour by revealing steps one or two at a time. You can still let them know what to expect from an exercise, but keep your exercise introductions high-level, and spare them the details until those details are actually needed.

## SAY, "YES, AND..."

Like with improv theatre groups, you want to say "Yes, and..." instead of, "Yes, but..." This doesn't just mean avoiding the word "but." Rejecting ideas in any way can hurt the egos in the room, halt brainstorming in its tracks and stunt the creativity of the group. When you use "and," it keeps the conversation flowing and allows participants to build off the ideas of others, which in turn leads to better and clearer solutions. In divergent thinking, no ideas are bad ideas... although, there are highly relevant, within-scope ideas, and less relevant or out-of-scope ones.

Practice saying things like, "That's a great starting point. How could we take that into the realm of [reiterate problem space/feasibility restrictions]?" Or try, "Interesting perspective! Can we connect that to other ideas we've heard?"/ "That's an intriguing idea. What if we built on it by... [offer a modification to direction]?" You should also make good use of the "idea parking lot" that I describe in an upcoming section. And you can go to the link at the end of this chapter for a resource focused on the rules of brainstorming.

### PREPARE BACK-UP ACTIVITIES

Make sure you have back-up activities. While most workshops move quickly and you often feel like you never have enough time, sometimes, you can be left with dead space if participants move quicker than anticipated. If this happens, you can find yourself in the awkward position of ending early, or coming up with some activities on the fly that aren't overly useful. I always like to have 1–2 extra activities in my back pocket that I'll walk participants through if time permits.

### WRAP UP STRONG

Even if things go sideways and you don't get to complete your last exercise, you should still lead the group through a succinct and reflective conclusion that ties things in a neat bow, dispels any lack of clarity and lets your participants walk away on a high note, with a feeling of accomplishment. It's a fact that people remember the beginning and the end of an experience more than the middle. A well-executed wrap-up can really make a participant's experience remarkable and memorable. It's an opportunity to show stakeholders especially that the hours they took out of their busy schedules were well spent.

A great wrap-up activity to do with stakeholder participants is to capture high-level next steps on a whiteboard and assign ownership. You can also discuss key takeaways, and ask them if there was anything they felt wasn't covered. Another great one is to ask them if they could choose one item from the day that they could move forward with and implement immediately, which one would they choose, and why.

## Workshop Time Management

An essential strategy for successful workshops is good time management. As designers, we tend to associate the term "time management" with strict deadlines and rigid product managers... but let's be clear: time management is your friend, especially when you've got a set agenda, a chaotic group of participants, and project stakeholders waiting to see tangible results.

Here are some tips to keep things on track and going smoothly:

- **Follow the agenda as diligently as possible.** Do your absolute best to get through all of your high-priority activities. It's crucial to respect people's time and avoid keeping them late. Give participants warnings when time is almost up on a specific exercise. Don't be afraid to cut an exercise short so you can save time for a more important one... but be discerning. If your participants are really thriving in a key exercise, consider skipping one of your planned items to give it more time. If you have really chatty participants that are holding up the show, tactfully intercept them so that you can keep the ball rolling.

- **Allow time for breaks.** Being a workshop participant takes a lot of mental energy (and coffee refills, usually). Build clear 10–15 minute breaks into your agenda, and a 30–60 minute lunch period if your workshop extends into lunch hour.
- **Find ways to get the group's attention.** Once the exercises start, it can be tricky to get everyone's attention and rein them back in. Put time limits on your breakout rooms, set a timer with a chime, or use some other creative signal (like flickering lights, if you're in person) to indicate when you need the group's attention.
- **Leave time for feedback, if applicable.** Depending on your activity and your attendees, you might need the groups to validate each other's solutions or ideas. Don't miss out on getting this data — it can sometimes be just as useful as the core activity itself.
- **Create an "idea parking lot."** Set aside some whiteboard space (whether physical or virtual) where you can "park" ideas outside the scope of your exercise, with the intention of picking them back up later. This technique will save you from straight-up rejecting off-topic ideas, allow your participants to feel heard and keep them on track. (Whether or not you actually revisit parking lot ideas depends on how much time you have, and whether those ideas become more relevant.)

**Action Advice:**

To avoid inaccurate, biased workshop data, do what you can to steer clear of group-think. When possible, start out your workshop exercises with solo brainstorming, then group your participants into small teams to share and build on each other's ideas. This will give each person a chance to reflect on their own before they hear everyone else's ideas and become influenced by them. Ensure that the "break-out" teams you assign are small enough that everyone will get to be heard. Teams of two or three sometimes work best in an online setting. For in-person workshops, limit groups to five people.

# Post-Workshop Follow-Up

Workshops are often used to inform and prompt next steps in your project — whether you're planning or conducting further research, beginning design storytelling or moving into design. So, be diligent in your post-workshop tasks. You want all of that work your participants did to go somewhere, and to improve your chances of actionable outcomes.

If you conducted an in-person workshop, make sure that you take pictures of everything. Before you leave the room, double check that you've captured images of all whiteboards, sticky notes and written notes. Zoom in on your photographs to make sure even the smallest text is legible in your photos. Then, use a scanning/transcription tool to convert the writing from all of the photos to text, so it's easier to analyse. Make sure that all your files and photos are clearly labelled and categorised in a way that you can easily reference them and anyone coming in from the outside can understand what they are.

After the workshop, I recommend that you debrief with your team and/or any other facilitators to call out common themes or moments of interest that stood out to you, and to discuss how you want to use the data. Afterwards, send a wrap-up email to stakeholders that includes key learnings from the workshop, as well as the immediate next steps that you've decided on together. Finally, create rough design artefacts or a preliminary report. These can be sent to your stakeholders as interim deliverables, to keep them engaged and looped in as you move forward.

# Conclusion

Growing into an impeccably organised and creatively energised workshop facilitator is one of those most effective ways that you can upgrade your research practice. With the right prompts and tactful handling, the workshops you conduct will become some of the most inspiring and memorable highlights of your career. Your stakeholders will get to see you shine, your participants will be more likely to help you in the future, and you might be the catalyst for some truly innovative ideas.

**Recommended Reading:**

Here are a couple of my favourite resources for developing great workshops. (*Gamestorming* in particular is a favourite book of mine!)

- *Gamestorming: A Playbook for Innovators, Rulebreakers, and Changemakers,* by Dave Gray, Sunni Brown and James Macanufo
- *The Art and Science of Facilitation: How to Lead Effective Collaboration with Agile Teams,* by Marsha Acker

**Online Resources:**

I've assembled a couple of resources at **designresearchmastery.com** that might help your workshop planning and facilitation.

What you'll find:

- Empathy Mapping Template
- The Rules of Brainstorming

# * Key Takeaways:

1. **Workshops are one of the most efficient methods for gaining context and generating ideas.** That's what makes them so versatile within your research project, and applicable at any stage of the design process. While they take significant planning, they're 100% worth it.

2. **In design research, the three highest-impact workshop types are:**

   - **Discovery workshops:** Conducted to gain more project context, help with research planning, and understand more about who your users are
   - **Co-design workshops:** Great for enabling creative solutioning, innovative thinking and co-creating deliverables and design concepts
   - **Validation workshops:** Used for evaluating, prioritising and refining research findings, deliverables, and design concepts or prototypes

   If, like most of us, you don't have the budget to conduct multiple workshops with users, you can get creative with combining workshop purposes and utilising stakeholder perspectives (as long as you remember that your stakeholders aren't your users!).

3. **A good "flow" is crucial to conducting productive workshops.** Plan a clear structure using frameworks, develop logical transitions and keep your instructions clear and approachable. Prepare back-up activities, say, "Yes, and..." and make sure to wrap up strong.

4. **Put care into your time management strategies and follow-ups.** Do whatever you can to stay on schedule and get through priority exercises. Use an "idea parking lot" for off-topic ideas and make sure to leave room for brain and body breaks. Lastly, ensure that you document everything that was written and created during the workshop, perform a proper team debrief, and update your stakeholders.

# 12

# MAKING SENSE OF DATA

## Analysis and Synthesis

"Supposing is good, but finding out is better."
— Mark Twain

# Introduction

Making sense of the data is where actionable insights are born. This arguably takes more brain power than any other step in the entire process, but it's necessary work, and it can be very inspiring and rewarding as you start to put the puzzle together.

There are so many things that you need to hold in your head at once: you need to grasp the business needs and product/service requirements at hand, deeply understand and empathise with your users and their experience, and develop a complex picture of the connections between all of these things. Then, you "make sense" by taking all of that knowledge about the current state, and using your imagination and creativity to translate that knowledge into truths and opportunities that both serve an ideal future state and tie directly to business needs. (And finally, presenting it all in a compelling way, with proof).

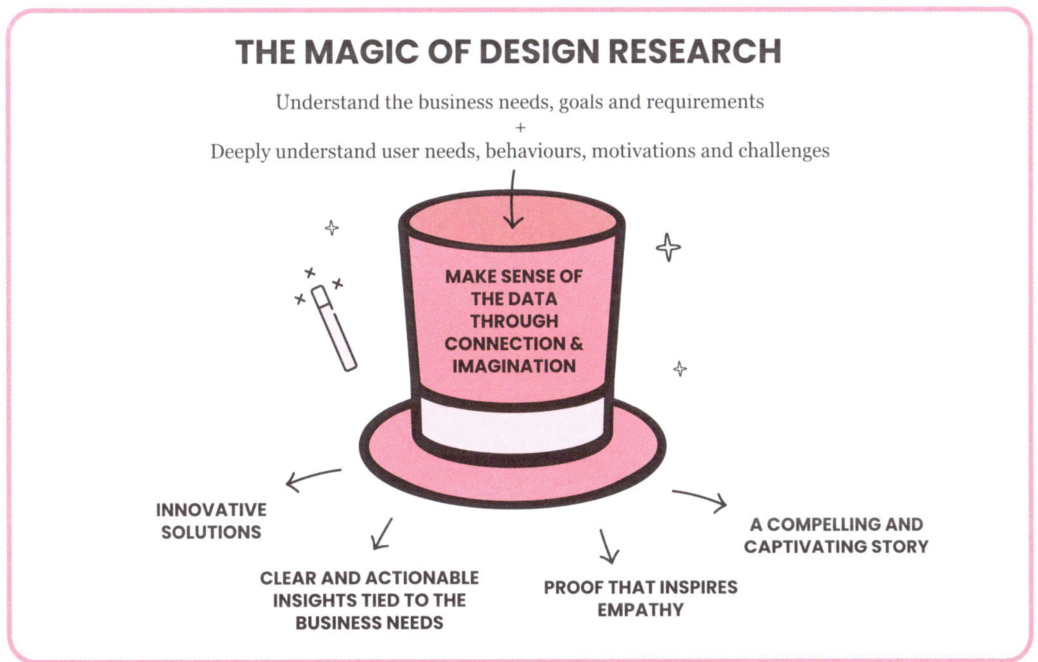

If you were to skip over this process and do a "quick and dirty" analysis (e.g. pulling out partial samplings of the data and drawing out loose themes without proper coding), you might end up favouring the findings you remember best, the ones that were expressed most clearly, or the ones that align best with prevailing assumptions.

You see, there are a few key stages where research fails or goes off-course. Often, it's because the research wasn't planned or conducted with enough care from the outset — stakeholders were never aligned with the plan, the research goals weren't accurate or specific enough and so the wrong data was collected. But many times, it's because the data analysis was rushed or just done incorrectly with no rigour, and the emerging insights weren't concrete enough to become the basis for any kind of decision-making. When this happens, products are created without a holistic view of users' needs and challenges, product launches see poor performance, and stakeholders get the idea that design research isn't worth the investment. I know many leaders who have lost trust in qualitative research because of bad experiences where this process was done wrong.

Other times, the data might have been collected properly and analysed properly, but no creative synthesis was involved, and so no compelling and innovative insights are produced. As a result, the findings fall on deaf ears, the reports don't "wow" anyone, and the needle doesn't move. To translate your research into real impact, you need to master all three processes: conducting research, analysis and synthesis.

In this chapter, I'll walk you through the analysis and synthesis processes that I've honed throughout my career and leveraged to create real change within organisations.

First, let's make sure we're all on the same page about what these process really are.

**Making sense of data:** This is the process of understanding the overwhelming mass of raw data you've collected, and translating it into something that's clear, actionable and highly relevant to the business as well as the product or service that you're studying. It includes two activities: data analysis and data synthesis.

> **Data analysis:** This involves organising, examining and configuring data in order to uncover themes and patterns that represent prevailing truths about the research participants and their experiences. In qualitative research, the analysis of data is rooted in grounded theory, which I'll cover in depth in this chapter.
>
> **Data synthesis:** This is the interpretation of the patterns and themes that you uncovered during analysis, done with the aim to answer your research questions and meet your research goals. This is the last step before you're ready to frame the actionable insights that will go into your final research deliverables, and, if you've done your job right, will also be carried forward as guidelines for smart and effective design decisions.

This is where you're officially entering the "define" phase — you've collected the data and now you're going to converge and make sense of it. In this phase, you're starting to define the problem area(s) and come up with insights that will inform the "design" phase. This is the fifth stage in the Six-Stage DRM Process.

Again, here's where that sits on the **Design Research Triple Diamond**:

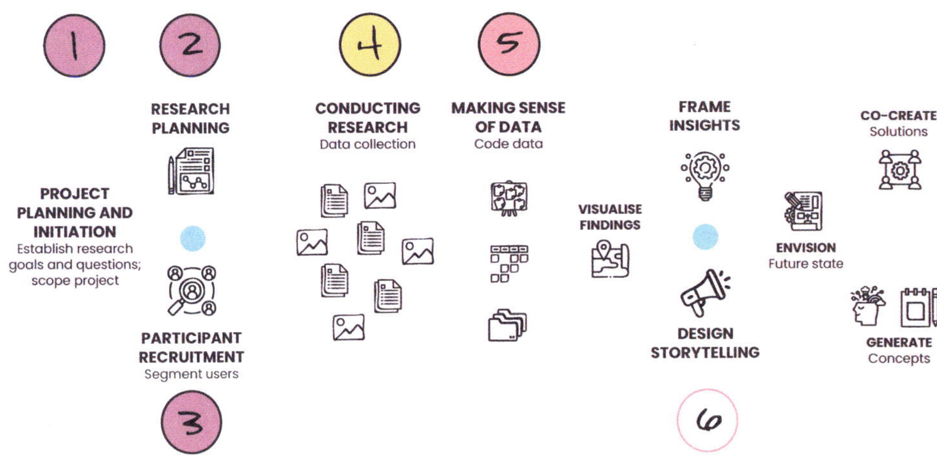


While they're technically described as separate activities, analysis and synthesis will eventually cross over in your brain, as you look over more and more data and start recognising patterns. So, even though I've laid out the steps in this chapter in a linear way, don't worry about trying to work in a "perfect" order. Making sense of data is iterative, just like design itself.

# Why Learn the Fundamentals?

Not all UX and service design practitioners havc a background in psychology or cognitive behaviour – and neither do I! There aren't a lot of on-the-job opportunities to learn the fundamentals of how to analyse data and pull out insights from the research that you can confidently stand behind when presenting to execs. Because of this, few of us are set up for success in making sense of data in general. This chapter was written to bridge that knowledge gap for anyone who needs it, so everyone can approach sense-making with the much needed rigour I mentioned earlier. I learned most of these processes while getting my master's degree, after reading a lot about qualitative research. This experience helped me understand that our work as design researchers isn't subjective. If done properly, it's actually a scientific approach that can produce new and very reliable insights.

It's true that AI is becoming more powerful and replacing many of the slow and time-consuming tasks in research, including data analysis and synthesis. Editing and reviewing your classified data is definitely quicker than doing it manually from scratch, and I recommend exploring AI-assisted workflows if you can. (A 60-minute interview transcription, about 15–20 pages of text, can take roughly three hours to analyse manually!)

**BUT, you still need to know the basics, so you can review what your AI tool spits out at you, and craft meaningful insights.** AI still needs to improve at finding nuanced connections between data points, which is an important part of properly identifying themes and drawing informed conclusions. Until this improves, researchers will still need to do some manual coding, and LOTS of thorough cross-checking, to ensure they're forming true representations of the data.

To conduct successful research, you need to take ownership over the quality of your work. Artificial intelligence is not perfect! And, most importantly, it will never be human… as I said in chapter 4, it's called "human-centred design" for a reason. Holding empathy for users and gathering context are necessary for making sense of data, and neither can be done through technology alone. This is where your true value lies.

If you can analyse your research data with all of the needed context and rigour, and synthesise it with creativity, empathy and thoughtfulness, you will be able to:

- **Influence business decisions with reliable data:** You'll have concrete qualitative data that's anything but "fluffy," that can provide sound, reliable direction for making real change.
- **Gain insights that lead to innovative product and service solutions:** You'll be uncovering unique opportunities that no one else has identified, creating paths to greater market share and ROI.
- **Make design recommendations that actually solve targeted challenges:** Your data will be rooted in real life context, and your insights will trigger "aha" moments where both user needs and business needs can be met, and an ideal future state can emerge.

The foundations in this chapter will enable you to double check the information that AI is giving you, and avoid relying on a robot to try and make truly meaningful, change-making connections and inferences between business needs and the needs of human users.

# Recommended Theory and Approaches

In the broader umbrella of research, there are a lot of different theories that you can use to extract insights from data. In research for human-centred design, we want to ensure that the insights we're extracting come directly from our collected user data, so that we're drawing on users' real human experiences — rather than making assumptions based on our own experiences. That's why you should use grounded theory. It's the approach I typically use.

**Grounded theory** is commonly used for analysing, synthesising and drawing conclusions from qualitative research data. In this theory, which was developed in the 1960s, researchers draw and present theories taken from the data they've collected, rather than using that data to modify pre-existing theories.

For you, this will involve going through the data from your interview transcripts, observation notes, etc. with an open mind, in search of themes and patterns that can uncover new truths about the experience you're studying. If you've done some research in the UX or service design space already, chances are, you've already used some version of grounded theory — it just doesn't usually get called by its original name outside of the academic world.

To apply grounded theory in your design research practice, you'll typically use an approach called "thematic analysis."

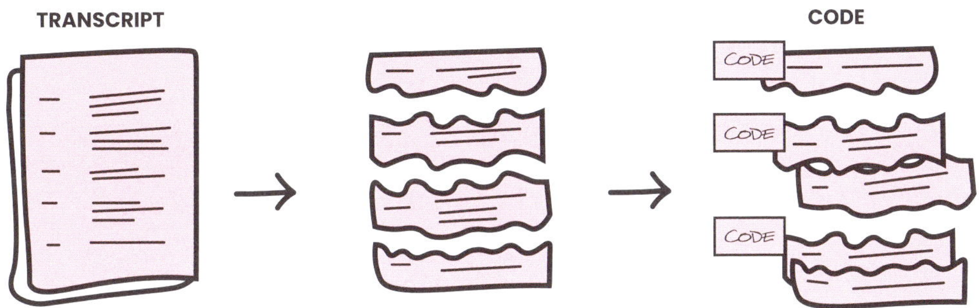


**Thematic analysis** in design research typically involves coding data and identifying similar thoughts (i.e. repeating ideas) across different participants and data points.

**Coding data** is the process of assigning rough "codes" to pieces of data (e.g. snippets of text) in your research notes and interview transcripts. These codes are made up of words that generally represent a pattern in your data, or what you think might end up being a pattern.

This approach is most practical when you have lots of data to go through, like when you're analysing 20 interview transcripts that are each an hour long. It's often done individually, with researchers dividing up the work, whether that translates to the actual coding or reviewing coding performed by AI.

Another approach that can be very useful as part of your larger grounded theory framework (and is possibly the most-well known) is affinity mapping.

**Affinity mapping** is the process of identifying related data points and grouping them by their similarity to each other. In design research using grounded theory, these data points (often represented by sticky notes in a workshop) will be thoughts, ideas and perspectives that come from different participants. You're mapping these ideas out, one idea per sticky note (virtually or literally), and grouping them close to each other based on their level of affinity. You then name the grouping, and this becomes a theme. This approach is best done in workshops with other project team members, users, or stakeholders. (Remember that the best way to foster stakeholder trust is to include them in each stage of your research project!)

However, I wouldn't recommend affinity mapping when you're trying to analyse larger amounts of data from interviews, observations and diary studies. It's a great method for speed and collaboration, but it can lead to missed connections and insights. Why? Well, compared to thematic analysis, it's much easier for ideas to get lost or be mapped incorrectly, because you're manually moving your sticky notes around. You also don't have the benefit of tagging a single data point with multiple themes or affinities, at least not without making several copies of each data point. (You can imagine how things might get very messy quickly.) Last but not least, it's harder to access the whole context of participant quotes because your sticky notes will have short-form summaries of the idea being represented instead of a direct excerpt from a user that you might get from a transcript.

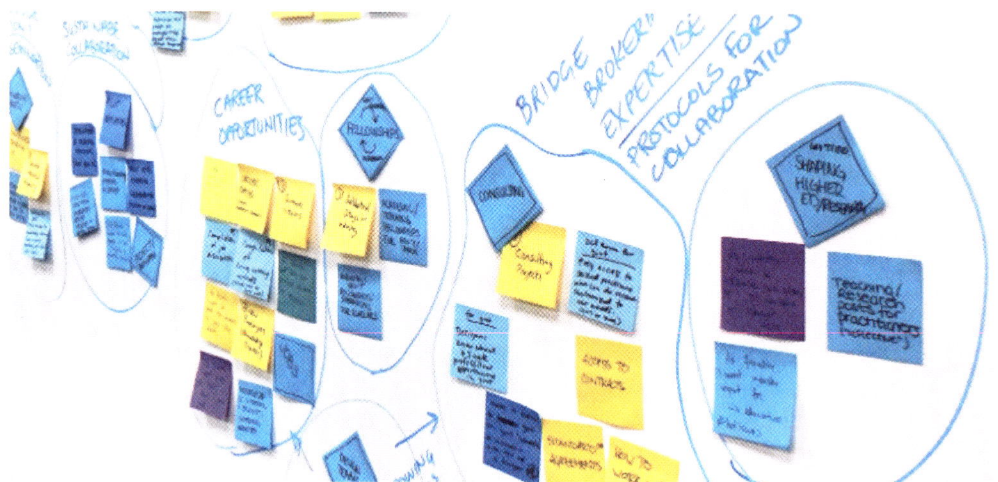


# How to Make Sense of Data

Now that I've gone over grounded theory and my recommended approaches for practicing it, let's break all of it down into approachable steps. The high-level process looks like this:

**PROCESS TO MAKE SENSE OF DATA**
(Using Grounded Theory)

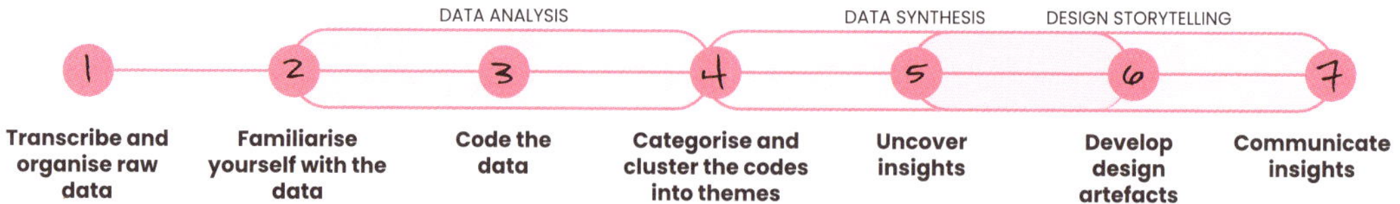


1. **Transcribe and organise raw data**
2. **Familiarise yourself with the data**
3. **Code the data**
4. **Categorise and cluster the codes into themes**

5. **Uncover insights** (finding themes through inductive and deductive reasoning, developing your insights)
6. **Develop design and research artefacts**
7. **Communicate insights**

This is the tried-and-true methodology that myself and my teams have used over the years, which has been proven to yield those game-changing insights that everyone hopes for when they set out to do research. The steps I've outlined use thematic analysis as a base, but I encourage you to also incorporate affinity mapping as part of a workshop in step 4, if it makes sense for your project. The last steps, "develop design and research artefacts" and "communicate insights" are a part of design storytelling, which will be covered in chapter 13.

Again, your digital tool may be able to execute for you on many of these steps, but understanding their order and what exactly each step is supposed to do will help you check your work, take ownership of the process and apply your strategic mindset to leverage, interpret and/or curate your tool's output.

**Action Advice:**

Revisit your initial research goals at key moments during the sense-making process. This will ensure that your insights are truly actionable and valuable for the business (and that you aren't falling off track). I recommend doing this before familiarising yourself with the data, after coding your data, and again as part of developing your insights.

Surprisingly, I do see a lot of projects go off the rails at this point. That's why revisiting your goals is a really important activity for success in research. It can be very easy to let the data lead you, to romanticise and theorise and delight in what you're uncovering. These are all good things, but it has to be done in the context of what the business actually needs. If you find some insight that is completely irrelevant to the business and over-rotate on it in your report, you'll frustrate or even anger your stakeholders —trust me, I've seen it happen more than once.

Remember that design research is research for the purpose of design, and design in our world is used to make things better for both our users and organisations. Your stakeholders are paying you to find out information to help them grow or fix key aspects of the business. You can't lose sight of this, especially not as you wade through the data and make sense of it.

Keeping your goals in mind will help you remember what kind of specific answers you're looking for.

As you move forward, consider grouping your codes according to each of your research questions or research goals. For example, imagine that one of your research questions is, "What are the key pain-points first-time home buyers encounter when making offers?" If you have codes called "multiple offers" and "pre-offer inspection," grouping data with these codes together could help you answer that question, since both ideas relate to submitting an offer.

Here's an example of grouped codes operating as tags within Dovetail:

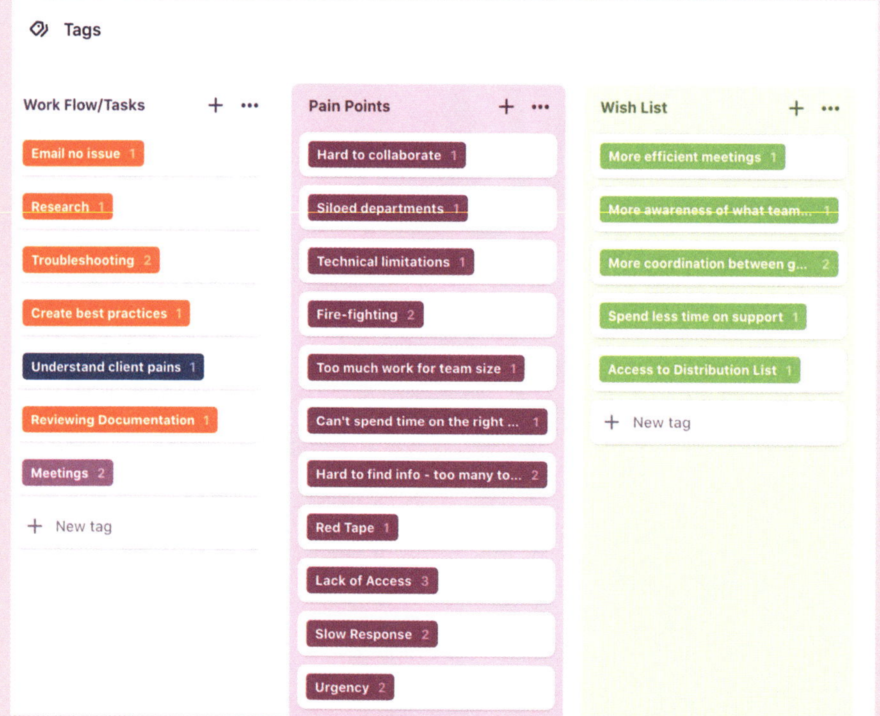


When you're pulling theories out of the data, focus on uncovering ideas that will be the most relevant and useful for your stakeholders in better understanding the users and making informed business decisions.

Of course, you don't want to skew the data to fit within your research goals — grounded theory, after all, means pulling theories out of the data, and not imposing theories onto the data. But, again, if you've done your research right and you've been asking users questions that fall within the scope of your research goals, the information you're left with will be highly relevant to those goals.

# TRANSCRIBE AND ORGANISE THE RAW DATA

Before you can begin data analysis, you first have to ensure that you've organised all of your raw data in a way that it's easy to access and analyse. While you're likely using one or several tools to help you do this, the point here is to make sure everything is captured.

Each of the research method chapters of this book include some tips for organising your data, but as a general rule, you should start by ensuring that all interviews, recordings, diary entries, and notes have been transcribed properly. You don't want to accidentally miss any of the valuable data that you spent painstaking hours collecting. Maintain consistent file labelling, so you and your team can quickly find what you're looking for, and keep tabs on what you have left to analyse, and what you've already analysed.

You should also use a **profile framework** to help you track which ideas came from which user groups. This is a spreadsheet that helps you remember who your participants were and their key characteristics (without using their names). Instead you'll use "p1," "p2," "p3" etc. to represent participant 1, participant 2, 3 and so on. Your files will all be labelled according to participant numbers as well in order to protect personal identifiable information.

A profile framework can be very useful in your data analysis because it'll enable you to slice your data by user group or by specific characteristics. For example, you may want to quickly pull out quotes and ideas from participants who lived in rural areas, to understand how their home buying experience differed from urban buyers. A profile framework can also help remember which user groups participants belonged to. ("Was p3 the doctor or the nurse?" / "What type of region did p5 live in?")

Now, depending on the digital tool you're using for your data analysis, your tool might have a special function for helping you tag, track and toggle on/off your user group information when you're examining data — in which case, you may not need this spreadsheet. But, if you do decide to build one, then you don't have to start from scratch. You can reference the participant recruitment tracker you built during your recruitment phase as a starting-off point.

Here's an example of what your profile framework table might look like.

| Participant # | Age Range | Location | Experience | Job Description |
|---|---|---|---|---|
| P1 | 30–39 | Urban | 0–5 Years | Nurse Practitioner |
| P2 | 40–49 | Rural | 10–15 Years | Doctor |
| P3 | 20–29 | Urban | 0–5 Years | Medical Assistant |
| P4 | 40–49 | Rural | 10–15 Years | Doctor |

When you go to report on your research at the end of your analysis phase, you'll need to show evidence to support your insights and findings. That's why it's crucial to keep track of which insights came from which participant quotes, snippets and data sets and why using the participant number (e.g. "p5") next to a quote is very important.

If one of your stakeholders asks you, "How did you come up with that?" you'll be able to quickly and easily reference the proof. The faster you can show accurate backing information, the more confidence your stakeholders will place in the research. Remember that your research is useless if your stakeholders don't want to take it seriously!

(**Note:** See the online resources listed at the end of chapter 7 for more on data privacy and personal identifiable information.)

## FAMILIARISE YOURSELF WITH THE DATA

Before you start making sense of your data, you should give all of it a high-level review, to jog your memory and get a general sense of what themes and patterns might crop up. I recommend re-reading research notes and transcripts and comparing your notes with team members' notes. Then you can discuss/brainstorm your predictions for high-level themes and patterns. For example, you might remember certain thoughts being repeated frequently by different users. From there, write down some of your predictions and potential codes you might use.

Don't wait until all of your coding is done to convene with your team. Putting your heads together at the start will help you get on the same page about what codes you might use, and it will ease the process of refining codes (explained in the steps coming up). By sharing your perspectives and understanding of the data, you can avoid making extra work for yourselves later on.

## CODE THE DATA

The most time-consuming step when making sense of data is coding. As I mentioned earlier, this involves finding relevant ideas and repeating patterns in the data, and classifying them with representative "codes". It's essentially a process of tagging snippets of text according to these codes. In design research, the purpose of this step is to identify common ideas in the data that speak directly to your research goals, and that reappear multiple times. This will help you define problem areas in the product or service you're studying, and it will help you group these repeating ideas into themes.

Example of coded text with tags in Dovetail:

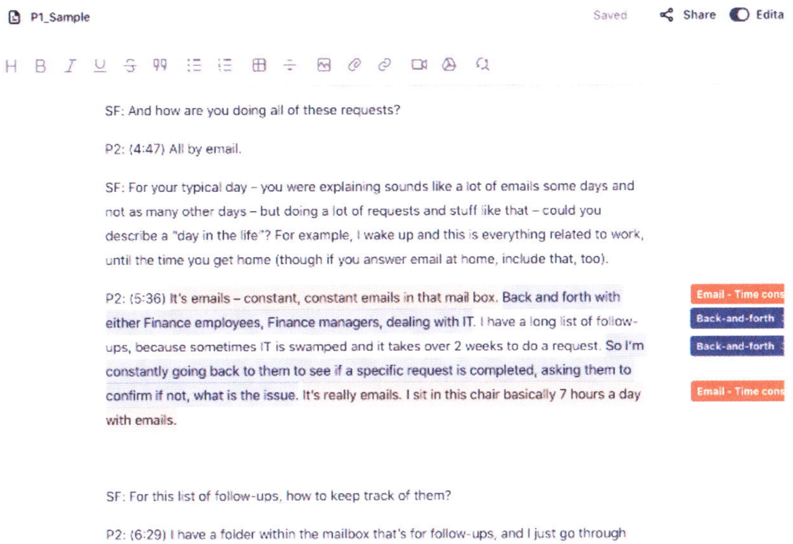


To classify and code your data, you'll start by highlighting and saving meaningful pieces of data. Then, you'll assign codes to these meaningful ideas as you go. Your codes don't have to be very imaginative or sophisticated — they just need to succinctly describe the main idea behind what the participant is saying.

**Example:**

Imagine that you're analysing data from users about pain points they're having with a safety compliance platform. You see that many participants have talked about struggling to reference the instructions simultaneously while they're filling out the form:

*"It was hard to fill out the inspection form efficiently. I kept needing to reference the instructions at the same time, but it would open a new window on my phone, and then I couldn't find the previous one. So I would have to click the back button several times, and then my information wouldn't be saved, so I'd have to start all over."*

In this case, you might create a code called "cross-referencing" and use it to tag any snippets of text similar to this one.

Next up are a few quick tips to help you — these are hard-learned lessons after hours upon hours of data analysis. Again, even if you've fully stepped out of the manual process of coding (via a digital tool), these are still good to know, so that you can check in on your AI tool's thinking process and edit its outputs as needed.

- **Process every sentence or paragraph that seems to contain a meaningful idea, regardless of whether it actually repeats.** You won't know if the idea repeats until you've finished classifying your data — just assume it does for now. You can worry about cleaning up your codes in the next phase.
- **Copy ideas directly from the text (without editing them!)** You don't want to paraphrase things that your participants said, if you can help it. There might be exceptions, like if you couldn't get an interview recorded and you had to take short-hand notes, but hopefully, that'll be a rare instance.
- **Keep your pieces of data attached to your participant numbers.** Keep your profile framework handy and make sure that any snippets of text have participant numbers attached (if they were removed or organised outside of the original transcript). That way, you can always go back and get more context if needed.
- **Only highlight text that explains the key idea, and that can be understood out of context.** You don't need to highlight an entire paragraph if only a couple of the sentences hold the idea that you think is relevant. Include just enough context that you can easily remember what the participant was talking about, without having to go back and read the full transcript or set of notes.
- **Not every word needs to be coded.** Only code ideas or sentences that are meaningful to your specific area of study and research goals. If your participant is going off-topic or describing something that's not relevant, don't code it.
- **Don't worry if you have more than one code per snippet.** For example, if your participant talks about using Uber, the ride-hailing app, and it's relevant to your research, you might code that snippet of text as both "Uber" and "ride-hailing app." Or, if you end up coming across mentions of Lyft and Bolt, too, then you might decide to turn the "ride-hailing app" code into a larger theme. If in that same snippet of text, your participant also talks about how Uber isn't available in their region, you might also decide to create a code called "service unavailable" or "service area."
- **"Unsure" codes can help to keep you moving when you get stuck.** Don't let perfectionism or indecision stop you in your tracks. If you're unsure at all about whether an idea is relevant to your research, err on the safe side, and code it just in case, using a word like "unsure" or "uncertain." Then, revisit these data points later on when you've analysed more data and the overall picture has gotten clearer.
- **Redundant codes are also okay at the start.** As you start coding your data, you'll inevitably have codes that are duplicative — maybe because you forgot you used a similar code elsewhere, or because in the moment, you felt like they would be important to differentiate. Don't get hung up on whether something is redundant or not. You'll have a chance to refine your codes in the next step.

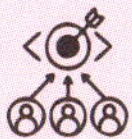

**Alignment Advice:**

Don't hold your stakeholders in suspense during your analysis phase... or in any phase, for that matter. Properly practicing grounded theory can take a few weeks, so it helps to give your stakeholders little updates about what you're finding so far. In the next check-in with them, drop in a couple of interesting details. "So far, several people are saying [x y z] and we're looking further into how this could be shaped into an actionable insight for the project. There's tons of potential in this data, and we're excited about it."

## CATEGORISE AND CLUSTER CODES INTO THEMES

Once you've gone through your interview transcripts and coded them, you'll need to group all of the repeating ideas together into themes. The purpose of this stage is to create a categorised database that you'll reference for developing theories during synthesis, and for gathering supporting evidence during design storytelling. It's a relatively straightforward step, but it does require some critical thinking.

You'll start by revisiting all your codes and refining them. Like I mentioned earlier, you might have some codes that are essentially duplicates and need to be combined or renamed, or that are closely related and should be given a new, broader code to make your analysis less complicated. For example, you might have a few codes representing participant ideas about different project management apps. If you coded each one with the name of the app (ClickUp, monday.com, etc.), and the difference between these apps isn't important to your study, you might want to re-code them as "project management apps."

Then, you'll group similar codes together into themes, creating higher-level buckets for all of the coded ideas. This will make it easier to reference supporting evidence as you form insights in the next stage. Depending on the approach you've chosen, this might involve literally re-arranging coded snippets from interview transcripts into new documents (one per theme), using affinity mapping to further group affinities of sticky notes into higher-level themes, or grouping codes/tags into columns that represent the higher-level themes.

## UNCOVER INSIGHTS

An **insight** is a profound and meaningful understanding of human behaviour that's born from the "aha" moment when you transform the data you've gathered from a problem into a potential opportunity. By this point in your design research project, you'll have reached a deeper understanding of your users' experiences, and you'll start piecing together enlightening perspectives on how to solve design-specific problems related to those experiences. If stakeholders act on these, they'll unlock transformative improvements to the product or service in question.

BUT, what about the times that insights get ignored by stakeholders? Well, that could be an issue with the way the insights are communicated but, I think it's often because the insights aren't "true insights" — in other words, they don't contain uniquely valuable information. They're either not relevant to your stakeholders' priorities and interests, not representative of the people you studied, not helpful in achieving the overall project's goals, or all of the above.

Your insights should always point to opportunities and actions that can improve the design of a product or service, and ultimately improve the experience of its users.

(**Note:** Pain points are still a critical piece of research that must be logged and included in a final research report. Your report will include a combination of key insights and key challenges that were discovered through your research. However, you'll want to clearly distinguish them from each other, both in your mind and in your design storytelling.)

In your report, you'll have a mix of findings and insights — both are valuable. However, they're often confused for each other. Findings typically represent a single theme that emerged from the data, like a pain point that occurred repeatedly across multiple participants. Insights combine findings together into a statement that can help prompt informed and sound conclusions about how to solve for a user challenge or need. Note that **findings can't act as insights on their own.**

To help illustrate this in more concrete terms, here's a comparison of what an insight is, and what it's NOT.

| What is an insight? | What is NOT an insight? |
|---|---|
| **A profound truth about how your users think:** They might think very differently compared to you or your stakeholders, for instance. | **A single data point:** In order to be considered representative of a user group, your insights must be created based on multiple data points that address a similar theme. |
| **A new way of understanding a design problem that challenges the status quo:** Maybe past updates and feature launches have been leading a product in the opposite direction of where it needs to go, and the insight illuminates that issue. | **A customer or user pain point:** The users you're studying will tell you what challenges they had during an experience, and while those challenges are considered findings, they're not insights in and of themselves. |

| What is an insight? | What is NOT an insight? |
|---|---|
| **A discovery of the "why" behind a user's behavior, need or challenge:** For example: why users are abandoning the free trial of an app; why they say they need integration with others tools; or why they're struggling to use certain features. | **Something a person has said they need or want:** Instead, it should express the underlying reasons and motivations behind those statements.<br><br>**A simple observation of a current state:** Real actionable insights will point toward recommended steps for improving a product and creating an ideal future state that solves for key needs and challenges you've identified in the data. |

I've provided some examples below of two findings and one resulting insight from the same project. (You might remember some of this subject matter from a diary study example in chapter 10.)

**Examples of Findings:**

1. *"While service providers would like access to a resource bank and more consistency in the assessments, they also need room for flexible lesson planning and options for teaching."*
2. *"Adult learners lead complex lives and have a variety of personal and family responsibilities, as well as other barriers that make it difficult for them to follow a formal schedule."*

In these examples, you can see that the findings identify patterns across multiple users, and they include details about their needs and challenges, and the "why" behind both.

**Example of an Insight (for the same project):**

Now, let's look at a real insight that was framed by synthesising these findings together into a **greater truth**:

*"Flexibility is key to successful learning programmes for adults. These programs must allow for and accommodate the diverse needs of adult learners, as well as the needs of the learning organisations and service providers that facilitate these programmes."*

This insight is framed in a way that points to an experience improvement, with specific requirements that would be needed to create that improvement.

Now that you understand what an insight actually is, let's talk about how you uncover them, since it's not as easy as summarising findings from your themes. Framing insights is one of the hardest skills to teach, but you'll become fluent in this way of thinking and writing with practice. To do so, you'll need a mix of empathy, connecting contexts, and different forms of reasoning. To point you in the right direction, here are three golden rules for synthesising insights in real-world practice.

1. **Always ask, "Why?"** This will help you get at the underlying motivations and unspoken or "latent" needs of the users you're studying.
2. **Focus on the problem or opportunity area.** This will help you ensure that your insights are relevant to your research goals, and that your insights point toward actionable steps related to your project's design goals.
3. **Channel empathy for the users and their experiences.** If you can ground your efforts in understanding the people that you're studying and how their experiences with a product or service are affecting their lives, you'll find it easier to take on their perspective and frame insights that are relevant to their needs.

| DEDUCTIVE REASONING | | INDUCTIVE REASONING | | ABDUCTIVE REASONING | | |
|---|---|---|---|---|---|---|
| What you saw or heard | + | What you understood from the data | + | What you interpret based on your experience | = | INSIGHT |

With this in mind, you'll also want to use three forms of thinking that typically go into data synthesis: **deductive, inductive and abductive reasoning.** Throughout a research project, you'll be engaging in all three types of reasoning. Above is a simplified look at what they each mean in comparison to each other, and how they add up to an insight.

I'll go over these concepts and how they fit together in more depth below.

**Deductive reasoning:** Deductive reasoning is a type of thinking where you start out with a general statement or hypothesis, and then measure that hypothesis against facts and observations taken directly from the research data (i.e. findings). As you start going through your data, you'll have certain hypotheses about where the key problem areas are. Those hypotheses will influence the way that you group your coded/mapped data into themes, and what connections you make between similar participant ideas.

> **Example:** "Rigid structures are often ineffective for groups with diverse needs and responsibilities."

**Inductive reasoning:** Inductive reasoning is the practice of discerning patterns and forming theories based on your understanding of the data. This is the part of synthesis where you're really starting to connect the dots and do some detective work. You're using your own understanding of the data and of the users you interviewed, observed or otherwise learned to figure out the motivations behind certain user behaviours or statements. Using this type of reasoning will help you pull together findings and frame insights that speak to common challenges and needs within or across the user groups you studied.

**Example:** "Adult learners frequently mention struggling with fixed schedules due to personal and family responsibilities."

By conducting research and familiarising yourself with the data, you've made yourself qualified to do this — you wouldn't be able to do it if you were coming in from the outside with no knowledge. Someone who just skimmed a couple of interview transcripts out of context isn't equipped to discern why a user did or said X, Y and Z. There's power in being a researcher and doing your job thoroughly!

**Abductive reasoning:** Abductive reasoning is the practice of inferring potential problems and solutions from the data, based on your lived experiences, your world views and the empathy you've developed for your participants by studying them. You'll engage this type of reasoning as you start to weave findings together and explore what the most relevant problems in the current state are, and what kind of ideal future state your findings might point to.

**Example:** "A lack of flexibility seems to be the best explanation for why learners are facing these struggles."

Once you have stellar insights generated through the systematic and rigid approach to data analysis and synthesis, the next stage is to create design artefacts from your research and communicate your findings and insights, through design storytelling— the last part of grounded theory. I'll cover this research stage in detail in the next chapter. That's where all of the hard work you've done will pay off, for you AND your stakeholders.

# Conclusion

While it can be intimidating and tiring, making sense of data is also one of the most rewarding processes of your design research project. It's the pivotal process that happens between conducting research and making an impact in your organisation. What you learn during this process will turn into impressive and informative discoveries that'll excite your stakeholders and inspire ground-breaking transformations of products and services.... that is, if you communicate your findings and insights in a convincing way. (More on that in the next chapter.)

# ✱ Key Takeaways:

1. **True design research analysis is rigorous and evidence-backed — it's never anecdotal.** Design research gets a bad rap when people take random pieces of raw research data and interpret it without context.
2. **AI-assisted digital tools have made analysis faster and easier, but you still need to understand the fundamentals.** Building stakeholder trust means owning your work and inspiring confidence in that work. This includes checking AI outputs thoroughly for subtle mistakes or oversights. And to find mistakes, you need to know how things "should be done."
3. **Grounded theory is the prevailing (and recommended) methodology for conducting design research analysis and synthesis.** Truly human-centred design is informed by insights that come directly from authentic and highly relevant user data. You can use a combination of thematic analysis and affinity mapping to put this theory into practice.
4. **It's important to keep your research goals top-of-mind throughout analysis and synthesis.** It's all too easy to get swept up in an interesting line of thinking and pattern identification that isn't actually relevant to what your stakeholders care about, or that falls out of the scope of your research and of what's actually feasible for your overall design project.
5. **An insight is not a finding or a data point.** It's a profound truth about your participants and their experiences, focused on the "why" behind a related behaviour, motivation or challenge. It's pulled from the data through careful analysis and synthesis using deductive, inductive and abductive reasoning.

# 13

# DESIGN STORYTELLING

## Creating Impactful Research Deliverables

“Inside each of us is a natural-born storyteller, waiting to be released.”

— Robin Moore

# Introduction

All of the work you’ve put into your design research project culminates in this step — the weaving together of the intriguing narrative that you’ve already uncovered through your research, told via words and visuals. For a lot of us, it’s the most fun part. It’s also one of the easiest parts to get wrong, because too many people see it as a simple assembly process. It’s not — it’s a storytelling process.

In order to effect change with your research, your deliverables and design recommendations need to be clearly communicated, compelling and captivating. You can do all of the research in the world, but without an artful, thorough and convincing approach to design storytelling, your insights will sit in a file folder to collect dust. No action will be taken, and your research will have been pointless.

Don’t drop the torch at the finish line! This is where you demonstrate to stakeholders that the discomfort of the “fuzzy front end” was worth it, because you’re empowering them with money-making business opportunities and with new knowledge that their competition doesn’t know about. I once had a client tell me that the design artefacts and insights report that I delivered to them six years earlier was still being used as the basis for training their entire design department. After hearing that, I figured if I could bottle up my design storytelling process and share how I’ve been doing it, it could be a game-changer for others in the field. That’s what I’m venturing to do in this chapter.

Design storytelling is the final stage of the **Six-Stage DRM Process**:

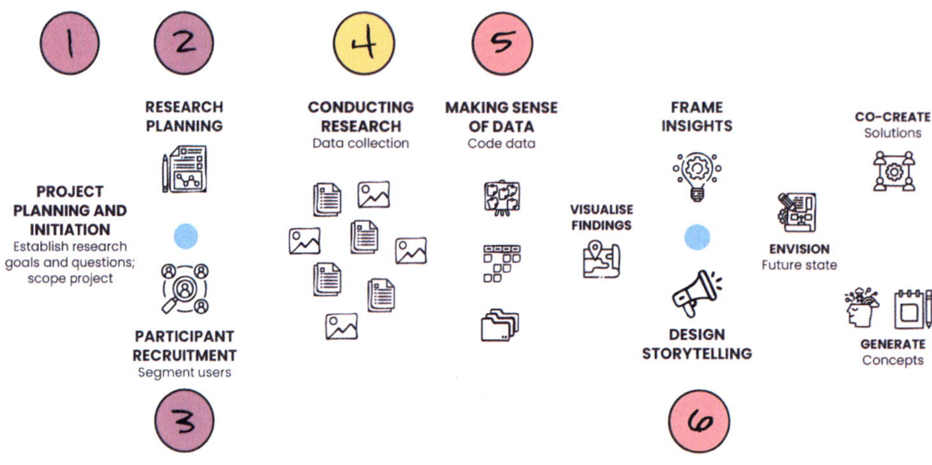


You've already made sense of your data, and you're leading your stakeholders toward something much more clear: a roadmap to their next product and service decisions. You're bridging that gap between the "define" phase and the "design" phase; you've just converged, and you're transitioning the project back into divergent thinking. In other words, you're guiding your stakeholders through the design problems and new insights you've identified, as well as the path to a better user experience.

# Great Design Storytelling

Effective design storytelling engages people, and ensures that those people take your research insights and suggestions seriously, so that you can influence their decision-making and inspire better products and services. Your deliverables can also build empathy for users among your stakeholders and team members and align them on next steps, so that your recommendations can move forward with a clear, unified vision that actually solves for user needs. You might even generate company-wide excitement about your research and action plan, which could live on well past the end of your project as a frequently referenced resource. If (or when!) this happens, your work could go as far as catalysing a major internal company shift from low design maturity, to a culture of embracing change and design-led strategy.

So, how do you create engaging deliverables that are respected as sources of truth?

**Know your audience.** This is a standard design principle: in UX and service design, you have to understand the users in order to create great user experiences. The same idea applies here. You have to understand the people who will read or review your deliverables — the specific stakeholders, team members, executives, etc. This will impact what information you include and the level of detail you provide. (More on this in the reporting section of this chapter.)

**Never underestimate the power of making things beautiful.** Design storytelling is, after all, part of the design process. Aim to make all reports and artefacts visually compelling through the use of images, diagrams, icons, colours and typography, and carefully plan the layout of your elements in a way that eases your audience through the information. Strategically manipulate white space to finetune the overall look of your deliverables as well as their readability. This is a key principle that often gets overlooked, because it's not seen as crucial... but it's definitely ideal. I have seen so many bad — or, dare I say, ugly — design artefacts, reports and slide decks that were too text-heavy, had no visuals, didn't use any breaks/slide dividers or otherwise didn't tell a clear story. Their overall effect was to either completely bore, overwhelm or confuse their audiences. You want to excite people, and feel them buzzing with anticipation as you move through your report and/or other representations of your findings. If you or someone on your team has the skills to make your deliverables beautiful, it can really elevate your work and encourage your stakeholders to share it widely.

**Infuse your genuine passion for the work (and use it as a motivator to outdo yourself).** This one is hard to teach, but I believe it's necessary for truly great storytelling. You can't do any of it halfheartedly. After weeks and months of planning, listening, drowning in data and dealing with different opinions, you are at the point where you get to tell the story of all the hard work. This is the best time of any design research project, and if you don't find passion here, then you're probably in the wrong line of work. If you are in love with the data and the study, and you actually care about the users and the problem you're trying to understand and solve, you will pour that passion into your report and your artefacts. You'll put serious consideration into the way you unveil that data, and your work will speak for itself. You need to be so excited to put everything together that this passion leaps off the page.

I've been passionate about every project I've worked on. Yes, there have been harder projects, where I couldn't do all the research I wanted, or dealt with difficult stakeholders. But I always saw value in the work I was doing, and I was driven by the opportunity to really change something and make people's lives better. To have a real impact and create better products and services, you have to see that opportunity in your work and believe in its potential.

**Think critically about the purpose for your storytelling.** Is your report or journey map or persona purposeful? Or, are you sharing information for the sake of sharing it, or just to show that you accomplished something? Is the information saying what it needs to say, based on your research goals? These are basic questions, but asking them can help you be more discerning about what you're putting on the page.

Every slide, every pain point, every piece of information you share should have an intent behind it. That intent should be to make the invisible seen — revealing latent needs, challenges, and design problems — so that people can start to work at fixing that siloed process, broken user experience, frustrating user flows, or that haphazard, confusing service. As you start building the deliverables that will tell the story of the data you collected, consider the reason you were asked to do the research in the first place, and make sure that it's addressed, and then some! While you were finding the answers to your main research questions, you might have uncovered some mind-blowing opportunities for innovation that your stakeholders weren't expecting — and that is the dream — but don't lead with those. Address the main research purpose first, so that you're at least satisfying the research goals that your stakeholders aligned on. (Otherwise, you'll frustrate them and start sowing doubt in the outcomes.) Then, you can showcase the new and interesting nuggets that your stakeholders didn't even realise were opportunities, and the insights that will make them dream up entirely new ways of doing things.

When you keep your eyes on your purpose, your artefacts and reports will be both practical and inspiring. They'll show stakeholders what they can do now to solve the immediate challenges with tangible, actionable recommendations, AND they'll point to innovative, unknown, and novel ideas that have emerged from the research that could completely reinvent the product or service in the future. They'll highlight how amazing these possibilities are, and inspire your stakeholders to work towards them. That is how you'll win with design storytelling.

## KEY ACTIVITIES IN DESIGN STORYTELLING

The design storytelling process involves a diverse mix of activities, and many of them can overlap. In a typical project, you'll have 3–4 weeks to wrap up your deliverables after doing your data analysis.

The key activities typically include:

1. **Developing design artefacts:** Including customer/user journey maps, service blueprints, ecosystem maps, etc., which illustrate the data from your research and can supplement your final insights report

2. **Crafting an insights report:** Drafting a formal, structured package of insights, quotes, challenges, positive points, examples, recommendations and other items that I'll cover

   Insights reporting also includes the processes of:

   - **Framing insights:** Taking the insights you uncovered in chapter 12 and "framing" them into enlightening, actionable information for your report

   - **Creating action plans:** Helping stakeholders take action on your insights and findings by laying out clear next steps

3. **Building feature roadmaps:** Bringing solutions and opportunities from your action plan and design recommendations together in a chart that prioritises potential new features and product improvements

This chapter is structured around these activities, with tips and tricks included to help your work really stand out.

As part of storytelling, you should ideally be holding co-design or feedback workshops with users or stakeholders, to validate insights, co-create deliverables and brainstorm solutions. (I covered these workshops in chapter 11.)

# Develop Design Artefacts

If you can't already tell from the way I described the passion behind my work earlier, creating design artefacts is one of my most favourite parts of the design process. You get to weave all of the pieces of data together in a visual masterpiece that makes sense of everything and brings strategic value to the business.

**Design artefacts** are documents or diagrams that visualise research findings in a way that's easy to absorb and appealing. They usually depict connections between the elements within a product, service or organisation that are having an impact on user, customer or employee experiences. They're great for depicting those connections and elements in approachable ways, whether you're trying to communicate complex processes, user experiences and interactions over time, user motivations and perspectives, or the current or future state of an experience.

No matter what, **your design artefacts should always be created based on research**, meaning they're proven, not hypothesised. In this section, I'll break down each of the most common design artefacts that you'll need to master for your future design research projects.

## PERSONAS

As you also know, **personas** are archetypes that represent the characteristics, values, motivations, behaviours, and pain points of specific user groups. In an average design research project, you might create 6–8 personas, one per user group.

Again, your personas should be based entirely on your research findings. Typically, they include things like a fictional name, image (stock or illustration), a descriptor (like a job title, if that makes sense for your project), a set age or demographic, a bio, and and the main motivations and pain points that this person would typically encounter while interacting with a product or service. Personally, I like to create task-based personas, which describe the tasks this type of user is trying to perform through a product or service, focusing on motivations and pain points specifically related to those tasks. Depending on your project, you might add in a few other factors or scales, like proficiency with technology, the tools or environments interacted with, and any other relevant characteristics. I also like to include a quote that sums the archetype up in a nutshell.

All of these traits and touches help to bring your persona to life. I've seen many superficial personas that don't provide enough detail, and that end up giving personas a bad name, because the intended audience (product owners, project teams, etc.) don't find them useful and never refer to them. And that's the whole point of personas — you want to make them so good that executives know their names and reference them in meetings: "What would Annie think about this?" "Would Jaden like this new feature?"

Here's an example of a real persona that I created as part of a client project that sought to understand the internal employee experience.

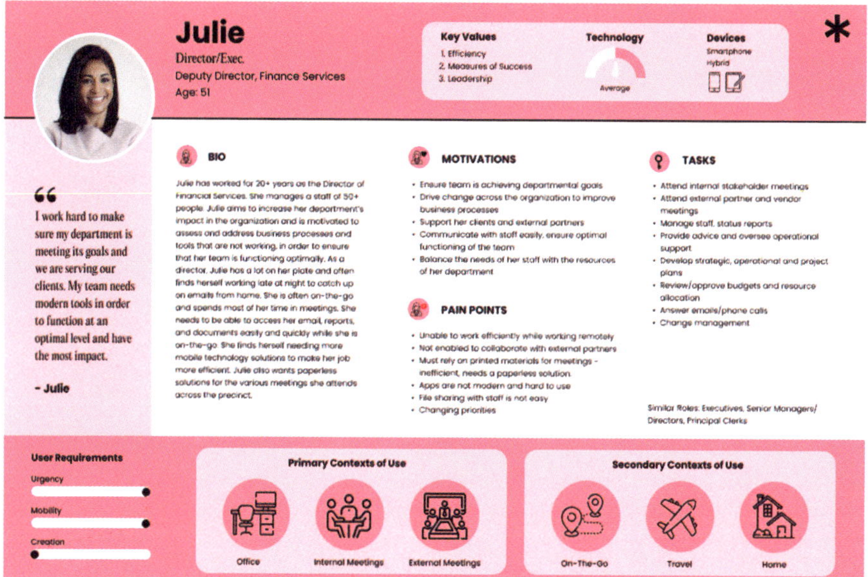

Sometimes, personas can be created based on assumptions. In these cases, what you're actually creating are called **proto-personas**. They can still be helpful as starting points to hypothesise when you don't have access to real users. However, they should always be labelled accordingly, and validated with real research later. Do NOT let your stakeholders confuse actual personas with proto-personas!

## CUSTOMER (OR USER) JOURNEY MAPS

A **customer journey map** (or "user journey map") is a chronological depiction of an end-to-end experience your users or customers have when they interact with a product, service or system over time. It's one of the most used artefacts, and one of my favourites in general, because of how practical it is in breaking down silos across departments and pinpointing where pain points occur along the journey. It becomes a single source of truth that brings everything together (all of the tasks, thoughts, feelings, pain points, opportunities, and more), in a way that's easy for anyone in an organisation to understand.

After creating many journey maps, I came to a structure that's easy to read and visually interesting, and that contains all the elements necessary for making user-informed design decisions. My journey maps always include: colour-coded phases (and sometimes sub-phases) of the journey, a timeline, user motivations or mindsets for each phase, detailed tasks and sub-tasks they accomplish, tools and technology, moments of delight (where things went well) and, most importantly, all of the pain points that relate to each task/subtask. If there's space, I'll often include a row of opportunities across the bottom that correspond to each pain point, or to a group of pain points. (I usually uncover these opportunities through a co-design workshop). Each journey map will be somewhat unique based on what you're studying, however I always recommend using colours to represent different elements, along with a legend — it'll make your map more engaging.

Below is an example of a customer journey map that I created for one of my clients. In this case, I mapped out a year-long journey where customers were onboarded to a complex software used for database-building. Specifically, I focused on how that experience led to either a renewal or abandonment of the product. Through the research, we hoped to reduce customer churn.

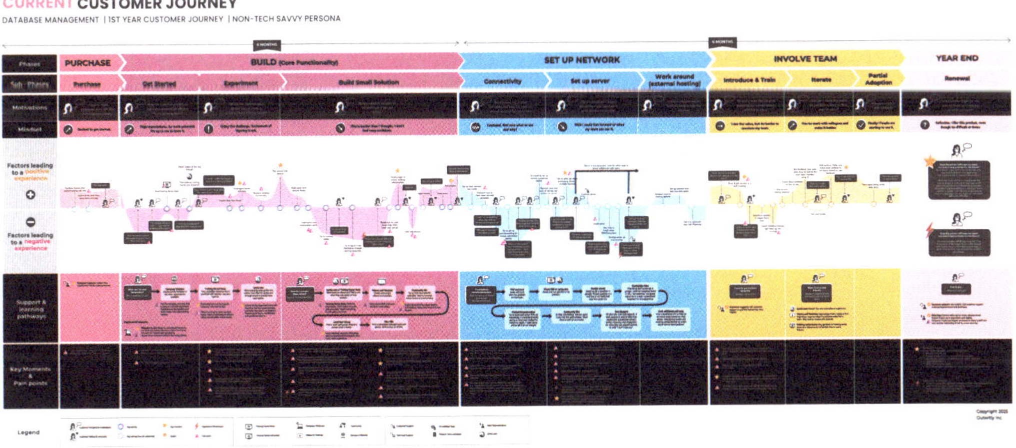


## SERVICE BLUEPRINTS

**Service blueprints** are key design artefacts used in service design. They're highly detailed, and they're typically used to visualise the actions taken by the customer or user while using a service, in full context with the front stage and back stage activities that employees do to support their journey. Sometimes, you might use service blueprints to depict systems or processes that don't have a front stage/customer-facing side, but that still require optimisation for better employee efficiency and reduced costs.

Service blueprints are very useful for:

- Pinpointing weaknesses in the current business processes and finding opportunities to optimise those processes
- Referencing a detailed breakdown of all the steps involved in a process that might need improvement
- Tying the customer journey together with the inner workings of the company
- Understanding greater complications and inefficiencies within your organisation

When you go to create a service blueprint, you should already have a deep understanding of the customer journey, which you'll have earned by conducting primary design research and mapping out that journey step-by-step. Then, you'll use that information to pinpoint an area or a process that is especially painful, and that might also be complex, duplicative, manual or siloed. The resulting artefact can illuminate how the process in question might be streamlined in order to deliver a better user experience.

In general, service blueprints will include these components: the customer journey or key user tasks (except at a much higher-level than what you depict on the journey map), a timeline/duration of activities, the front stage activities (done by employees that directly touch the customer), the back stage activities (done by employees who are out of the customers' view but support the front stage staff), sometimes the behind-the-scenes activities (done by internal teams or individuals who enable the broader service infrastructure), and lastly, the pain points that are felt by any of the people (or "actors") during any of the activities.

Let's look at a simplified example of a service blueprint that I built for a project that required a deep-dive into a payment process that was impacting the user experience. Service blueprints can be much more in-depth than this, but this example shows you the broader structure.

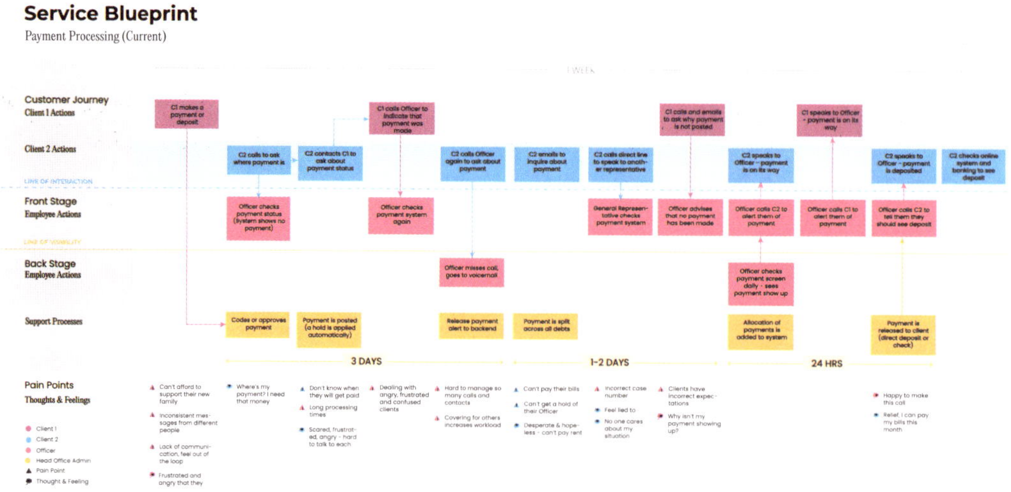

**Service Blueprint**

Payment Processing (Current)

Customer Journey
Client 1 Actions
Client 2 Actions
Front Stage
Employee Actions
Back Stage
Employee Actions
Support Processes
3 DAYS
1-2 DAYS
24 HRS
Pain Points
Thoughts & Feelings

# ECOSYSTEM (AND STAKEHOLDER) MAPS

**Ecosystem maps** and "stakeholder maps" are diagrams that show the relationships between the different factors impacting (or impacted by) a product, service or system you're designing or improving. These factors can include people, places and things involved, like stakeholders (both internal and external), partner organisations, users or customers, products, services, programmes, etc.

In general, I think that ecosystem maps are most useful in the early stages of the project initiation, where you might be trying to learn more about the organisation. You could build one as part of a workshop with stakeholders, and then finalise it right afterwards as an early deliverable, or save it and include it as part of your deliverable package at the end of a project.

Each map tends to look very different, because the things you include and the way you organise them on the map will vary based on the needs of your project (i.e. the reasons why you're creating the map in the first place). Below is an example of an ecosystem map I created to depict all of the organisations, stakeholders, partners and other factors that impacted a student learning experience — moving from those that had the biggest impact on that experience, outwards to those that had an indirect impact. (Even those with indirect impact need to be considered as part of a system redesign).

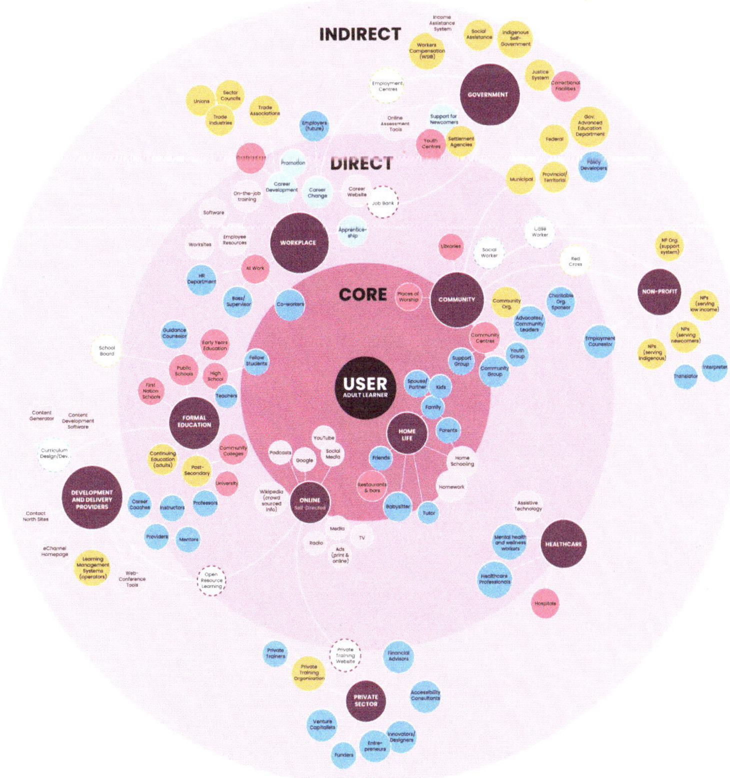

# STORYBOARDS

**Storyboards** are design tools that literally illustrate the user experience in a sketch or comic book style. They're often made up of panels that depict a person accomplishing a specific goal through the use of a product or service. This form of storytelling helps stakeholders picture the experiences being studied, without having to imagine them. They can be helpful to convey how a future state of service or product (or an entirely new one) could function, and the experience users could have in the future. Or, they can also be used to show the current state. Because they're made up of images and they illustrate the thoughts and feelings of the user in a literal story, they're great for engaging stakeholders, getting them excited and helping them build empathy for the user.

For illustrative purposes, this storyboard example depicts the experience of using a new ride-hailing app and how it would fit into someone's life.

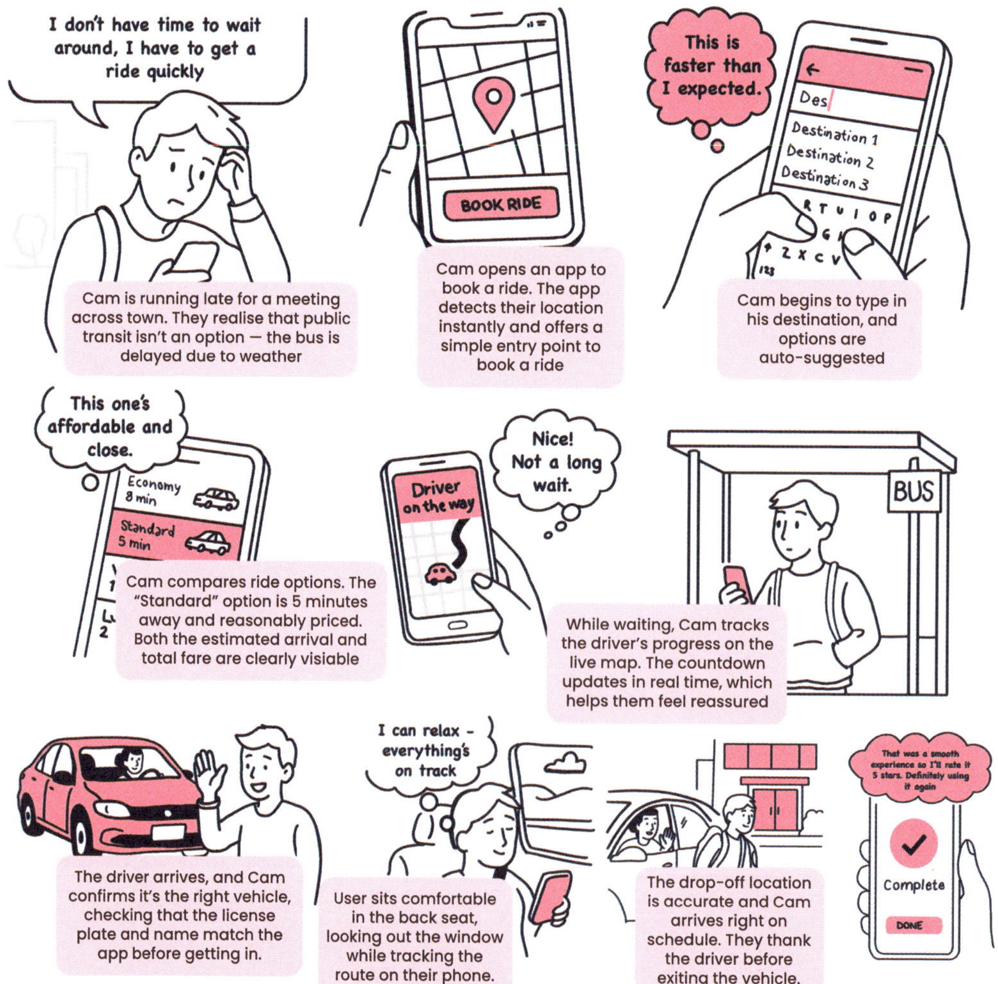

## DESIGN ARTEFACT USE CASES

While there are many more types of design artefacts, the five I just listed are the most important to have in your toolbox as a design researcher who wants to create real, meaningful change within organisations and become a champion for human-centred design and design-led business strategy.

Here's a chart that will help you compare the best uses and scenarios for these artefacts, so that you can make the most of them.

| Design Artefact | Use It To... | When You Need To... |
|---|---|---|
| Customer or user journey map | • Highlight areas for improvement in the current experience<br>• See the end-to-end journey that customers experience with a product, service or system<br>• Break down organisational silos that impact a user across their journey<br>• Link pain points to the specific part of a process or journey that's broken/needs improvement<br>• Compare and prioritise issues based on what steps, processes or departments are contributing to the most pain points | • Gain a broader, end-to-end understanding of a chronological customer experience<br>• See a play-by-play of how your customers are experiencing a specific aspect of a product or service<br>• Clarify where things are going wrong during the customer journey |
| Service blueprint | • Gain a detailed view of actions being taken across a service<br>• Identify inefficiencies in the current business processes<br>• Link the customer journey and its pain points with the inner workings of the company<br>• Find opportunities to optimise processes and address those pain points | • Map out an internal business process that has different employees working front stage, back stage and behind-the-scenes<br>• Understand the "why" behind business process inefficiencies<br>• Build on a solid understanding of the customer journey to investigate the root cause within the organisation |

| Design Artefact | Use It To... | When You Need To... |
|---|---|---|
| Persona | • Build empathy for the user<br>• Help teams understand and align on who you're designing for<br>• Reduce self-referential assumptions (where stakeholders and/or teams think that they can innately understand the user without doing research — these situations come up a LOT)<br>• Satisfy the needs of "the many" (one persona might represent the needs of potentially thousands of people)<br>• Create a shorthand for referring to certain user groups (using fictional persona names, like "Julie" in the earlier example)<br>• Inform human-centred design and development (through all of the effects listed above) | • Gain a much deeper understanding of your users<br>• Educate team members or clients who are less familiar with their users, and/or who don't typically interact with users<br>• Design a product or service that will serve many different user groups with different needs and challenges |
| Ecosystem map | • Gain a holistic view of an entire system or organisation<br>• Identify the internal and external stakeholders who may need to be consulted for research or decisions<br>• Prioritise the elements of a system to improve<br>• Understand how the different people and elements in a system will be impacted by the outcome of a better experience or a change to that system | • Design for a system that is multi-faceted and complex, involving many different stakeholder groups (e.g. large enterprises and government organisations)<br>• Account for all of the people who will be impacted by a change or a new experience (when you don't currently have a single source that tells you this)<br>• Familiarise yourself with all of your stakeholders in the "discover" phase of a design project |

| Design Artefact | Use It To... | When You Need To... |
|---|---|---|
| Storyboard | • Convey a true-to-life scenario of the current experience<br>• Provide a visualisation of the ideal future state of an improved experience<br>• Exemplify issues and opportunities in a current or future experience (to help team members and stakeholders understand them in context) | • Help others understand a current experience that's hard to imagine without imagery<br>• Create an entirely new product or service that has never existed<br>• Share a new design or proposed solution with people who were less involved in the research |

## Communicate Insights: Crafting the Report

An **insights report** is an important document that clearly summarises the insights generated by a design research project. While the insights are a key feature, the most effective reports will also summarise the research methodology, challenges, kudos, and other findings that put these insights in context. The purpose of this report is to take your stakeholders through what your research uncovered and point to recommendations and next steps for the design phase.

It's the one document that will be referenced again and again by the project team. It serves as a definitive record of your particular study, including all of your major and minor discoveries. If you play your cards right, it will live way beyond the timeline of the individual research project... meaning that the impact of your work will continue long after you've moved on. You want your stakeholders and the project team to really absorb the takeaways from your report and take them to heart, so that your recommendations are acted on. It should provide a mix of high-level thinking and attention to detail.

**Your insights report should have a beginning, middle and end (see below).** This will make it more memorable and easier to absorb. You'll start with a broad overview, then get into more detail, and conclude by summarising the biggest takeaways and laying the groundwork for future action. To be truly effective, every one of your insights reports should include the elements on the next page.

## REPORT STORYTELLING

**WHAT YOU DID / WHERE YOU STARTED**

### BEGINNING

1. Executive Summary
2. Project Overview
3. Research Goals
4. Research Overview (Methodology)

**WHAT YOU FOUND OUT / WHAT THE PROBLEMS ARE**

### MIDDLE

5. Key Insights
6. Top Challenges
7. Top Kudos
8. Other Findings

**WHAT TO IMPROVE / WHAT TO DO NEXT**

### END

9. Design Recommendations
10. Action Plan
11. Conclusion (Next Steps and Future Research)
12. Appendix

Think of your audience as being made up of **skimmers, dippers and divers:** executives who are very busy and will only skim the core facts, people who are somewhat involved in the project and will look further into your insights, and the key players with key responsibilities who will comb through your report from cover to cover.

Considering this, you should reveal the complexity of your research like an onion — in layers — the first layer shows the high-level headers and ideas, so that a skimmer could simply browse the deliverable or report and get the gist of it. Then, you add the next layer of detail for the dippers, who will want to see some broken down bullet points revealing more info on the key insights.

The third layer goes even deeper for the divers, who are typically the digital architects and business analysts actually responsible for executing the recommendations and changes you propose. They'll need a level of detail that's thorough, complete with the little details, like where in the onboarding process users got tripped up, how many times they called support, and what exactly happened on each of those calls.

Executives will never care about all of those little details...but each of these types of stakeholders might be looking at the same design artefact or report, so everyone has to be able to get what they need out of it. Executives especially are prone to become bored or lose interest if the high-level information isn't immediately readable and engaging to them, because they're focused on the bigger picture, i.e. what actually matters to the business from a strategic perspective.

Next, I'll break down each elements of a great insights report.

## 1. EXECUTIVE SUMMARY

This single page summarises all of the high-level information executive stakeholders need to know about what research was conducted and what information was found, as well as general recommendations. I recommend that you use a combination of icons, headers and subheaders to help make this page skimmable.

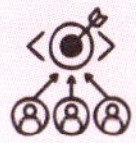

**Alignment Advice:**

You might be asked to present your report to very different groups on totally separate occasions. In cases like this, I recommend creating different versions of your report — a shorter one for executives, and one that's more detailed for business analysts or product owners who will want all of the nitty-gritty details. (In fact, if you have the time and/or you know you're catering to multiple stakeholder groups, I'd recommend doing this across the board, even without being asked.) You might also decide to provide more detail on certain topics than others, depending on the interests of each group. Yes, it's more work, but it could make the difference between a disinterested reception of your report, and an excited, eager one.

## 2. PROJECT OVERVIEW

The project overview provides a brief introduction to the project and the research. This should be easy to put together using information from the project initiation document (PID) you assembled during the project initiation stage.

If there were any assumptions or biases made during the research, you should also identify them here, as a disclaimer. For example, maybe some bias could have been introduced when you were observing users and taking your own notes based on their experiences. Or maybe you couldn't interview one of your user groups because of time constraints, or you had to use a proxy user in place of a real user in certain cases, so there are gaps in the research. Get all of that out in the open here, so nothing gets misconstrued or becomes an unwelcome surprise.

(**Note:** This shouldn't be the first time your stakeholders are seeing or hearing about these biases. Ideally, you'd have let them know as the issues came up in the project.)

## 3. RESEARCH GOALS

This section reminds stakeholders (or others reading your report) what the initial research goals were for the project. This sets the tone and provides context for later sections when you'll dive deeper into your findings and insights, and the work you did to uncover them. Again, you should be able to draw this information directly from your initial research plan.

## 4. RESEARCH OVERVIEW (METHODOLOGY AND PARTICIPANTS)

The research overview outlines the methodology/approach, usually over a few slides. It indicates whether you used desk research, interviews, observations, etc., how many participants from each user group were included in each method, the duration of each research activity (e.g. 5 days of observation; 60-minute interviews), and an explanation of the overall methodology. I also like to explain human-centred design or the double diamond process at a very high level for folks who are new to this type of work. You might think that this section seems superfluous, but it's important to include because it shows that there was rigour behind your work. It provides executives in your audience that extra layer of confidence in the insights, so that they can use those insights as a basis for decision-making.

## 5. KEY INSIGHTS

In the last chapter, I went over the basics of insights — what they are, what they're not, and how to uncover them in your research data. In your final report, you'll need to actually frame and present those insights in a formalised way that includes all the essential details, appeals to the eye, and doesn't overwhelm your reader.

- **Title and tagline:** Concise and clear
- **Description:** Explains the insight and related challenges
- **Solutions and recommendations:** Reveal opportunities based on the data
- **Proof and examples:** Taken directly from the research
- **Icons and colour:** Make it memorable

This core part of your report should feature 5–10 key insights drawn from the data that practically address your research goals and questions. They should be profound and unique truths, and, as I've said before, they shouldn't just be raw findings. I like to include these at the start of the report to really "hook" stakeholders, but you can also include them after your main research findings and challenges. These will become a part of your action plan (which I'll explain coming up).

I've provided an example of a framed insight in the study on adult learners I referenced in earlier chapters. This is a page pulled directly from a final insights report. You can see that each element listed above is present:

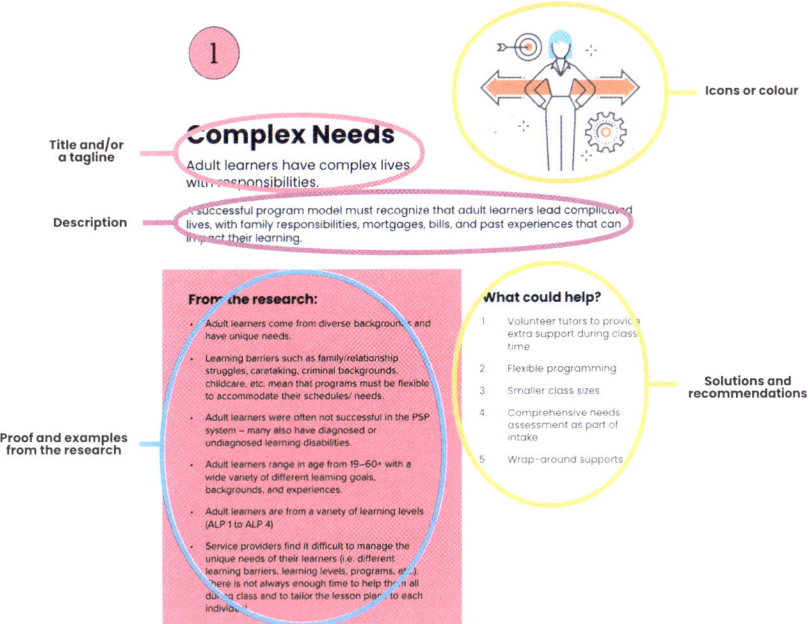


An insight is only an insight if it's actionable. Again, the purpose of design research is to find areas of improvement and innovation. If you're just rehashing the current state, then you've only done half of the work. What I mean is that you need to describe the insights in such a way that stakeholders and other team members can easily understand the opportunities you've uncovered, their relevance to the project and how they could connect to possible solutions. If you create an insight that feels wishy-washy or vague, your audience will struggle to make the connection between what you're saying and what needs to be changed in the product or service. To make an impact, you have to be extremely clear, and make it easy for that change to happen.

## 6. TOP CHALLENGES

Along with your insights, you should include a section that summarises the 5–10 top challenges or pain points that emerged through the research. These should be things that you heard over and over again and really stood out as being problematic — which would also have a strategic impact on the business. "Top challenges" are the most frequent AND most relevant challenges (based on the business context). For example, if your client or organisation said that high call volumes and the drain on their support team were big drivers for the research, be sure to include any pain points that emerged which could provide some help in solving those issues. If you've done your job right and followed the steps in this book, all of your research findings and challenges will be relevant to the business. But, you want to take that extra step to think critically about which pain points you choose to elevate here. It'll show that you're a strategic thinker. The challenges you choose to highlight will be the ones that gain the most attention. You have the power! Use it wisely.

## 7. TOP KUDOS

This section cushions the impact of hard-to-hear challenges by showcasing positive feedback about the experience. It helps to keep stakeholders excited by what they're hearing from the data and understand the good that already exists in their product or service. (Nobody wants to hear that an experience is 90% or 100% horrible, even if that might sometimes be true to your highly trained or biased eye.)

## 8. OTHER FINDINGS

Not all of your note-worthy research findings will fit neatly into your main insights, challenges or kudos. This section provides an opportunity to mention other relevant and intriguing patterns in the data that add to a holistic understanding of the research. This could be where you include less frequently heard findings or less impactful findings, or ideas that were not directly tied to a research goal.

You might also include overall customer perceptions about the product or service and satisfaction ratings.

## 9. DESIGN RECOMMENDATIONS

Your design recommendations form a "laundry list" of clear and tangible opportunities for addressing challenges that might be secondary to the most fundamental design problem(s) identified in the research. I usually dedicate 2–3 slides for this content.

**Every single insight and challenge you include in your report, big or small, should be accompanied by a corresponding design recommendation.** The most relevant and potentially innovative solutions and recommendations should be included in your action plan (which I'll go through next). But your list of design recommendations should include all of the "low-hanging fruit" — the more obvious or surface-level opportunities and solutions that don't directly relate to the central innovative digital transformation that you might be proposing, but that will still make some level of impact and add value.

For example, if you look at the image of an action plan coming up in the next section, you'll see that it contains unique ideas for the big "buckets," or main areas of concern, like communication, support, payments, etc. These five areas were prioritised in the action plan because they emerged from the research as the most painful by far, severely impacting and deteriorating both the user and employee experience. The action plan suggested that the service would completely change for the better if these main areas could be addressed. (For each one, I then provided new and novel solutions.) BUT, beyond these main areas of concern, there were a lot of other issues and ideas that came out of the research, so I listed those as part of the greater recommendations section, which acts as a larger to-do list for overall improvements.

## 10. ACTION PLAN

I created the concept of an action plan when I realised just how mind-numbing some research reports can be. Few have any real conclusions to come to at the end, and instead, they just provide a condensed brain dump of everything you heard earlier in the report. The many executives I've witnessed reacting to reports weren't interested in that kind of thing. They wanted tangible actionable steps, and beyond that, something unique and innovative. This was something I realised I could deliver, because of my design thinking skills and my ability to distill complex information into exciting and new solutions that I knew could really make an impact. That's why every report I've created since, and every report my team creates, has an action plan.

This is invaluable — I can't emphasise it enough. If you want to make an impact with your research, if you want to affect real change, if you want people to sit up and notice you and the research you did, action plans are the way to do it. They summarise everything you learned and all of the creative thinking you went through to solve those issues in a few slides that will get passed around the organisation for months and even years to come. They identify and categorise specific steps, ideas and design recommendations that came out key insights and challenges from the research. They take the intangible, "fuzzy" aspects of research and make them tangible and actionable. I typically include 3–6 action areas, descriptions of the insights and related challenges that will be addressed, and 3–5 actionable recommendations per action area.

To assemble your action plan:

- List out all challenges and insights that came from the research.
- Prioritise your challenges and insights with your stakeholders.
- Brainstorm opportunities and solutions for the highest-priority challenges and insights.
- Group those opportunities, concepts and solutions into high-level themes. (These become your action areas.)
- Narrow down your list of opportunities and solutions. Choose the ones that are most feasible and have the most potential for impact.
- Write formal descriptions of your action areas and clearly indicate your recommendations.
- Dress your action plan up with memorable visuals.

You can also do this in reverse — you can group your challenges and insights into high-level themes, translate those into action areas and then come up with recommendations for each action area.

Here's an example of some action plan sides that I created for a project about spousal support payments.

## 11. CONCLUSION

The wrap-up of your insights report succinctly summarises everything in your report. It also provides immediate next steps and areas for future research. The next steps you include here shouldn't be the same as your design recommendations. Instead, you should highlight the immediate tasks required to keep the ball moving on the project — meetings to book, timelines to discuss, design teams to brief, etc. You may not be in a position to determine the next steps and owners, so use your judgement and defer to the process that makes the most sense for your situation.

As far as future research, you should provide a list (prioritised in order) of those areas you think should be investigated next. These suggestions should come from any research gaps or outstanding questions you have, maybe because there were user groups you didn't get to study, or because a key process that was adjacent to your main research themes revealed itself as something worth digging deeper into.

## 12. APPENDIX

This final, optional section features extra sources of information that are interesting and relevant to the research but didn't "make the cut" in your main report. I almost always include one. If you have too many great data points and you don't have space to include them all in your main sections, an appendix can help you add value to the report that anyone (especially the "divers") can read further into. You might provide additional quotations, more details on the research methodology and how recruitment was done, or you might even include the profile framework I described in chapter 7. These sources will serve as quick and convenient references if your stakeholders have questions about additional findings, or if they ask for additional proof.

If you're attaching design artefacts to your final insights report, ensure that you include slides or sections that point to these artefacts, and set some context for them. Depending on what they cover, they might slot into sections 5–9 of your report.

# Build Feature Roadmaps

Feature roadmaps are more specific than action plans — they're used in product management to support the development of websites and applications. They translate design research insights into literal steps (and features) for product design and development. (This type of deliverable is only applicable in product design, UX design and the digital transformation of services.)

I find it a surprisingly rewarding activity to wrap up all of the work that's been done. This is where you, the researcher, get to connect the dots from what you heard to what will be done about it in the design. Most often, your feature roadmap will be created in collaboration with a product owner, after your action plan has been reviewed by your stakeholders. Then, you can use the approved recommendations from that plan to inform the list of features your team is going to create or update.

To create an effective feature roadmap, you should:

- List out all possible features that need to be designed, built and/or updated.
- Rank features by effort level. How much time and resources will it take to design and build?
- Assign a priority level based on how "painful" something was for your users, whether it's low-hanging fruit, and whether it would make a significant and strategic impact to the product or service.
- Add a column for the status/stage of design and development you're in.
- Add a column for ownership.
- Assign dates in a Gantt format showing when things will be worked on and how long they will take (like the example on the next page).

(**Note**: Priority ranking should always be done with stakeholders and product team members — not in isolation.)

Here's a hypothetical sample of a Gantt-style feature roadmap. This format is great for tracking multi-step initiatives that overlap across a clear timeline.

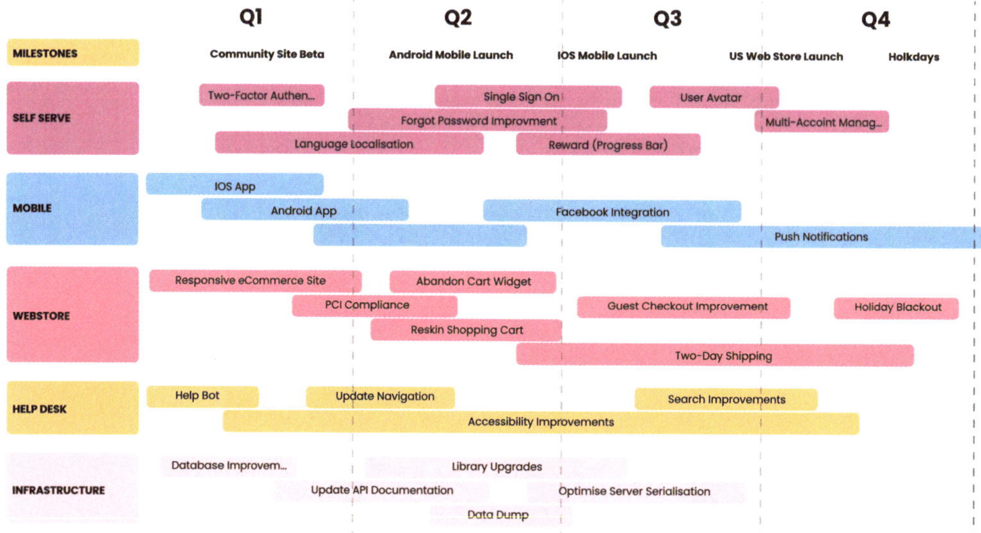


If your project isn't quite at the stage of development where a roadmap makes sense, then at the very least, I recommend that you create a spreadsheet (or database) of all the pain points you heard, ranked by severity/frequency, along with a corresponding solution. That way, when the project is ready to move to design and development, stakeholders can reference your database or spreadsheet as a jumping off point for their feature roadmap.

### Design Research in Reality: *Studying and Influencing the "Middleman" Experience*

One Outwitly project sits in my memory as a particularly proud accomplishment in terms of presenting insights and seeing them acted on.

We followed the exact process outlined in this book. We conducted a ton of research (interviews, observations, workshops), all focused on understanding the end-to-end experience of third-party intermediaries and sales representatives. From the synthesis of that research, we developed and presented an action plan that identified three core areas for innovation. These ideas were so exciting to the organisation that they asked us to do an executive roadshow. For the next four months, we delivered presentations of our research artefacts to different executive groups across this Fortune 500 company — and keep in mind, there were a LOT of teams at that level.

Our work connected these typically siloed groups, inspiring them with ideas for the future and immediate areas for action within their own product and service domains. We gave long-overdue visibility to a user group that had been largely underserved, and highlighted the challenges they faced in their work — all in a way that clearly tied user needs to business needs, revealing unique, revenue-generating opportunities they had never thought of.

This kind of outcome is a huge triumph for design researchers. You get people excited. You show them what's possible. You create visibility for the good work — the important work. You make users happy and help the business make money.

Every project should aim for this. This particular project even changed key activities on the company's long-term roadmap, which had been set years in advance. The changes were better for the users, better for the business, and ultimately, it meant better products for everyone in that market.

## Tips for Better Insights Reports

Since your insights report is typically your star deliverable in design research, I had to include my best hands-on tips tailored specifically to knocking them out of the park.

### DESIGN IT FOR NEWBIES

Keep in mind that even after you formally present your report, it might be passed around later on to other groups who have no familiarity with your research or the background of the design project. That's why you should always pretend that whoever will be reading your report or reviewing your design artefacts has little to no context or knowledge of the research. Write and design them in a way that anyone in the organisation could pick them up and quickly understand them.

The people reviewing your deliverables should have zero confusion whatsoever about what research activities were performed, why you performed them, who and what you studied, the current state of the product, and what next steps you recommend. You should also include the most essential contextual information in your section summaries, in case they get taken from the report and shared by themselves. Think about what information would be needed for each slide or page to stand on its own.

### DISTILL AND SIMPLIFY

Some researchers come onto the UX scene after being trained in formal scientific/academic settings, and they overload their reports with crazy amounts of detail. These types of reports can be incredibly dense and take hours to read — hours that your stakeholders don't have to spare, and will refuse to spend.

- Focus on high-level information, key insights and need-to-know facts.
- Be concise in your wording.
- Avoid cramming multiple subjects into one slide or section.
- Limit your supporting evidence to 2–3 quotes or clips per point.

- Restrict yourself to an approachable length.

## SUMMARISE FIRST, THEN ELABORATE

At the start of every new section in your insights report, include a slide or page that provides a high-level summary of the information coming up. Include diagrams to represent these summaries whenever possible — they can help distinguish your central points.

Here's an example of a diagram I included on a summary slide:

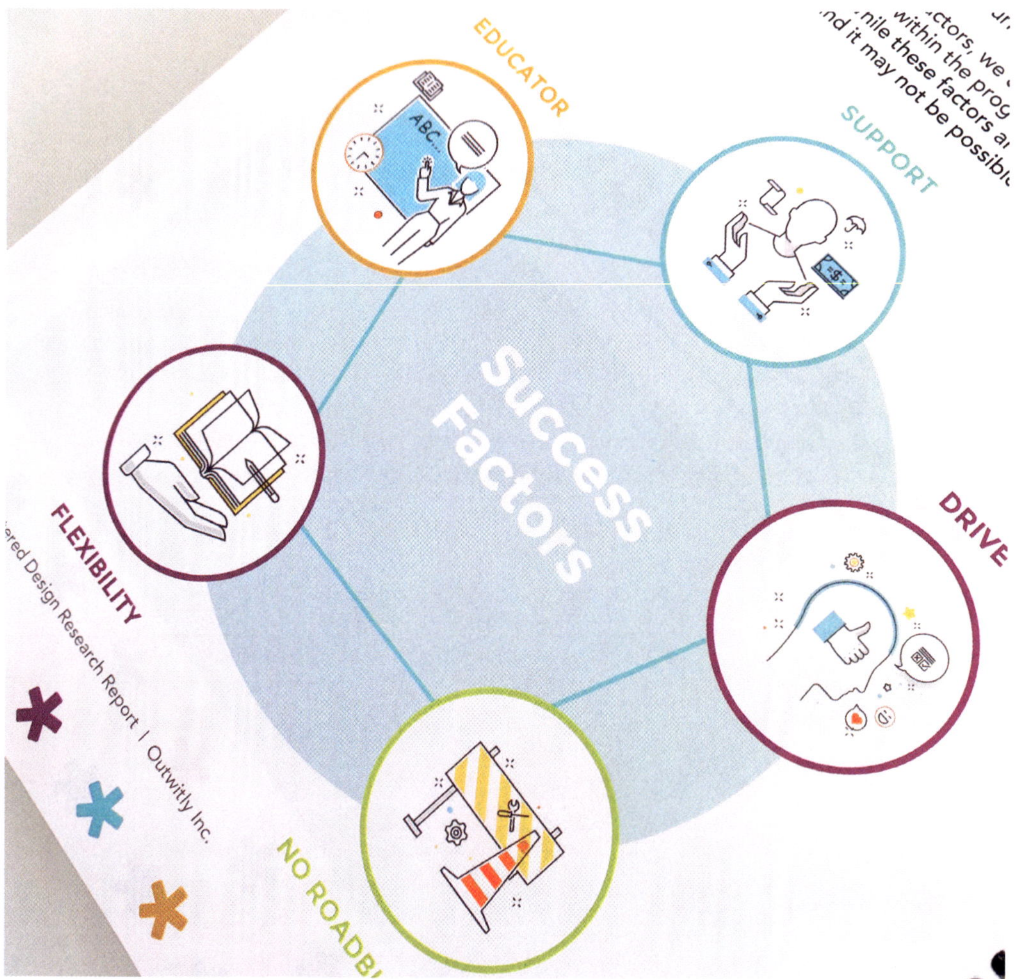

## USE GROUPINGS

Categorise and group similar pieces of information together, number them, and give your lists clear headings. For example, you might give them names like, "10 Key Insights," "15 Top Challenges," "5 Core Areas of Improvement," etc. This will reduce overwhelm and ease your audience's experience while reading, because they'll be able to scan your report quicker and understand how much information to expect in each section. (You may have noticed that throughout this book, I've made use of clear heading and subheading hierarchies to smooth out the reading experience.) Use bulleted lists instead of bulky paragraphs whenever possible.

## EVOKE AN EMOTIONAL RESPONSE

For your deliverables to be meaningful and memorable, they need to strike an emotional chord with your audience. You can achieve this by showcasing real-life examples of your participants (including photos, video clips, audio clips, or written quotes from your research with users), that show the related impact on the product or service, whether good or bad.

The beauty of design research is that we can grab real verbatim quotes and other evidence to give more meaning to what we're reporting on. This helps to draw stakeholders in and activates their empathy as they learn about the specific challenges, pain points and benefits that their users have been experiencing.

## MAKE IT ACTIONABLE!

As you're creating your design artefacts or insights report, it's important to shift from a mindset of problem-finding to one of problem-solving. Focus on identifying how to innovate and/or improve the product or service. You were focused on problems earlier on in the process, but your report isn't just feedback on the current state — it's meant to encompass an ideal future state and actionable steps. Design storytelling should inspire your audience to take action. Every challenge and insight should be balanced with an opportunity, and your audience should walk away full of ideas for how to move forward. Otherwise, all that beautiful work you painstakingly assembled throughout your research project will reach a dead end.

Of course, your suggested design solutions don't have to be fully formed — they will get iterated on and polished in the design phase. But, you should strive to make your recommendations as clear as possible, so that no in-between or prefacing is needed to move on to design.

# Conclusion

Up until design storytelling, you were the one being convinced of what truly matters the most in your area of study — your stakeholders, users and/or subject matter experts were sharing their challenges, concerns and pain points, and you were absorbing it all like a sponge. Now, in the design storytelling stage, it's up to you to do the convincing. You've worked tirelessly to analyse, synthesise and frame your findings into actionable insights that you know could dramatically improve the experience of a product or service, and lead to real change and ROI. Do yourself, your team, your participants and your organisation justice by telling an engaging story that takes decision makers along for the ride, inspires their empathy and motivates them to take meaningful action.

# * Key Takeaways:

1. **The purpose of design storytelling is to inspire improvements to an experience, and point stakeholders to aspirational ideas and achievable action.** As a design researcher, it's your job to translate overwhelming amounts of data into solutions with clear-cut roadmaps. This is the strategy piece that becomes invaluable to your stakeholders.
2. **Truly successful design storytelling caters to its audience and embodies design principles with purpose and passion.** Your information, wording and content should be beautiful, well-structured, and it should evoke emotion.
3. **The most useful design artefacts are created and reviewed in collaboration with stakeholders/and or users.** Participation increases engagement, excitement and buy-in for the research.
4. **Memorable design research deliverables should have a beginning, middle and end.** In your reports, start with an executive summary and project overview, then move through all of your insights, top challenges and kudos, and wrap up with recommendations and an action plan.
5. **Your insights reports and design artefacts should be able to stand alone.** They should be foolproof, provide context and evidence, and express all information in widely understandable terms.
6. **All of the content in your deliverables should be accessible to skimmers, dippers and divers.** Think of your deliverables as having layers like an onion, where your diverse audience can choose to either read the headlines, get the key details, or investigate every step you took.

# 14

# DESIGN RESEARCH RISING

## The Future of Design Research

*

"A rising tide lifts all boats."
— John F. Kennedy

# Introduction

Once you've mastered the principles and strategies in this book, what's next? And what does the future look like for the discipline? For this last chapter, I'm going to share the deeper, big-picture motivation behind this book, my hopeful (and achievable) vision of design's role going forward, and some important career advice to leave you with. First, let's start with the deeper motivation.

I envision a world where designers and researchers are the last roles to be cut when there are layoffs... where design teams are consulted any time an organisation faces operational challenges, and stakeholders and decision makers bring designers into strategic product and service conversations first. What if those were the norms? How would this all manifest in the products and services we interact with as users, customers, citizens, and as humans in general? Our experiences would be less clunky and frustrating, for one thing. We'd be more efficient as a society, and we'd all be a lot happier.

So, why hasn't this bright future arrived already? The answer: Not enough people understand the value of design research and human-centred design... not yet.

**Design research hasn't peaked — it's still rising.**

When you're uncovering opportunities and catalysing innovation, there's no ceiling. But before design research can elevate human experience to greater heights, we have to elevate design research much higher in the eyes of the world.

The work of elevating design research is going to require passionate, self-assured people who can adapt to change while also advocating for the true "magic" of the work.

The fact is, the industry has faced big challenges recently. At first, there was a rapid rise of design and research jobs in the tech sector, leading to a "boom" of design bootcamps exploding onto the scene, with tons of people jumping into UX design, UX research or service design... only to be hit a few years later with mass tech layoffs, to have their value questioned in every meeting, and now to face the "threat" of constantly advancing AI.

Understandably, so many designers and researchers are getting perpetually burnt out, becoming skeptical, and feeling helpless, like nothing they try will change things. We get knocked down over and over again by the overbearing product owner who doesn't believe us, the rigid and dogmatic scrum master, the challenging stakeholder, or the bad product we try and try to fix with no results, because all our suggestions fall on deaf ears. I get it, because I've been there.

BUT, I believe this skepticism keeps our discipline small. It disempowers us and prevents us from having the impact we so desperately want to have on our world. We all want to see the products and services we work on improve, and we want to provide meaningful experiences for the people who interact with them. To attain this consistently and to see our industry rise, we need to accept these challenges at face value and — as painful as it can be sometimes — examine ourselves, how we've been working, and start the change with us. Where are we coasting because we're fed up? Where are we ostracising ourselves with jargon and rigid "process" that nobody outside of design can relate to? How can we be the ones to break the ice, rather than waiting for someone else to do it?

It starts with your mindset and the daily choices you make to understand and correct your thoughts. As I mentioned in the beginning of this book, you have to focus on what you can control first, before your circle of influence and your impact can expand. Mindset is everything for an extraordinary career and life. We need to think critically about how we perceive the world, and decide to shift our perspective when we aren't getting the results we want.

This isn't talked about enough in our industry — but as someone who has worked hard over more than a decade to create a better life and a multi-million dollar business, I can say that my mindset, and my willingness to change that mindset, have been the key to success. That's why I'm going to quickly share with you the **CTFAR** framework. It comes from The Life Coach School, and it's something a cherished business coach taught me.

**C** = Circumstance **T** = Thoughts **F** = Feelings **A** = Actions **R** = Result

Here's how it works: All circumstances are neutral — if you think about it, they're all just facts. If you were intentionally left off of a meeting, for example, that's still just a fact, until you start having thoughts about it. Our thoughts about a circumstance lead us to have certain feelings, and those feelings lead to certain actions, which then have a result, intended or not. In this way, our thoughts can become a self-fulfilling prophecy. The trick is to reframe. See the two example scenarios in the chart on the next page.

| | **Scenario 1** (Unintended, Negative Thoughts) | **Scenario 2** (Intended, Positive or Neutral Thoughts) |
|---|---|---|
| **Circumstance** | The Product Owner left you off of a meeting invite related to the next feature launch. | The Product Owner left you off of a meeting invite related to the next feature launch. **(The exact same circumstance as scenario 1.)** |
| **Thoughts** | "How dare they not include me? That was on purpose. They're trying to exclude me from the team and turn them against me. Now, no one's going to listen when I say we can't design based on assumptions." | "The PO left me off the meeting by mistake. I should check-in with them and see how I can bring value to the meeting in a way where the PO feels supported." |
| **Feelings** | Angry, frustrated, worried | Calm, confident |
| **Actions** | You email your boss to complain that you were left out. You act hostile towards the PO in future meetings. | You have an honest chat with the PO from a positive place, you get added to the meeting, you attend it on aligned terms, and you add value to the meeting and to the PO. |
| **Result** | You start to withdraw from work and breed distrust in the team and discord | The team who attended the meeting is more aligned, trust has been fostered between you and the PO; you establish yourself as a "value-add" team member. |

You can see how in the first scenario, any person who had those thoughts about being left out would feel angry and frustrated. It's not a "you" issue, it's just that your unintended thoughts (caused by an unexamined, instinctual reaction) have led you to have certain feelings about an otherwise neutral circumstance.

Here are a few other examples showing ways that I would reframe the pessimistic thoughts I mentioned at the start of this section.

| **Unintended, Negative Thoughts** | **Intended, Positive or Neutral Thoughts** |
|---|---|
| "AI is getting so good, it's going to take over my job. I will no longer add value." | "Advancements in AI could make me even better and more efficient at my job. Research will be conducted faster and it will be easier for me to get buy-in as a result." |

| Unintended, Negative Thoughts | Intended, Positive or Neutral Thoughts |
|---|---|
| "No one ever listens to me. It doesn't matter what research we do, it won't change anything." | "This research is important and it has the power to impact the entire direction of this product. I can show them how." |
| "They don't believe in my work. I'm so sick of showing up every day and hitting a wall, where they don't let me do research, and we just design based on assumptions." | "I'm uniquely qualified to show them the value of this work. It's exciting to know that there's so much opportunity for improvement. I should share that passion and excitement with them." |

Doing this will change the quality of your life and the work that you do. It'll also allow you to create more impact through your research. (Of course, there will always be unreasonable people, but that's why you focus on educating your potential allies first — see chapter 3.)

# What (or Who) is Behind the Mastery?

A significant percentage of this book was dedicated to giving you step-by-step guides and tips for your toolbox. I gave you practical ways to: grow your influence and communicate the value of your work; plan and lead design research projects that yield unbiased, robust data and truly actionable insights; and hone your design storytelling so that your design recommendations become building blocks for true innovation in the products and services you study.

Of course, anyone can pick up a book or a checklist and follow instructions. A true "design research master" stands apart because they're committed to:

1. **Pushing for excellence in their craft:** Embodying "Action" strategies in new creative ways to make the most meaningful impact possible in their day-to-day work, and evolving those strategies as new technology, challenges and opportunities come onto the scene
2. **Building meaningful relationships:** Sticking with "Alignment" strategies no matter the circumstance, and approaching every stakeholder or team member they meet with equal respect, empathy and patience, as well as an understanding that everyone has needs, challenges and fears

That's why I've included "Alignment Advice" and "Action Advice" throughout this book. **The work of inspiring action and aligning stakeholders takes a certain kind of person.** In the end, my ultimate goal is not just to enhance the way we do design research... it's to pave the way for more (and better) design projects. Each person who becomes a design research master is representing the discipline, and painting a picture for the world to judge.

# The Emerging HCD Unicorn

**Let's redefine (and future-proof) the concept of the "unicorn" in this industry.**

In my journey of growing Outwitly, first as a design consulting firm and then as a UX staffing agency, I've slowly been building a vision of a powerful practitioner archetype with every ideal trait I've seen embodied in this field, all assembled into one package.

You've probably heard of the UX unicorn before — a rare "full-stack" design practitioner who can wear an incredible number of hats. That unicorn goes beyond the "T-shaped" practitioner (who has deep knowledge in one area, and broad knowledge in many other areas). They excel in multiple areas of product, like UX design, UI design, design research, facilitation, prototyping and sometimes even front-end development.

But career longevity, success and industry elevation is not just about diversifying your skills. The higher we keep setting our goals, the more power we'll be able to harness in amplifying the value of our work across markets and sectors, even as the world rapidly changes. So, how do we keep on rising, and demonstrating the power of design and design research?

To answer this question, I've put together a new avatar to represent the people who will rise in the face of our current challenges, and help our discipline rise with them.

The new "HCD unicorn" is:

## EMOTIONALLY INTELLIGENT

Their ability to read a room and understand emotions is what makes them a crucial catalyst in human-centred design. Like I said in chapter 1, AI can't empathise the way that a HCD unicorn with a high emotional quotient (EQ) can. AI might be able to predict or identify emotional reactions (with varying accuracy) based on prompts that contain user data. But the HCD unicorn will always be best at setting participants at ease so that they open up more — sensing when to probe further on a subject, and holding the fears, needs and challenges of user groups and stakeholders in their head all at the same time when synthesising insights or designing concepts.

They can confidently navigate company politics, and they're also stakeholder whisperers who know how to pinpoint motivations, identify concerns, invite stakeholders into conversations, and integrate their ideas into processes. They bring together and align people with wildly different viewpoints and priorities, and they involve users in co-creating solutions that make waves and speak to people's hearts.

## MAGNETIC

The HCD unicorn becomes a magnetic force that draws in opportunity, innovation and fascination with their work. The opposite of rigid, they're not just open to new ideas and opportunities — they actively pull these things toward them because they've established a reputation for respectful, engaging and even exciting collaboration.

They're excellent facilitators who can make workshops into memorable experiences, they promote synergy between design, research and product teams every step of the way, and they're always finding ways to add value to the teams around them. They have that "Je ne sais quoi" that makes people think that they're a rare personality or that they have some secret power, but in reality, they just genuinely see the benefit of working together, and, with experience, they've figured out how to create optimal collaborative environments. They engage the CTFAR framework and focus on keeping a growth mindset, setting off a positive feedback loop that brings authentic joy to their day-to-day life, and unleashes higher levels of creativity.

When you approach your work this way, people will always want to have you around. They'll seek out your opinions, they'll ask to collaborate with you, and they won't be afraid of how you might react in a certain situation.

## MASTERFUL

This type of person is a true master of their work, committed to deep excellence in their craft and how they deliver projects. They also understand that "mastery" isn't really a fixed state, and that there's always further to go.

They commit to:

- **Pushing for bigger breakthroughs and higher quality:** They aim to improve by 1% every day, and pushing for every workshop, artefact, or insights report to be even better than the last. They literally ask themselves, "How can [the current deliverable] be the best one I've ever done?" This exercise might feel cheesy, but it actually pushes people's brains out of autopilot, and into brainstorming improvements.

- **Growth through learning:** Their work always evolves, because there's always more to learn from others, from books, from technology and from their own "failures."
- **Sharing their knowledge and experience with others:** They aim to elevate the industry as a whole, because they understand that knowledge-sharing is how we upskill each other and benefit from each other's experience. (If I do a better job, and you do a better job, more people will realise how much they need us, and there'll be more opportunities for everyone.)

If you do all of this, you will be one of the people that stakeholders call up and ask for advice. You will be invited to the "big rooms," and you will get a chance to not only say your piece, but actually help determine the way forward.

## STRATEGIC

Powerful design strategy comes into play when you've worked to research and understand the complete context of the problem you're addressing and all of the factors involved (resources, people, sentiments, trends, needs, challenges, etc.), and you use that information to tie your project back to the business and its needs. The magic of design research is in this connection between your research and the business, from raw data, to insights, to innovation, to ROI.

An HCD unicorn is always strategic, and thoughtful about the research and design work, constantly asking, "Does it add value?" "Is it useful?" "Is it feasible?"

When you know the business and where it needs to go, and you understand the users and their unmet needs, you can use your creative mind to connect the dots and propose strategic solutions and recommendations that are invaluable to your stakeholders. It's in these moments of "connecting" your thoughts, the merging of the left and right brain, where design strategy shines.

## STORYTELLER

Ultimately, the new HCD unicorn is a compelling, captivating storyteller. Storytelling is key to elevating the industry, and it's an art you need to be good at to communicate anything effectively.

Part of being an amazing storyteller is helping others see your vision. People in this field are naturally creative, and our gift is that we can see how much better something could be. In order to be properly heard, we need to convey that vision and excitement for the future in a way that's not only connected to specific goals, but that's also captivating and alluring to stakeholders... so much so that they look at the "stories" we tell about our research or design decisions and they think, "Wow, if we could create that, we would be unstoppable as a company. Let's get to work." This is the kind of power that changes roadmaps and can reroute the direction of an entire department.

This unicorn understands how to connect to an audience, and not just through design. They can infuse the kind of storytelling magic that forges connection, whether that's directly in their work, or in their working relationships.

Don't assume that I'm talking about somebody else. Anyone can become an HCD unicorn. Maybe the term "unicorn" first came up because they're thought of as fictional, or hard to find. But let's shatter that. Let's just take the "magic" part, and lose the "rare" part. Let's make the idea of an HCD unicorn so prevalent that the narrative goes from, "Wow, that one practitioner is amazing" to, "Wow, this practice is amazing."

# The Bridge Between Humans and Tech

As I mentioned earlier (and as you no doubt know), many people have been worried about AI replacing them entirely. But, the fact is, **AI is going to continue creating even more opportunities for interactions between technology and humans** than there are today. And that means your role is not going anywhere... actually, it's going to become even more significant.

As designers and researchers, we have a bigger part to play in the creation of our world.

**I believe we are the bridge between humans and technology.**

Think about how heavily we all interact with pre-AI technology — we do it all day long for our jobs, and then we're on our phones all evening long. We're always connected to some form of software, designed by someone like us. With AI, it's a whole new type of evolution in interaction. Instead of passive use, there's active, two-way engagement with an intelligent machine. This is already making interactions more dynamic, and it's going to create more "wicked problems" that will require design thinking and strategy to solve. As these types of interactions multiply, organisations are going to need more people like us to bridge the gap — examining those interactions, pushing to understand the latest advances and strategising about how to improve them, so that they offer even better experiences for humans.

The unknown can be scary, but if you can get past the fear (again, using that CTFAR framework I introduced earlier), you can bet that life will reward you with some fascinating challenges and exciting outcomes.

## A Force to be Reckoned With

Before I sign off, I need to make sure you know this: your voice matters.

Too often, talented design practitioners shrink back from people who challenge their ideas, unsure whether their work is "important enough" to champion. But you know what you're talking about, and your opinions can be absolutely pivotal. The skills you've cultivated — empathising, strategising, storytelling, etc. — are exactly what the world needs now, especially as new technologies shift the landscape.

So, speak up in the rooms where decisions are made. Talk about users. Talk about their very real needs. If you work on building trust and you express yourself with clarity and conviction, your insights will be heard.

Stop doubting. **You can make people's lives better.** Even if the world doesn't always say "thank you," the impact will speak for itself.

So, own it, and inspire others to do the same.

# Acknowledgements

This book came to life thanks to the support, patience and creativity of so many people. First, I want to acknowledge my husband, Chris — thank you for always being in my corner, for encouraging me every step of the way and for holding down the fort during the long writing and editing sessions, especially those extra bedtime shifts with the kids.

Over the past decade, I've had the privilege of working with incredible clients whose projects, challenges and insights have shaped me as a researcher and leader. I'm grateful to each of you for those opportunities and experiences. You've helped me grow and you've empowered me to foster growth in others, so that more people can feel the joy of fueling human-centred design.

I'm continuously inspired by the talented contractors and the wider community of practitioners in Outwitly's network — your passion and engagement drives me to do more, share more, connect more, and push for the elevation and recognition that the UX and service design industry deserves. To my amazing core team at Outwitly — thank you to every single one of you for your patience while I poured time and energy into this project, and for continuing to show up with excellence and care. Zuna Amir Dhanani, my brilliant designer, thank you for your tireless creativity and your willingness to work through countless versions and details to make this book visually beautiful. Rachaela Van Borek, my deepest thanks for your hard work, late nights and dedication over the last two years. From day one, you were there to help shape the proposal, organise my thinking and move this project forward with clarity and intention. You helped me bring my voice to the page. Your thoughtful partnership allowed me to stay focused and actually make the time to finish this. I'm endlessly thankful for everything you brought to this journey — this book wouldn't have happened without you.

My heartfelt appreciation also goes to BIS Publishers. Harm van Kessel and Anneloes van Gaalen, thank you for believing in this vision from the very beginning and for guiding me through this process with such thoughtfulness.

# Index

## A

A/B testing 49–50
accessibility 164, 168–169, 180
action advice 8, 71, 83, 101, 116, 124, 129, 171, 188, 196, 206, 251
action plan 141, 185, 189, 221, 223, 237, 238, 240–242
AEIOU 151–152
affinity mapping 82, 185, 193, 204–205, 212
agenda 145, 148, 151, 153, 191, 195, 196
AI (artificial intelligence) 3–5, 20, 80, 105, 172, 178–179, 202–203, 204, 211, 249–250, 253, 255
alignment advice 8, 60, 84, 99, 125, 143, 145, 157, 163, 178, 190, 212, 234, 251
analogue 43, 163
analysis 45, 52, 89, 118, 126, 150, 155, 168, 169, 175, 176, 178, 179, 189, 200–212 (See also "data coding" and "thematic analysis")

## B

back-ups 108, 122, 126, 195
bias 80, 84, 103, 113, 115, 116, 119, 138, 143, 190, 196, 234
brainstorm 81, 86, 97, 118, 144, 185, 193–194, 197, 208, 224, 238
British Design Council 44

## C

case studies 20, 39
champions 18, 21–22
influence
  circle of concern 12–14
  circle of control 12, 15, 26
  circle of influence 12–15, 17, 22–23, 25, 249
  focus on your craft 15
co-design workshop 6, 48, 51, 185–186, 226
coding data (See also "analysis" and "thematic analysis")
  coding 82, 204, 205–207, 209–212
  familiarise yourself with the data 205–206, 209
combining research methods 87–88 (See also "mixing methods")
company politics 18–21
consent 107–108, 118, 123–124, 127, 138
converging 45, 193, 201, 221
CTFAR 249, 253
cultural probe 146–148
customer journey 121, 124, 129, 225–227, 230

## D

data saturation 84, 91, 100–102
data triangulation 50, 81, 83– 85, 88, 91
day-in-the-life 82, 121, 146
debrief 145, 157–158, 176, 197
decision makers 13, 21–22, 30–31, 71–72, 101
deliverables 15, 30, 52, 61, 62–64, 88, 184, 185, 187–188, 197, 220–245
design artefacts 39, 64, 90, 146, 187–189, 197, 206, 219–231, 242, 244
design leadership
  advocacy 14
  diplomacy 18, 29, 132
  collaboration 23, 82, 92, 96, 118, 191–193, 205, 240, 253
  communication 6, 23, 24, 67, 70–72, 130, 154
  working in the open 26
design maturity scale 5, 18
design phases
  discover (or "discovery") 44–45, 48, 87, 183
  define 44–45, 47, 48, 87, 185, 201, 221
  plan and implement 44–45, 49
  prototype and test 44, 48, 87
design research
  5 Cs of Effective Research Goals 79, 81
  bad rap 3, 46, 218
  definition of design research 47
  magic of design research 5, 254
Design Research in Reality
  *Escalation Hesitation* 68–69
  *First Impressions Matter* 154–155
  *Half-Baked Buy-In* 67–68
  *Impostor Participants* 104–105
  *Physician's Journey For Better Patient Outcomes* 140–141
  *Probe to Powerful Metaphor* 147
  *SaaS 30-Day Trial* 166–167
  *Studying and Influencing the "Middleman" Experience* 241–242
  *Understanding Grocery Shopping* 165–166
  *Understanding the Adult Learning Experience* 164–165
Design Research Triple Diamond 53, 56, 76–77, 95, 202
design squiggle 46–47
design thinking 238, 255
desk research
  desk research 17, 21, 87, 88, 97, 110
  document review 49

jurisdictional scan 49
literature review 48, 49
town hall 20, 39
trends analysis 49
diary studies
traditional vs. digital 163, 168–170, 180
trigger types (in-situ reporting; signal reporting; snippet reporting) 170–172, 180
discovery workshop 70, 81, 87, 183–186, 189
diverging 45–46, 183, 193–194, 221
double diamond 44, 53, 235

## E

ecosystem maps 228, 231
emotionally intelligent 253
empathy 29, 36, 39, 130, 163, 203, 215, 216, 221, 231, 244
empathy mapping 29, 36, 184, 185, 197
evaluative research 48–49, 54, 58, 59, 61, 183, 187–188
exploratory research 48, 58, 59, 61, 181, 183

## F

facilitation 29, 132–133, 182–197
field research 50, 51
findings 213–216, 237 (See also "insights")
future state 122, 185, 203, 214, 224, 229, 232, 244
fuzzy front end 46–47, 220

## G

generative research 48, 51, 58–61, 183
governance 23, 57, 69, 70
grounded theory 203–205, 207, 212, 216
growth mindset 253
guerrilla research 139

## H

HCD unicorn 252–255
human-centred design ("HCD") 3–5, 17, 43, 203, 235, 248, 252–255

## I

ideate 45, 183, 185
incentives 36, 89, 104, 105, 106, 109, 168, 172, 177, 179
insights
abductive reasoning 215, 216
deductive and inductive reasoning 206, 215, 216
framing insights 45, 212–216, 223, 235, 242–244
what is an insight 213–214
insights reporting
appendix 239
design recommendations 186, 222, 223, 237, 239
executive summary 234
insights report 83, 84, 90, 223, 232–239, 242–244
other findings 222–223, 237
top challenges 236
top kudos 237
interview probes 117, 120, 123–126 (See also "question types")
interview protocol
protocol 116, 123–126, 129, 131, 133
welcome script 123

## J

journey map 82, 121, 129, 184, 185, 187, 225–226, 227, 230

## K

kick–off 65, 67, 69, 70, 81
key performance indicators
KPIs 16, 32–34, 35, 156
analytics 32, 84, 93, 96
benchmarks 21, 32, 33
churn 31, 32, 33, 35

## L

latent needs 50, 51, 136, 162, 215 (See also "unspoken needs")

## M

mixing methods 51–52 (See also "combining research methods")

## N

no-shows 104, 105, 108, 126, 127

## O


observation frameworks 151–153
observation types
  contextual inquiry 48, 85, 137, 138, 154
  fly–on–the–wall 50, 138
  shadowing 50, 85, 137, 139


## P


participatory research 48, 51, 183
personas 82, 87, 172, 184, 224–225, 231
pilot interviews 38, 127
POEMS 152–153
pre and post interviews
  pre- and post-observation interviews 144, 145, 151
  pre- and post-diary study interviews 168, 176–177
primary research 48–49, 86, 87, 183, 189
privacy
  data privacy 90, 107, 109, 208
  data storage 90, 107, 109
project charter 70
project initiation document 67, 70
project scope 53, 57–62, 78, 95, 143–144
proto-personas 184
prototyping 44, 45, 48, 49, 86, 87 188


## Q


qualitative data
  qualitative 32, 50, 84, 86, 100–102, 163, 201, 202, 203
  rigour 46, 201, 202, 203, 235
  robust 51, 83, 162, 177–179, 251
quantitative data 32–33, 50, 54, 84, 86, 96
question types
  question types and samples 120–122
  double-barrelled and single-barrelled questions 120
  ideal experience questions 122, 125
  leading questions 116, 119, 121
  open-ended questions 118–119
  probing 85, 113, 117, 120, 123–126, 129, 130, 131, 132, 147 (See also “interview probes”)
  rated scale questions 122


## R


ramp up 52, 57, 69, 71, 115
rapid prototyping 45, 188 (See also “prototyping”)
recruitment
  2x2 user group matrix 97
  participant tracker spreadsheet 99–100 107
  profile framework 208, 211, 239
  recruitment criteria spreadsheet 99, 107
  screener 104, 108
  screening questionnaire 107–108, 109
risk mitigation 57, 65, 65–67, 70, 71, 72, 73, 126, 183, 194
ROI
  return on investment 5, 32–33, 34, 39, 188, 203, 254
  churned revenue 32
  getting to market faster 35
  market share 203, 34
  retention 31, 35


## S


scheduling 52, 57, 61–66, 70, 72, 89, 90, 107, 108, 117, 126–127, 145 157, 171
scoping 53, 58–61, 95
secondary research 48, 49 (See also “desk research”)
self-reporting 50, 51, 147
service blueprint 226–227, 230
Six–Stage DRM Process 42, 52–53, 62–63, 76, 112, 188, 201, 221
soft skills
  soft skills 29
  active listening 130, 132, 133
  navigating personalities 131–132, 191
  rapport 119, 121, 124, 130, 132
  read the room 29, 153–154
stakeholder interviews 17, 69–70, 87, 114–115
stakeholder management
  stakeholder management 4, 11, 84–85, 178
  blockers 72, 128
  business needs 15–18, 20
  escalate issues 67, 68
  expectation setting 23, 46, 64, 76,
  fears 37–38, 40, 83, 127, 183, 188, 193, 194, 251
  jargon 16, 20, 30–31, 79, 249
  objections 35–36
  preliminary report (or “early findings”) 64, 71, 197
  raise flags 24, 67, 71, 72
  status update 67, 71, 127, 128
  talk in terms of results 31
  transparency 24, 72
  trust 3, 22–24, 46–47, 56, 65, 67, 69, 71, 76, 84, 115, 125, 127, 143, 143, 157, 188, 250

stakeholder maps 228
stakeholder workshops 17, 183–187
subject matter expert 62, 69, 97, 115, 145
surveys 50, 59, 60, 86, 87, 88, 96, 102, 106,
synthesis 113, 201–202, 203, 205, 206, 212–216, 236

---

## T

target audience 95–96
thematic analysis 204, 205, 206, 209–212 (See also "analysis" and "coding data")
transcribing 113, 118, 197, 205, 208–209

---

## U

unspoken needs 50, 85, 87, 136, 215 (See also "latent needs")
usability testing 38, 44, 49, 101, 105
UX unicorn 252

---

## V

validation research 38, 44, 104
validation workshop 187–188

---

## W

WIP (works–in–progress) 24, 71
workshop (See also "co–design workshop," "discovery workshop," "validation workshop" and "stakeholder workshops")
  workshops 70, 86, 87, 102, 182–197
  bodystorming 48, 51
  design charrettes 48, 51
  hopes and fears 183, 193, 194
  hybrid workshop 186, 189